The Diaspora Strikes Back

In *The Diaspora Strikes Back*, Juan Flores flips the immigration process on its head: what happens to the home country as a result of the constant streams of emigrants and remittances flowing in from abroad? He looks at how "Nuyoricans" (Puerto Rican New Yorkers) bring challenges and changes to Puerto Rico, introducing salsa music, hip hop and inner-city New York culture to the Caribbean island. While he focuses on Puerto Ricans, Dominicans and Cubans the model is broadly applicable. Indians in London, Japanese in Sao Paulo, Turks in Berlin, Mexicans in Los Angeles, all transmit such "cultural remittances" back to their home countries, often with dramatic consequences. This ongoing process is both massive and global, and Flores' account is relevant across disciplines.

Juan Flores is a professor at New York University.

Cultural Spaces Series

Edited by
Sharon Zukin, Brooklyn College and the City University Graduate Center

Books in the series

THE DIASPORA STRIKES BACK

Caribeño Tales of Learning and Turning

JUAN FLORES

First published 2009
by Routledge
270 Madison Ave, New York, NY 10016

Simultaneously published in the UK
by Routledge
2 Park Square, Milton Park, Abingdon, Oxon OX14 4RN

Routledge is an imprint of the Taylor & Francis Group,
an informa business

© 2009 Taylor & Francis

Typeset in Adobe Garamond and Helvetica Neue
by Florence Production Ltd, Stoodleigh, Devon
Printed and bound in the United States of America
on acid-free paper
by Edwards Brothers Inc.

Library of Congress Cataloging in Publication Data
Flores, Juan, 1943-
    The diaspora strikes back : Caribbean Latino tales of learning
and turning / by Juan Flores.
        p. cm.
    Includes bibliographical references.
    1. Return migration – Social aspects – Puerto Rico.
    2. Puerto Ricans – Migrations.   3. Puerto Rico –
Emigration and immigration.   I. Title.
JV7382.F56 2008
304.8'7295073 – dc22   2007052005

ISBN13: 978–0–415–95260–6 (hbk)
ISBN13: 978–0–415–95261–3 (pbk)
ISBN13: 978–0–203–89461–3 (ebk)

ISBN10: 0–415–95260–3 (hbk)
ISBN10: 0–415–95261–1 (pbk)
ISBN10: 0–203–89461–8 (ebk)

CONTENTS

LIST OF ILLUSTRATIONS

Cover image: "Salon de calle", artist Carmelo Sobrino

SERIES FOREWORD

The *Cultural Spaces* series presents in-depth, sociological portraits and interpretations of people and places in constant change. Some authors look at geographical spaces like cities, neighborhoods, industrial districts like "Silicon Alley," and even buildings like New York's World Trade Center site. Other authors write about the social practices that develop around modern spaces—the "branding" of New York City to overcome an image crisis in the 1960s and 1970s; the invention of highway billboards in the 1920s when Americans geared up for long-distance driving; and the creation of consumer goods in the late nineteenth century home, museum, and city. The common element these authors share is a desire to document tensions between elite cultures and the cultures of the streets—between "high" and "low" culture, political domination and countercultural style, and conventional and unconventional cultural forms.

The Diaspora Strikes Back allow us to look at the new face of immigration—circular migration between home country and host country—in an unconventional way. Though we know that immigrants bring the cultural norms and values of their home country with them, we rarely pay attention to the ways of looking and thinking they bring back with them when they return home after years of living, working, and raising a family overseas. These migrants travel with a double baggage: the culture they were born into at home, and the culture they have learned and created in their host country. When they return home—some, after spending their entire working life in the host country—they bring back the original culture they left with, many years ago, which is now old-fashioned, but they also bring back the way of life they have learned in their host country as well as the hybrid or fusion culture they and their fellow immigrants have created to survive and thrive there. In contrast to the economic remittances, or money, that immigrants send home, they bring with them *cultural* remittances.

Those who did not leave home are not always glad to see this new culture. In fact, they may be quite critical of the return migrants, who want to teach them new musical styles, a new language, and new forms of political protest. Gradually, the return migrants and those who did not leave home forge yet another new culture, a fusion of styles and values that the migrants bring home and the residue of tradition.

To show how this new culture is created, Juan Flores treats us to first-person stories from the Caribbean migration of Puerto Rico, the Dominican

Republic, and Cuba. This migration stream has a long history in North America. It is connected with the Atlantic slave trade, the expansion of the United States' influence throughout the western hemisphere, and North America's drive to industrialization, and then to factory shutdowns and outsourcing, in the 20th century. But the Caribbean migration is also connected with salsa, merengue, and hip hop—three powerful cultural forms that, themselves, have traveled the circular passage from the Caribbean to the U.S. and back to the islands. These cultural remittances show us the "other" face of immigration in *The Diaspora Strikes Back*.

Sharon Zukin
Series Editor

ACKNOWLEDGMENTS

I have been thinking about this book for many years, and have talked about the themes of culture and return migration with hundreds of people. I would like to thank all of them by name for their generous help in all aspects of the work, but will limit myself to those with whom I spoke most directly about this subject.

I begin with the storytellers, those wonderful Puerto Ricans, Dominicans, and Cubans in a range of different places and from many walks of life who were willing to sit with me and tell their stories. I thank them for helping me ground my thinking in the real lives of real people. I regret not being able to name each of them individually, but here are those who expressly said that they were willing or even wanted to be mentioned by name: Aracelis Román, Ariel Fernández Díaz, Loira Limbal, Venus Castro, John Sánchez, José Irizarry, Iris Toro, Sebastián Ramírez, Josefina Báez, Chiqui Vicioso, Richard Hernández, Kaity Trinidad, José Rodríguez Calderón, Guillermo Ayala, and Victoria García.

In addition, I thank the following friends, colleagues, students, and other acquaintances for their ideas, suggestions and comments on all or parts of the book manuscript as it developed: Gerard Aching, Paul Austerlitz, Josefina Báez, Daisy Cocco de Filippis, Jorge Duany, Arcadio Díaz-Quiñónes, Marcos Dimas, James Early, María Fernández, Nancy Foner, Víctor Fowler, Pablo Gastón, Stuart Hall, Rafael Hernández, Bill Kornblum, George Lipsitz, René López, Gerardo Mosquera, Juan Otero Garabís, Deborah Pacini Hernández, Gina Pérez, Luis Eligio Pérez Meriño, Lydia Puchi Platón, Guillermo Rebollo-Gil, Raquel Rivera, Francisco Rodríguez, Mayra Santos, Susanne Stemmler, Silvio Torres-Saillant, Marén Uriarte, Victor Viesca and Esther Whitfield.

I am grateful to Sharon Zukin for inviting me to submit my work for inclusion in her "Cultural Places" series, and to Steve Rutter, Beatrice Schraa, and Mhairi Baxter of Routledge Press for guiding me through the publication process. Research grants from the National Endowment in the Humanities and from the Professional Staff Congress at the City University of New York allowed me the time I have needed to do the research, travel and writing of the book.

Finally, I am always most deeply indebted to my wife, Miriam Jiménez Román, for her constant and loving guidance and indispensable help in the conceptualization and all other aspects of this challenging project. As my friends always tell me, "con Miriam pegaste la lotería!"

"Marielena" in Knee Socks, Puerto Rico, 1968.
Photographer unknown. Permission Iris Toro.

INTRODUCTION: *CARIBEÑOS,* COUNTERSTREAMS AND CULTURAL REMITTANCES

Marielena was 15 when her family moved back to Puerto Rico. It was 1965, and she found it hard getting used to her new surroundings after growing up in the South Bronx. With all the romantic illusions she held about her enchanted island homeland, she felt unwelcome and sadly disappointed. She and her sister were ridiculed by the other kids at school and in the neighborhood, for the way they looked and spoke and everything about them. "What am I?" they asked themselves. "Am I really Puerto Rican the way I always thought, if here there are Puerto Ricans laughing at me and calling me gringa and treating me like a slut? Am I Americana after all, when up there I was always treated 'different,' and where I was even proud to be different? I was deeply confused, and felt lost." It was the most painful experience of her life, but she did struggle through it, and made adjustments while never losing her dignity and pride in herself.

"As time passed and we found our way around a little, they started to accept us, and give us a chance. In fact, after a while we even became popular. We still had our own unique style, that stood out, but they began to think it was cool, and admired it and imitated us. You know, the way we walked, jitterbuggin' and all, and our hair with the zig-zag cut and pony tails, and our music, rock and roll and Motown and Latin soul. And I was proud of all that, 'cause you know, I came to Puerto Rico at a rebellious age. They challenged us, but we challenged them back, too. I wasn't about to give up my diddly-bop for no one, I was proud of the blackness in me, even though I was blond with blue eyes. So, they started to like our style, they wanted to learn about it and act that way, too. Like me and the other Nuyorican kids in the school and in our neighborhood. 'Cause as time went by there were more and more of us. And there was salsa, and there was Pedro Pietri and

Nuyorican poetry that they started to hear about, partly from us. This is the stuff we brought with us."

And so, with time, Marielena went from being the butt of ridicule and insults to being a teacher, a mentor in cultural ways that the kids on the Island wanted to learn. "So I remember one time during free hour when I was in high school, we were listening to music and practicing dance steps. And I was doing some moves to something, I think it was the Wobble or one of those dance crazes of those years, or maybe it was some Joe Cuba record, some boogaloo, and I remember those same kids that used to bring us such grief coming over and saying, 'Oye, enséñame ese paso!' 'Hey, show me that step!' I'll never forget it, how the tables turned, '¡Enséñame ese paso!'"

Looking back, she realizes that her battle was worth it after all: "Because of my experience, and the same experience that a lot of other New York *boricuas* have lived through here, the new generation of people here are more tolerant. We have taught them, by example and from what we have said, to accept people as they are, to be less narrow-minded, and to know racism and prejudice when they see it, just as we learned it on the streets of Nueva York."

* * *

The theme of this book first occurred to me during several visits in recent years to the Puerto Rican city of Mayagüez, where I had been invited along with a few other Puerto Rican writers from the States to offer readings and discussions of our work. Surprisingly large and animated crowds attended the events, and cheered us on as we read not only in Spanish, but in English and in that widely practiced switching of codes, Spanglish.

The audience seemed hungry for the voices and images of Puerto Rican communities in U.S. urban settings, and to relish that bi-cultural mixture of nostalgia for their ancestral island homeland and assertive pride in the fabled "mean streets" of the Bronx and other inner-city neighborhoods in the United States. They went wild when Tato Laviera read his poem "nuyorican," where he speaks directly and defiantly (and in Spanish) to his beloved Island, and especially the lines "Now I return, with a *boricua* heart, and you, / you scorn me, you look askance, you attack the way I speak, / while you're out there eating mcdonald's in american discotheques, / and I couldn't even dance salsa in san juan, which i / can dance in my neighborhoods full of your customs." Or when Mariposa performed her signature poem, "Ode to a Diasporican," with its proverbial chorus, "No nací en Puerto Rico, / Puerto Rico nació en mí" ("I wasn't born in Puerto Rico, / Puerto Rico was born in me.") We felt like rock stars.

As I was to learn in the lively receptions that followed the readings, and in those joyous days spent in discussions on the Island, many of my new-found friends turned out to be the college-age children of return migrant families. They all seemed to share some version or other of the same familiar story of rejection and disillusionment on their arrival "home," along with a strong affective identification with the big-city life they had left behind in the United States. They felt marginalized by the Puerto Rico they encountered, yet at the same time entitled to assert themselves and take full part in the life of the society. Their ambivalence and divided loyalties were reminiscent to me of what I knew of expatriate communities, or even more interestingly, of the similarly marginalized and similarly self-assertive Nuyorican diaspora in New York. The way that they hung out together and shared a sense of group belonging in an often unaccepting environment made them seem like a diaspora, or actually a kind of reverse or return diaspora within the homeland society itself. We joked, and made up the term "Re-asporican." To me it was a startling twist on the questions of Latino identity and everything I had been studying and writing about for decades.

I also observed their interaction with friends and family who had never left the Island, and with their uneasy and bewildered teachers, parents, and other authority figures. I noticed that the "Re-asporicans" frequently found themselves confronting and challenging stubborn assumptions about all kinds of hard-set cultural values: what it means to be Puerto Rican, what is an acceptable language of public discourse, how to relate to one's blackness and African heritage, the traditional roles and life-choices of women, and a range of other pressing social issues. I also observed the responses of their peers and others who were at home on the Island, and it became clear to me that, as in Marielena's story, along with the disdain and fear the returnees typically evoked there was also an admiration and even emulation of their ways and ideas. The "stayees," "los nativos" as they were sometimes called, thought the Re-asporicans were cool and liked their style and way of looking at things. There was not only interesting cultural contact going on here, but the seeds of change, some covert and reluctant, some vocal and quite public.

Here, I thought, in this fascinating, highly charged collision of distinct but intertwined experiences, lies an important key to the future of this country, and of many countries and regions of the world. Some major social changes must already be underway, and many more in store, because of this intense intersection of transnational desires. Such a dynamic and suggestive zone of cultural contact is surely worth a closer look and some creative analysis.

* * *

In many parts of the world, return migrants and their children are bringing significant changes and challenges to home countries, and thereby altering the direction and impact of cultural and political flows that result from international migration and diasporic settlement. Whether it is Turkish or Spanish "guest workers" returning from long-term stays in Germany,

Japanese Brazilians moving "back" to Japan, Mexican immigrants in the United States taking active part in the civic life of their hometowns, or Dominicans shuttling between San Juan or New York and the Dominican Republic, returning emigrant nationals ("remigrants") of many countries bring cultural ideas and values acquired in diaspora settings to bear on their native lands or that of their forebears, often with boldly innovative and unsettling effect. While these and related social phenomena have received growing scholarly and journalistic attention in terms of political economy and global migration, most studies continue to focus strictly on money remittances and transnational community formation by way of civic activity, entrepreneurship, and institutional development.

What most gripped my attention, however, was what I have come to call "cultural remittances," that is, the ensemble of ideas, values, and expressive forms introduced into societies of origin by remigrants and their families as they return "home," sometimes for the first time, for temporary visits or permanent re-settlement, and as transmitted through the increasingly pervasive means of telecommunications. Thus, after years of studying, teaching, and writing about migration and the resultant cultural changes and continuities in receiving or host societies, I was now eager to explore a new and unknown side of the same phenomenon: the reverse flow or "counterstream" resulting from massive circular and return migration and the ongoing remittance of cultural values and practices through friends, relatives, and the media.

The history of Puerto Rican migration, community formation, and returning home provides an especially rich field for studying modern-day processes of transnational identity formation, trans-locality, circular migration, and diasporic communities, and will therefore serve as the primary and paradigmatic case in point in this book. In the Puerto Rican case it is possible to examine such processes as they unfold through several generations of social history and play out in highly charged political and cultural contexts. For over thirty years a diasporic, "Nuyorican" identity location has been staked out, and circular migration has become a prevalent mode of movement, Puerto Ricans thus anticipating by a decade or more experiences undergone by millions of transnational migrants around the world. The re-entry of thousands of Puerto Rican families, many of them born and raised in U.S. cities, has had an enormous though largely uncharted impact on the Island society, such that assumptions about the meaning of national culture itself, and intersecting issues of territory, citizenship, language, gender, race, political representation, and social class, are of necessity addressed in new ways.

This often unwitting and unintended cultural challenge—which I encapsulate with the term "the diaspora strikes back"—has a particular edge because it is lodged not by "foreigners" imposing their ways in accord with reigning systems of international power, but by "one's own," as it were, fellow Puerto Ricans who continue to claim full-scale membership in the national community but whose life-experience has had the effect of differentiating them from their Island-based compatriots in myriad ways. Contrary to their illusions and expectations, returning home has been a sobering moment for many Nuyoricans, causing them to feel like "strangers in the ethnic homeland" (the title of one book on return migration of Japanese Brazilians). They are outsiders and "others" whose presence all too often spurs resentment, ridicule and fear, and even disdain and social discrimination with clear racial and class undertones. Yet at the same time, their presence also elicits fascination, engagement, and change. With all of the ambiguities and complexities involved, and though difficult to measure with any precision, this highly charged cultural encounter has unquestionably had an unsettling and de-centering effect both on the remigrants themselves and on the cultural realities and assumptions in the home countries and regions.

The Puerto Rican case is of course idiosyncratic in some important ways, perhaps most of all because of the abiding colonial relationship under which its entire migratory movement and diaspora formation have transpired. The longevity, volume, and working-class composition of the migration and return migration are among the most salient consequences of this political and economic dependency, as is the intensity of its transnational and cross-cultural connections; perhaps most obviously, the U.S. citizenship status of all Puerto Ricans differentiates them from other Caribbean and Latino groups. Nevertheless, I would hold that rather than merely exceptional, and in some ways precisely because of its exceptional qualities, Puerto Ricans serve as an excellent focus by anchoring me in a paradigmatic and especially illuminating instance of transnational life and culture.

In thinking through my Mayagüez encounters and extending them with further study, I rapidly came across a wide array of congruent and contrastive experiences of co-ethnic "remigrants" and "cultural remittances" in other countries. Dominican and Mexican stories would appear to be closest to those of returning Puerto Ricans; while I do treat the Dominican experience here, the Mexican case, and the whole idea of Chicano culture haunting the traditional Mexican imaginary, while obviously of central concern for any consideration of U.S. Latino life, is so huge that it really requires a study in its own right. Other illuminating parallels can also be found among West Indians, African Americans returning to the south (as captured by Carol Stack in her book *Call to Home* (1996)), Filipinos and Koreans, Japanese Brazilians, and Turkish and southern European "guest workers." In reference to earlier stages in American immigration history, the largely overlooked drama of European return migration has also been addressed in more recent studies, as in Mark Wyman's *Round-Trip to America* (1993), and that of African Americans returning to Africa in James T. Campbell and David Levering Lewis's *Middle Passages* (2006).

But for the sake of focus, the Puerto Rican experience is the privileged example in this study, as is New York City the central diasporic location for that and so many other transnational communities historically and in our times. Of course no such case can be taken in isolation, so that to assure the generalizing power of my analysis I identified the Dominican and the Cuban experiences as offering the most promising lines of contrast and comparison. The Hispanic Caribbean, the three Spanish-speaking Antillean islands with huge, vibrant Caribbean Latino enclaves in the United States, are as closely linked in their common cultural heritage and regional location as they are distinct in their political status and migratory and diaspora histories. I refer to this tri-national focus of my analysis as "Caribbean Latinos," or to use the Spanish word, "*caribeños.*"

Combining as it does close family resemblances and sharp political divergences, the Caribbean Latino experience thus makes for an ideal testing ground for the study of transnational cultural flows and interactions. All three countries endured four centuries of Spanish colonial rule, which involved the virtual extermination of the indigenous Arawak populations and importation of millions of enslaved Africans. In differential ways, all demonstrate a troubled relation with that African heritage, and all have spent the past century under the direct and overweening sway of U.S. imperial power, which has included the formation of huge diasporas in North America. On the other hand, in addition to differing processes of national formation, their respective relations to their imposing northern neighbor exemplify the full gamut of modern-day political possibilities, from direct colony (Puerto Rico) to neo- or semi-colony (Dominican Republic) to tenuous breakaway from the imperial orbit via revolutionary socialism (Cuba). As a result, while the three diasporas bear many commonalities and intersections, making them almost seem like one pan-ethnic Caribbean Latino community in various historical periods, closer inspection shows them to make for very diverse historical realities. The same may be said for the processes of return migration and remittances, such that it is only by marking off those discrepancies that one can speak meaningfully, as I attempt to do, of a single "Caribbean Latino counterstream."

The longest-standing, most consistent and voluminous of the three migratory, diasporic, and return experiences is the Puerto Rican one, which is ample reason for allowing it a certain pride of place among the three instances. The Dominican case bears closest comparison with the Puerto Rican one over the past forty-some years, but that massive diasporic presence has been more recent and the cultural changes under study more abrupt, both differences attributable to the differing relations of colonial power at work. While the flow of cash remittances to the Dominican Republic has been far more abundant and that of challenging cultural transfers more abrupt and sharper, there has been far less migratory return, especially of a long-term or permanent kind.

The most anomalous of the three is of course the Cuban experience; demonstrating their compatibility within the analytical model I seek to develop will be the most obvious challenge to the validity of my argument. Historically, Cubans were the main protagonists of Spanish Caribbean exile in the nineteenth century, and shared close inter-diasporic connections with Puerto Ricans through the first half of the twentieth. But the 1959 revolution and its aftermath have meant the veering off of the Cuban community from the Puerto Rican and Dominican, and indeed an exceptional status within the larger "Latino" pan-ethnicity in recent generations. While the transfer of cash and other material goods has been ample and consequential and the ideological challenge posed by the exile community as extreme as can be, there has been virtually no return migration and resettlement in the homeland. Nevertheless, between many and meaningful temporary visits and incessant communication between diaspora and homeland locations, a cultural counterflow has definitely been evident all along and, as in the other two cases in point, has been a thorn in the side of the traditional homeland culture in terms of the reigning values, ideological perspectives and expressive means.

But the main reason for including Cuba and not, say, Mexico or Haiti or Panama, is not because of such direct commonalities, nor even its belonging to the Hispanic Caribbean family of national experiences. The idea is that if an analogous experience can be established in such a diametrically opposite situation, the line of analysis may then be applicable in a wider and more universal way. What I hope to show is that the "cultural remittances" entering and so consequentially affecting Cuba in our times stem not so much from a nationally defined and specified diaspora, but from broader Caribbean and Afro-Atlantic diasporic sources also influential in contemporary Puerto Rican and Dominican counterstreams. In other words, the process is indirect and oblique in the Cuban case, the diaspora and its cultural diffusion effectively disengaged from its explicitly national moorings and comprised of an already transnationalized mix of multiple cultural traditions.

* * *

The Caribbean Latino diaspora and its varied relations with the home countries and region is thus the geo-cultural location for my study. I attempt to characterize this space and its historical trajectory in chapter 3, and then ground it with narrated life-experience and creative expressions in the remainder of the book. Before arriving there, though, it is important to address the key theoretical issues of diaspora and cultural "return" and set forth my own understanding of these complex concepts and social processes. What is a diaspora? What is a "transnational community" and what is new about modern-day transnationalism as compared with earlier instances of local and global migrations and transformative cultural contacts? What can be said of cultural migrations between diasporas and homelands, and especially of the impact of return flows of people and their diaspora-forged cultural experiences and values?

I seek to address such and other related questions in chapters 1 and 2. In offering a critical review of previous scholarly and journalistic accounts, I was surprised to find myself bringing into dialogue two integrally tied but as yet relatively disconnected theoretical discourses; that is, I realized that the vast theoretical literature on diasporas and transnational communities rarely dealt directly with the phenomenon of migratory return or the impact of remittances, and that the equally expansive studies of return migration and even remittances bore little if any explicit relation to the comparatively newfound fields of diaspora and transnational studies. By implication I am proposing that the two discussions be brought into interaction with one another so as to arrive at a more coherent approach to contemporary transnational experience.

In addition to thus conjoining these two theoretical discussions, I also draw out my own points of emphasis so as to best set the stage for the evidence presented in the remainder of my study. My two main interventions have to do with the issues of power and of the cultural, both of which have in my view received inadequate attention in most theoretical reflections on diaspora and diasporic return. In thinking diaspora, we need to make clear which social sector of the home and host societies goes to comprise the given diaspora community, and what international power relations motivate and condition the diasporic formation. The phrase I take as the title of chapter 1, "thinking diaspora from below," signals my focus on working-class and economically based migratory movements and diasporas, and on colonially defined relations among home and host societies. The social and cultural worlds forged of such experience—which I refer to with the playful phrase "créolité in the hood"—is an expression of these structured relations of power, and therefore resist or at least go to qualify the idea of some generic diaspora reality. In different ways, all three *caribeño* diasporas exemplify these coordinates of transnational power, and the cultural goods moving between homeland and diaspora locations need to be understood as—to take the title of one pertinent book—"streams of cultural capital."

I have also found that previous study of these relations has tended to focus inordinately on political and economic, or more broadly sociological, aspects, and to treat the cultural dimensions in minimal or marginal ways. While motivations for migratory movement as well as the relative placement of migrant communities clearly have economic and political sources, it is in its cultural manifestations that diaspora life and return can be understood in its human, experiential qualities, and differentiated at more specific, idiosyncratic levels. I also argue that when scholarly writers do take up cultural considerations, they generally conceive of "culture" in limited and often individualistic terms of social behavior and attitudes. Likewise, they take a narrow view of "politics" as civic consciousness and participation. Issues of ideology and collective challenges to traditional values and social identities usually get short shrift when they are not totally absent, while the humanistic sense of culture having to do with creative expressions and styles has no role in the analysis. The vast literature on the ubiquitous contemporary phenomenon of remittances provides ample examples of these shortcomings.

It is in terms of power and the cultural that I introduce the concept of "cultural remittances," perhaps the guiding idea of my book. In doing so, I hope to expand on the term "social remittances" as developed by anthropologist Peggy Levitt in her book *The Transnational Villagers* (2001). Scholars have long been saying that it is not just money and financial capital that are transferred in the multiple cross-border transactions of today's society, but also values, ideas, beliefs and a host of other features of social life. Levitt did the welcome service of injecting this insight into the used and abused concept of "remittance," and thereby provided a handy term for a whole range of transnational studies. However, I contend that her theoretical innovation fails to live up to its potential because of the methodological and philosophical limitations of her notion of the cultural. In order to recognize that the non-monetary aspects of today's "remittances" may bear even greater consequences than the "cash transfers" to which most of that discussion is limited, and indeed to understand the potential deeper significance of all "transfers" emanating from diasporas, our notion of culture needs to embrace collective, ideological, as well as artistic meanings of the term.

* * *

With these theoretical and historical bearings in view, I then seek to ground my ideas by providing evidence in the form of personal life-stories and instances of expressive creativity. I think of the "Tales of Learning and Turning" that make up Part 2 as the heart of the book, the narrative fulcrum on which the more abstract and interpretive efforts turn. My commentaries included before and after the tales themselves ("Introducing the Tales" and "Reading the Tales") are intended to explain how they came into being, and what conclusions or insights I suggest might be gleaned from them as illustrations or illuminations of my main arguments and the social phenomena under study. The tales are based on interviews I conducted in a range of sites over several years since around 2000, and especially in 2006 and 2007. I have changed the names, arranged them chronologically (and alphabetically for ease of reference), and reorganized each tale so as to enhance its dramatic appeal and draw attention to those experiences most germane to the present study. The result is a rich and engaging tapestry of Caribbean Latino lives as real people from different walks and stations of life navigate the joys and challenges—the intensive "learning and turning"—of transnational cultural reality. In this context it is also intended to serve as an archive or database of evidence for the controversial theoretical and interpretive perspectives set forth in the remainder of the book.

Indeed, in Part 3 I make frequent cross-reference to the stories so as to connect and associate my reflections on poetic, musical, and artistic innovations with this qualitative experiential data. Some of the writers and performers who illustrate the "Style Transfers" of that part are also storytellers of "learning and turning" experiences, and I am therefore obliged (with their permission, of course) to blow their cover, as it were, and reveal their biographical identities. In chapters 5 and 6 and in the Coda, "Bring the Salsa," "Open Mic," and "Visual Crossings," respectively, Puerto Rican cultural history forms the point of departure and most fully substantiated case in point, in part because it is the longest-standing and in part because of my own greater familiarity with that experience. Clearly, I view the emergence and assertion of a "Nuyorican" field of group identity and creative expressivity in the later 1960s and early 1970s as the benchmark of the cultural ground-shift of central interest here. Nevertheless, it becomes evident that, despite the marked variations among them, Dominican and Cuban experiences may well bear even more radical implications for social and cultural change than the Puerto Rican case itself. In all three national instances, and in the pan-national regional framework, the Caribbean Latino cultural counterstream has the effect of de-centering national, ethnic, and racial identities, and of redefining the sources and catalysts of cultural innovation.

Though salsa and Nuyorican poetry, both from the 1960s and early 1970s, are my primary examples of "remitted" culture forms, it is hip hop, since its diffusion as of around 1990, that serves as the main conduit of cultural styles forged in the diaspora that then exert such a challenging and even subversive influence in contemporary Puerto Rico, Dominican Republic and Cuba. That diffusion has of course been global in scope, and the presence of hip hop in the Caribbean is obviously part of a broader transnationalizing process. One difference, however, is that in the Caribbean Latino case the bearers of that traveling stylistic modality are themselves ethnic diasporans from those very nations, and many stem from the very social location and context in which hip hop originated; some of them, in fact, especially in the Puerto Rican case, were among the actual creators of hip hop from the beginning.

Furthermore, it is becoming ever clearer that hip hop is the stylistic current most closely identifiable with contemporary globalization. It is perhaps the aesthetic remittance par excellence because it emerged just when financial remittances became the most visible, tangible manifestation of transnational social relations in our times. Thus, in addition to being the uncontested lingua franca for youth cultures all over the world, it is also serving as the main vehicle for cultural solidarity and contestation. Its eminently subversive role, the assertion of which might seem counterintuitive and even questionable when limited to the U.S. context, is blatantly evident when transferred to other national and regional cultural realities. Though the commercialized, domesticated and ideologically venomous qualities most familiar in the U.S. setting do of course spill over to the close neighbors in the Caribbean, the radical democratic impulse that characterized hip hop in its inner-city beginnings still infuses much hip hop in the Puerto Rican, Dominican, and most of all in the Cuban context.

* * *

I have arranged the three parts of this book in a sequence that makes most sense to me. I have placed first a definition of terms, an extended theoretical reflection about diasporas and cultural return, along with a discussion of the cultural history of the Caribbean Latino transnational space and cultural "counterstream." This more abstract and reflective exposition is then given personal and narrative substance, or experientially "grounded," with representative life-stories with which any reader anywhere can identify. And then in the last part, building on that theoretical and ethnographic foundation, I interpret new cultural traditions and practices. Cultural remittances from below, as elaborated conceptually and as narrated in the oral histories of those who live them, take the form of stylistic transfers capable of exerting an innovative and catalytic influence on the course of national and regional histories. They illustrate in a cogent way how the cultural dimension of human experience can involve remarkable agency and power, and often embody profound lessons in democratic and cosmopolitan values and social practice.

Little did Marielena or my friends in Mayagüez know that their "Re-asporican" stories would open up a whole new world to me. Thanks to them I have been able to develop an extensive network of helpful and generous people whose life-stories give me confidence in the tenability of my ideas, however controversial, and in whose very personal, unique experiences I recognized patterns and interfaces with those of countless others that I encountered directly, by word of mouth, or in my research. Of course there were many others whose views or life-experiences diverged from those patterns, or even contradicted them, people who fit neatly into the home society on their return, or whose presence or "remittances" go to reinforce the status quo there more than to challenge or unsettle it. But I believe that the lives I describe, while sadly understudied, are actually much more common in today's transnational reality, where the working poor far outnumber the more privileged migrants, exiles, and returnees, both at home and abroad. It is to these remigrants, starting with the twenty-two who have shared their life-stories, that I dedicate my book.

PART 1:
CONCEPTUAL BEARINGS

**Wall graffiti in Barrio La Cuarta,
Ponce, Puerto Rico, 2005.**

Photographer José Irizarry. Permission
José Irizarry.

1 THINKING DIASPORA FROM BELOW

Lines of Definition

Diaspora has the ring of antiquity, yet the term is a favored keyword of contemporary social theory and public discourse. The word conjures up images of the exodus of the ancient Jews and the scattering of Africans with the Middle Passage, but modern diasporas are transnational communities of the most unprecedented kind. The age-old idea holds a place of privilege in the fashionable vocabulary of globalization, border theory, and post-colonialism. While attempts to define and delimit diaspora abound, consensus has been elusive at best. Until the present generation, the "ideal types" and virtually exclusive referents were the Jewish and the African diasporas, and even the latter usage, as pertinent as it is to reflections on modernity, is of surprisingly recent vintage.[1] But nowadays, as of around 1990, anything can be a diaspora, from a food club to a graduating class to a far-flung viewing audience, such that only the minimal sense of dislocation or displacement, as suggested in the etymological metaphor of scattering or sowing seeds (*-sperien*) across space (*dia-*), seems to circumscribe in any way this sprawling and variegated semantic field. Appropriately, there has also been contestation over the very relativism and indeterminacy of such displaced, scattered usages.

The reason the idea of diaspora has so fired the contemporary critical imagination is surely that it is about movement, travel, change on the basis of contact, interaction, and the transfer of context and concept. The ancient origin of the word serves as an abiding reminder that these have been human experiences from time immemorial. But its current appeal and multiple meanings attest to massive demographic movement and resettlement at an unprecedented scope and scale, and the need to elaborate names and concepts with which to organize our knowledge of those new conditions.

Rather than defining and demarcating diaspora per se, or enumerating necessary traits or preconditions, the most fruitful way of getting a theoretical handle on diaspora is to suggest taxonomies and periodizations, with a special interest in "new" or "global" formations of more recent times. What were the primary motives for departure and dispersal? Which sectors of society felt impelled to pick up and leave? What were the circumstances of their geographical movement? How long have they been in their new location and under what conditions have they been living? What relation do they maintain with their personal or ancestral homeland? How do they identify themselves relative to where they are, where they came from, and where they are going? Such are the questions that surface immediately upon approaching any specific diaspora, and invoke some key insights on the subject. Instead of aiming to state what diasporas are, more fruitful lines of inquiry are directed at determining how they are, where they are in time and place, and what sets of relations condition their existence.

One such new understanding is that diasporas are not about fixed states of social being but about process—what is clumsily but usefully called diasporization, that is, how diaporas come into being and develop over time. The life of any given diaspora starts not with the arrival of people to the host setting, but only when the group has begun to develop a consciousness about its new social location, a disposition toward its place of origin, as well as some relation to other sites within the full diasporic formation. It takes time to emerge, and time brings changes, such that what was true of a diaspora at one point and place in its history may not hold for a later stage or different location within the overall experience. In this respect generational differentiations are of central interest, in terms of both individual lifespan and longevity of collective presence in the diasporic setting.

Another guiding notion is that understanding a diaspora is about looking at that group relationally, rather than in isolation and strictly in its own terms. That is, we need to analyze its existence vis-à-vis the home country or region, the new or host setting, as well as in view of its own internal complexity and contradictions. While diaspora has been seen as "a naming of the other," studying any specific diaspora involves a naming of what is other than that diaspora, what is non-diaspora in the sense of communities whose realities are defined not only by the fact of displacement but by long-term native residence in homeland or host society, or by assimilation. Yet diasporic relations are not only external in this way, but also internal, in regard to the crosscutting hierarchies of class, gender, racializing influences, and other determinations.

Further, modern diasporas and diasporic identities are not singular and exclusive, nor limited to a group or individual sense of social placement. Rather, individuals or groups may pertain to several, often intertwining and sometimes even contending diasporic formations at once, a phenomenon variously referred to as "overlapping diasporas" or a "diaspora of a diaspora."[2] Such is the case, for example, of "Dominican Yorks," Dominicans living in New York City, who belong at once to African, Caribbean, Dominican, and, a bit more controversially, to "Latino" diasporas. Thus even the familiar axes of home and host, sending and receiving, departure and arrival and return are immensely complicated and nuanced under present conditions of transnational mobility and flexible citizenship. Diasporas do not correspond to neatly circumscribed social units but tend to be messy and ragged at the edges.

A further key insight, and here the ideas of Stuart Hall and Arjun Appadurai have been of seminal importance,[3] is that the cultural experience of diasporas is shaped by the dialectic of continuity and change, tradition and disjuncture, the extension and prolongation of inherited cultural backgrounds on the one hand, and ruptures and innovations stemming from life in the new setting on the other. In much thinking about diaspora, undue emphasis tends to be placed on one or the other of these paired processes, either on continuity and tradition or on change and disjuncture, such that the resulting analysis suffers from either a primordialist or an integrationist cast. Both of these misrepresentations run askew of the complex, multi-directional dynamic specific to diaspora cultural experience. Terms like hybridity, transculturation or creolization typically figure in this theoretical balancing act and help to navigate the slippery interpretive terrain of transnational cultural interaction.

Again, it is essential to specify context and contingency when considering these guiding premises. To talk persuasively about diaspora one must identify when and where. That is, at what stage in the historical experience of home and host societies, and of their relations, and more broadly in the course of international history, did the diasporization process set in and unfold? Aside from geographical and historical context, specificity also entails location within the taxonomy of possible diasporas. The plural is important in this regard, since theoretical reflections on diaspora characteristically include the delineation of types or kinds, generally marked off according to the primary motivation behind the departure from the homeland, and conditions of subsequent displacement or dispersal. Perhaps the most elaborated of such typologies is that of Robin Cohen in his overview, *Global Diasporas* (1997), where differentiations are drawn between "victim diasporas" (Jewish, African and Armenian), "labour and imperial diasporas" (Indian and British), "trade diasporas" (Chinese and Lebanese), and "cultural diasporas" (Caribbean), among others.[4] Another common mark of differentiation is the individual or group composition of the resettling population, such that the founding issue of the journal *Diaspora* in 1991 refers to diasporas formed differentially of and by immigrants, expatriates, refugees, guest-workers, exiles, and "overseas and ethnic communities." Such demarcations, according to the editor of that influential publication, Khachig Tölölyan, go to comprise the "semantic domain" of diasporas, "the vocabulary of transnationalism."[5]

As helpful as such classifications are for sorting out the polysemous phenomenon of diasporas, checklists of traits or defining motives tend to be like apples and oranges. Looking at Cohen's groupings, for instance, aren't "labour" and "imperial" too often polar opposites of one another to be grouped together? Aren't "labour" often also "victim" diasporas, and "imperial" often also "trade" diasporas? Aren't they all, as well as the sorely missing category of "religious" diasporas, also "cultural diasporas" in many ways? Further, as for Tölölyan's catalogue of displaced persons, isn't there a risk that diaspora formation then becomes synonymous with migration per se, or with "travel" (in James Clifford's language), the term thereby losing all uniqueness and specificity?

Enumerating types of diasporas, then, though a necessary and generally helpful exercise, can only compound the elusiveness of the concept if not qualified by further distinctions. Nevertheless, although his engaging and often cited essay "Diasporas" stretches the idea to the limits of its implicit relativism, it is Clifford who points a way out of the taxonomical quagmire. A different approach to definition by checklist, he suggests, "would be to define the field diacritically. Rather than locating essential features, we might focus on diaspora's borders, what it defines itself against . . . . Diasporas are caught up with and defined against (1) the norms of nation-states and (2) indigenous, and especially autochthonous, claims by 'tribal' peoples."[6] In other words, whatever diasporas are, they are decidedly not forged in obedience to the anti-cosmopolitan, assimilationist ideological claims of nation-states, nor is their constitutive claim that they were "here all along." Over against these conceptual and experiential "borders," diasporas are by definition trans-national, resisting both the jurisdictional confines of the nationally bounded polity and the territorial rootedness to a single location.

Prisms of Power

Both of these important conceptual demarcations indicate that diaspora exists in relation to power, whether national or international, whether primarily political or economic. The varied motivations for geographical displacement, and the diverse constituents of the given diasporic population, may all be ranged according to whether the diaspora formation in question occurred as a wielding of social power or the subjection to it. Furthermore, since the act of displacement intrinsic to diasporic experience is typically (even if not axiomatically) attributable to conditions of oppression and violence, diaspora most commonly connotes subordination and marginalization rather than collective or individual empowerment. Indeed, Clifford conceives of diaspora so centrally in terms of disempowerment, or what he refers to as "common historical experiences of dispossession, displacement, [and] adaptation," that he actually identifies "significant areas of overlap" between diasporas and indigenous communities. Interestingly, though he had appeared to draw the two in stark contrast, when factoring in the dimension of social power Clifford recognizes diasporic dimensions to tribal alliances and visions at a national and international level.[7]

Thus the migratory movement that initiates diaspora formation, as well as the continued tie to homeland which marks off diaspora from immigrant or exile experience more generally, both stem from the asymmetries of transnational power rather than from transnationalism per se. The combination of being "from elsewhere" and being socially disadvantaged in the new setting conspire to challenge the hegemonies engendered by these asymmetries, and to devise alternative lines of communication and community as forms of conscious or unconscious resistance. The understanding of diasporas in their discrete particularity as well as comparatively presupposes a diagnosis of social power both in its international sense, that is, as exerted among and between national economies and states, and within each of the sites of diasporic presence. Where do the sending or home society and the receiving or host country stand relative to the wealth and power of the world's nations? Where does the diaspora constituency stand in the structures of domination prevailing in each of the societies within its migratory orbit? The range of permutations is wide, from relatively empowered countries or regions spinning off some fraction of its privileged or its working classes, to impoverished societies being drained of some of their budding elite or casting off some portion of their redundant poor. When thus viewed through the prism of power, diasporas exemplify these options and every configuration in between, the extreme on one end being imperializing settlers from rich lands, and on the other the settling of persecuted refugees and unskilled laborers from the colonies and post-colonies. But in any and all cases it is the interplay of local, national, and international domination that should most appropriately and effectively serve as the touchstone for classifying and comparing diverse instances of diaspora experience.

By power is meant, first and foremost, economic and political power, the sheer financial wherewithal and governmental–military might required to propel masses of people into geographical movement and then keep them far from their place of origin no matter how deeply they might miss it and hope to return. Such is the basic, constitutive force underlying the overwhelming majority of today's diasporas, which in spite of all divergence from the Jewish and African prototypes remain fundamentally "victim diasporas." But in order to sustain the gravitational pull of large-scale migration and the magnetic force field that retains people in this ambivalent, insider-outsider status, effective ideological and cultural suasion is of course indispensable as well. The social imaginary of the migratory destination and new diasporic abodes must be made attractive enough to draw and retain people, but not that attractive that they might fashion themselves, however imaginatively, as internal or native to those adopted locations. When the basic lines of the reigning political economy are sufficiently normalized and taken for granted, as under the present globalized regime, the role of ideology and culture becomes central in the creation and perpetuation of diasporic conditions. It is perhaps for that reason that Robin Cohen's historical survey of "global diasporas" culminates in "cultural diasporas" as that kind of transnational formation most representative of contemporary social realities on a world scale. The example of Afro-Caribbean peoples migrating en masse and settling in diverse urban sites in the United States, Canada, Britain and elsewhere serves to illustrate in a paradigmatic way what the experience of diaspora is most representatively about in the present historical era.

In light of these explanations for the present-day currency of the diaspora concept, new and alternative forms of classification and typology suggest themselves that correspond to location within the global cultural economy and in relation to the social identities forged out of diasporic life. For instance, it is crucial to differentiate along class lines, however roughly, and to distinguish between what we might call "diasporas of privilege" and "diasporas of deprivation." Though they are all diasporas, it is not the same thing to be considering, on the one hand, those comprised mainly of professionals, entrepreneurs, and endowed political exiles whose transnational experience is aimed at or results in an increased accumulation of cultural capital, and on the other hand the more widespread and numerous communities formed of labor migrations and impoverished refugees.

Related to such differentiation according to relative advantage or empowerment at an international level would be a sense of diasporas ranged along other axes of power. Most evidently, there are those forged out of colonial or semi-colonial or post-colonial relations in contrast to those commonly referred to as "trade" or "imperial" diasporas, where the colonial asymmetries cut in the other direction. Congruent with this kind of contrast would be such constellations as "racial" or racialized diasporas, where racial oppression and identity formation play a key role in the entire formative process, from motives for dispersal to social position within the host society. A further delineation, both among and within diasporas, would be what we might call "gender(ed)" and "sexual(ized)" diasporas, the latter sometimes colloquially referred to as "sexile," where women's or homosexual experiences account for important dimensions of the diasporic reality. Finally, with regard to the sheer range or span of unifying identities which go to constitute varied diaspora formations, we might mark off "civilizational," "regional," "pan-ethnic," and "ethnonational" communities, as exemplified by the African, Caribbean, Latino, and Dominican diasporas respectively. It bears repeating, of course, that as was true of other classificatory schemas, most historical diasporas fit into many of these categories at the same time, the advantage of this alternative taxonomy being that the types are more directly in line with modern-day social conceptualizations and structured relations of power.

What's New about "New Diasporas"?

The newfound interest in and study of diasporas, and the virtual re-coining of the word for modern-day usage, clearly corresponds to the emergence of economic and political conditions that generate the unprecedented proliferation of this kind of social formation. While African diaspora studies (by that name) may be traced to the 1960s, the explosion of diaspora-speak came as recently as the early 1990s, coinciding with the ascendancy of postcolonial theorizing and the ubiquity of the term "globalization" in modern-day public and academic parlance. But probably the closest terminological accompaniment to diaspora in its renewed use is transnationalism, to the point where the "new diasporas" are commonly referred to as "transnational diasporas." The immediate caveat of course is that diasporas are and always have been, by definition, transnational—without transnational relations and demographic movement there would be no such thing. It is also clear and warrants emphasis that transnationalism is really nothing new but has characterized regional and world relations in many prior periods of social history.

In discussing immigration to New York City, for example, Nancy Foner entitles an article (published in *Diaspora* (1997)) "What's New About Transnationalism?," and begins, "Transnationalism is not new, even though it often seems as if it were invented yesterday . . . . While there are new dynamics to immigrants' transnational connections and communities today, there are also significant continuities with the past." Yet Foner herself, while highlighting cogently the many continuities and thereby effectively helping deflate the hype about the presumed novelty of today's conditions, is equally effective in identifying the "new dynamics," that is, "just what is new about the patterns and processes involved in transnational ties today."[8]

The same caution, and the same balance between precedence and innovation, is called for in thinking about diasporas. At times it is the thinking that is new, more so than the social phenomenon itself. For example, Paul Gilroy's *The Black Atlantic* (1993), the most cited book of all on the subject of diasporas, ranges widely historically, and delves deep into the past. Yet it is clear that Gilroy is thinking about the African and other diasporas in a new way, his analysis and vocabulary bearing the strong imprint of British and African American cultural studies of that period. But one can also speak of "new diasporas," the title of an important book (1998) by Nicholas Van Hear which is in some ways a sequel to Cohen's *Global Diasporas* (1997) in that it picks up where Cohen leaves off (and is even the follow-up entry in the same book series). Identifying the "new" period as the end of the Cold War, as of the later 1980s, Van Hear describes the many unprecedented features of contemporary migration patterns and densities as they issue from revolutionary developments in communications technology and transportation facilities unimagined in earlier historical periods. These sweeping changes,

along with the loosening of some demographic constraints and the ideological instabilities resulting for the post-Cold War impasse, have unleashed
major migration flows, and what he terms "migration crises," in many parts
of the world. It is out of this cauldron of rapid and extreme shifts in the
present configuration of world power that Van Hear sees the emergence of
"new diasporas."

What most emphatically marks off "new diasporas" when compared with
those of earlier periods is the intensity and reciprocity of the ties between
emigrant or exiled populations and their countries of origin. Transnational
connections have always been a defining part of diaspora existence, so much
so that in his seminal article "Diasporas in Modern Society" featured in the
inaugural issue of *Diaspora* (1991), William Safran offers six conditions
for the existence of a diaspora and all of them have to do with the relation
to the homeland.[9] But that relation has grown so much in its variety, depth
and range that Van Hear, for one, frequently has recourse to another term,
"transnational community." He considers that term more inclusive than
diaspora and more closely in accord with today's "new" patterns of transnational formation and of ever more unified fields incorporating homeland
and life in the host society or societies. While earlier concepts stressed "myths"
of homelands and "long-distance nationalism" sustained by communication
and cash remittances to families, the "new" situation capsulated in the phrase
"transnational community" evidences the near collapse of the social distance
between the two poles of diasporic life and the merging of homeland and
host land into a single arena of social action and determination.[10] Notably,
Van Hear characterizes the present demographic and structural remapping
in terms which are of direct relevance to the lines of analysis which I develop
in this book. "[I]f diaspora formation has accelerated in recent times," Van
Hear suggests, "so too has the unmaking of diasporas, seen in the *regrouping*
or *in-gathering* of migrant communities of dispersed ethnic groups. Like the
formation of diaspora, these regroupings may involve voluntary or involuntary movements of people back to their place of origin. . . ."[11]

Accepted notions of diaspora, formulated in earlier times and with earlier
social processes in view, are now being subjected to considerable revision with
the emergence of alternative or even contrary tendencies in the nature of translocal social arrangements. For Alejandro Portes, "transnational communities
are in a sense labor's analog to the multinational corporation," traversing
and transgressing national boundaries to such a degree and in so many ways
as to "shake up" social hierarchies in all locations of diasporic presence,
including both host country and home society. "The rise of transnational
communities," claims Portes (and he does not even use the word diaspora)
"represents the most novel facet of contemporary immigration," forcing the

birth of new notions of citizenship and community. As a result, contemporary social analysis is dedicated in significant ways to tracking what Portes calls the "social aftershocks of the transnational metamorphosis."[12] It is clear that the vantage point of such analysis must itself be multi-local, as well as highly sensitive to the play of power across national borders and traditional class and political hierarchies.

It is telling that in spite of Portes' striking phrase identifying the new diaspora configurations as "labor's analog," his and most other work on transnational connections and transactions have to do with entrepreneurial and electoral successes rather than with more organic working-class or subaltern struggles. Story after story in the research literature relates the impressive achievements of immigrants in their upward mobility, and their taking advantage of economic and political asymmetries so as to assume elite or privileged status in their home countries. Conversely they are also seen to use their homeland's resources to gain footholds in the host society. What had appeared a "from below" perspective of resistance to transnational hegemony turns out to be a documentation of real or potential success stories in tune with the imbalances of global and national power.

A somewhat extreme but symptomatic case is Yossi Shain, who in his book *Marketing the American Creed Abroad: Diasporas in the U.S. and Their Homelands* (1999) portrays the influence of Mexicans and other diaspora ethnicities as operating basically in tandem with imperial ideological agendas. It is significant that in making his case Shain refers approvingly to work by Roger Rouse, Robert Smith, Portes, Nancy Foner, Luis Guarnizo and many other researchers and commentators whose work is generally informed by internationalist and democratic orientations, but who nonetheless tend to view the nature of diaspora-homeland-hostland relations in similar terms and tones. With all the wide variety of emphasis and cases in point, the tenor tends for the most part to be one of triumph against the odds, and potential conciliation between nations and communities. Frequently, the talk is about what Portes calls "transnational entrepreneurs," who may be "labor's analog to the multinational corporation" in terms of their status at the time of arrival but whose entire trajectory within the diaspora is one of economic ascendancy in accord with the terms and social ethic set by those very multinational corporations. Indeed, in some accounts "transnational practices" are equated with, and reduced to, what is called "transnational entrepeneurship."[13] As Portes puts it when asking what engenders today's transnational communities: "it is the social and economic forces unleashed by contemporary capitalism—many of the same ones, in fact, that allow corporations to move manufacturing plants from one country to another."[14]

Views from Below

Transnationalism from below, grassroots globalization, vernacular cosmopolitanism—these are some kindred phrases now in circulation in public discussions of contemporary social and cultural dynamics that suggest a class-differentiated and dichotomized understanding of these larger-than-life processes more often viewed as monolithic. That is, there is countervailing pressure to the globalizing, transnationalizing forces driven by hegemonic economic and political power and its monopolistic command of technology. According to terms like "from below," "grassroots," and "vernacular," there is also a common person's and quotidian experience of that same engulfing world structure and a new sense of social agency that is on the ground— lived by people and communities with no proprietary stake in systems of power and command.

A major scholarly contribution to this alternative idea of globalization and modern-day transnational communities is the book of that title, *Transnationalism from Below* (1998), edited by Michael Peter Smith and Luis Eduardo Guarnizo. The editors and included authors seek to ground the discussion of transnationalism in the everyday social practices of working-class "transmigrants" (the term here for diasporans), their negotiation of life in multiple locations and variegated systems of political and economic power. Again, many if not most of the contributions point to successes at grassroots entrepeneurship as the most striking instances of working the transnational system, yet the intellectual agenda of the book is defined by the metaphor of vertical differentiation, "from below," and described in cautious but unequivocal terms: "Identities forged 'from below' are not inherently subversive or counter-hegemonic. Yet they are different from hegemonic identities imposed from above. The process of subaltern identity formation is a process of constant struggle—a struggle in which discursive communities produce narratives of belonging, resistance, or escape."[15] The editors make it clear that the identity politics of greatest interest to them are those articulated in the context of transnational grassroots movements, collective social practices that "may reduce power asymmetries based on gender and race, and even promote solidarity based on these dimensions. . . ."

With varying inflections, the ideas of "grassroots globalization" as set forth by Arjun Appadurai, James Clifford's "discrepant cosmopolitanisms," and "vernacular cosmopolitanism" as defined by Stuart Hall, Homi Bhabha and others correspond with the "from below" perspective and indicate the need for a differentiation in the analysis of diaspora and transnational community along lines of class, status, and cultural capital.[16] The first of these, "grassroots globalization," calls attention to the non-hegemonic role of NGOs and what Appadurai calls "the research imagination," as a widespread globalizing effort. The concept of "vernacular cosmopolitanism" as set forth by Homi Bhabha,

Stuart Hall and others argues that "vernacular ethnic rootedness does not negate openness to cultural differences or the fostering of a universalist civic consciousness and a sense of moral responsibility beyond the local."[17] Both formulations lend themselves to a critical understanding of the "triadic trans-local relation . . . that links transmigrants, the localities to which they migrate, and their locality of origin." The grassroots, vernacular, "from below" approach helps to point up the many diaspora experiences that diverge from those of the relatively privileged, entrepeneurial or professional transnational connections that have tended to carry the greatest appeal in scholarly and journalistic coverage. That approach, guided by a concern for subaltern and everyday life struggles of poor and disenfranchised people, also allows for special insights into ongoing issues of racial identity and gender inequalities that are so often ignored or minimized in the grand narratives of transnational hegemony.

But even with this class-sensitive orientation toward transnational relations, there are two further aspects of diasporic realities that tend to get overlooked or slighted: that of culture, and that of generation in the sense of age. Two excellent essays in the *Transnationalism from Below* collection provide valuable examples of these theoretical and analytical gaps. In his included article "Transnational Localities," and more extensively in his book *Mexican New York* (2005), Robert C. Smith provides his often-cited case study of the intricate transnational activities of working-class Mexicans in the swelling diaspora of New York City and in their places of origin in the Mexican state of Puebla. Extending on the pioneering ethnographic work of Roger Rouse and cited as a paradigmatic example by Alejandro Portes in his influential discussion of transmigrant life, Smith's close-up observation and penetrating analysis of cross-local political and civic activism, and especially the intensive involvement of diasporic "Mexyorks" in public works projects in the tiny fictitious town of "Ticuani," has been an eye-opener even for the most imaginative theorists of transnational relations. Smith also takes up issues of gender and provides interesting commentary about racial attitudes as they move between the two sites of this vibrant transnational geography.

Despite the rich and wide-ranging consideration of the bi-local "Ticuani" experience, however, there is disappointingly little regard for its cultural dimensions, that is, for changing definitions of national and ethnic identity, ideological considerations of race, gender, and sexuality, and the impact of diasporic life on the forms of cultural expression representative of the community. How much more would the reader learn by also knowing about these aspects of the Mexico–New York transnational nexus, that is, how the group experience in the New York City setting is affecting those ethical and aesthetic values and the way that the "Ticuanis" understand what it means to be Mexican, or Poblano, or "Ticuani," in view of the re-territorialization of the entire group and its traditions.

Some sense of that added analytical interest of diaspora's cultural dimension is evident in another engaging contribution to the *Transnationalism from Below* collection, the essay "Belizean 'Boyz 'n the Hood'" by Linda Miller Mattehi and David A. Smith. Subtitled "Garifuna Labor Migration and Transnational Identity," this ethnographically based study introduces us to the transnational world of the Belizean community in Los Angeles and in Belize City, and particularly the criminal gang activity of Garifuna youth and its chilling impact on the home society when they are deported. The focus on youth allows access to aspects of transnational life not represented in Smith's discussion of Mexican New York, and provides a far less sanguine view of the changes wrought on transmigrant experience at the hands of hegemonic globalization. Here again, though, the cultural dimension gets short shrift, in the form of the voices of the "boyz" themselves and their relation to their African American and Chicano counterparts, as well as in other respects. The political economy of the experience is presented well and in historical depth, but the reader is left with the impression that something is "done to" these unknowing youths, and that they in turn "do something to" the unwitting and helpless home society in Belize. Greater attention to the dynamics of urban youth culture would surely enliven the motivations and self-definitions of the young protagonists of these events, and counteract in some important ways the criminalizing tenor of much of the narration and recounted public opinion. Clearly there are other sides and consequences to this eerie story of ruinous diasporic invasion, a story that in fact is endemic to public attitudes toward youth whose values were supposedly corrupted and corroded in the urban diaspora settings where they grew up.

"Créolité in the Hood"

Since the advent of transnational studies the analysis of diasporas entails, more than ever before, cultural interpretation. In the words of the "manifesto" in the inaugural issue of the journal *Diaspora*, it "must pursue, in texts literary and visual, canonical and vernacular, indeed in all cultural productions and throughout history, the traces of struggles over and contradictions within ideals and practices of collective identity, of homeland and nation."[18] Robin Cohen in *Global Diasporas* goes so far as to classify today's "new diasporas," in distinction to earlier trade, victim, labor, imperial and other modes of transnational life, as "cultural diasporas." In this most contemporary kind of diaspora, the multiple forms and trajectories of translocal cultural movement become the core of diasporic reality and the benchmark of all differentiation and specification among diverse transnational communities.

Cohen also maintains that the cultural changes and interactions characteristic of diaspora life and its transnational impact are most saliently present among the youth, whose very lives center on the transculturation and hybridization of new identities resulting from trans- and cross-national social practice. Cohen highlights this reciprocity between the focus on culture and the centrality of youth by citing his collaborator Steven Vertovec, who points to some of those very aspects of diaspora experience that have gone unheeded in much previous work on the subject:

> Aesthetic styles, identifications and affinities, dispositions and behaviours, musical genres, linguistic patterns, moralities, religious practices and other cultural phenomena are more globalized, cosmopolitan and creolized or "hybrid" than ever before. This is especially the case among youth of transnational communities, whose initial socialization has taken place within the cross-currents of more than one cultural field, and whose ongoing forms of cultural expression and identity are often self-consciously selected, synchronized and elaborated from more than one cultural heritage.[19]

It is thus precisely the "boyz [and girlz] in the hood," young people in today's urban diasporas, who need to be centered in analyses of contemporary transnational communities. The inner-city reference to "the hood" serves as an indicator of class position, racialized marginality, and relative subalternity. Clearly, it is the cultural expressions and identity politics developed and articulated by diasporic youth that are of special interest in contemporary diaspora studies.

The word "creole" or "creolized" often surfaces in discussions of this cultural world of the new diasporas. Interestingly, it is a word, and a process, traditionally used to refer to the Caribbean region and its syncretistic cultural formation out of the mix of African, European, indigenous, and other civilizational lineages. As mentioned, Robin Cohen in his typological overview considers as prototypical of the new, transnational diasporas those comprised of Caribbean peoples settling in the urban centers of the U.S., England, France, Canada, and other enclave sites. In a highly instructive (and little-known) autobiographical essay by Stuart Hall, "Creolization, Diaspora, and Hybridity in the Context of Globalization," (2002) the idea of creole or creolized culture is cautiously dislodged from its very Caribbean and classical African-diasporic geographical and historical specificity, and its often narrowly linguistic denotations, and inserted into the contemporary, postcolonial context of massive transnationalized and globalized social relations.

Speaking as a member of the post-war black diaspora in Britain, Hall proposes a parallel between the histories of diasporas and of creolization. He contends that, just as there are two models or stages in the history of diaspora formations—first those of the "classical" Jewish and African exoduses and in recent times those resulting from modern migratory movements—so there are also two historically differentiated moments of creolization, one during the cultural formation of the Caribbean region and the other with the diasporic movement of Caribbeans (and others) to colonial and postcolonial metropoles. As Hall puts it, the experience of "the new communities from the postcolonial world who have migrated to the center of the metropolises of the West . . . has given new conceptual life to the concept of 'diaspora'."[20] The millions of people of African descent who, like Hall himself, have come to live in new diaspora settings, are in his words "twice diasporized," and, he might add, twice creolized as well. Hall shows how the terms "diaspora" and "creole" have become deeply and mutually imbricated as descriptions of contemporary cultural life on a global scale.

The idea of creolization and "le créole," then, for centuries referentially rooted in the English and French Caribbean, has by now become a global discourse, a way of naming the kind of cultural fusion and hybridization typical of highly diasporic urban settings in the metropoles.[21] Orlando Patterson, among others, devotes a good deal of his bold remapping of world regions to his notion of "cosmopolitan creolization," mentioning by way of examples "the creation of wholly new cultural forms in the trans-national space, such as 'New Yorican' and Miami Spanish."[22] The Martinican poet and cultural theorist Edouard Glissant, though his notion of *créole* is still primarily directed at the African diaspora, provides a rich and nuanced conceptual apparatus for understanding transnational cultural interactions. His intriguing coinages like "détour-rétour," diversion-reversion, and "points of (historical) entanglement" are easily applied to the new forms of creolization resulting from modern-day migrations and settlement.[23]

The word creolization, though, despite its historically and regionally embedded usage and its salutary emphasis on process rather than state of being, is a rather unwieldy one, and is perhaps overloaded with cultural specificity. The less familiar term "créolité," on the other hand, is decidedly less so on both counts. It not only rolls off the tongue in a more compact and graceful way, but it is actually a neologism of our times, having emerged in the 1980s as a step beyond the overly essentialist negritude movement of an earlier generation and the assimilationist tendency of the Francophile heritage descending from Aimé Césaire and others. In the hands of the "créolistes," the rambunctious Martinican writers Patrick Chamoiseaux, Raphael Constant, and Jean Bernabé who took their lead from Glissant, *créolité* comes to be characterized as an "annihilation of fake universality, of monolinguism, and of purity" (*La créolité est une annihilation de la fausse universalité, du monolinguisme et de la pureté*). Though specifically directed against the continuing dominance of French culture and language in the Antilles, this programmatic orientation as set forth in their highly publicized manifesto *In Praise of Créolité (Eloge a la Créolité, 1989)* brings the *créolistes* directly in line with the general thrust of vernacular cosmopolitanism and other efforts to emphasize the local, the particular, and the "mixed" in the face of universalizing and homogenizing globalization.[24]

Créolité, then, and so as to emphasize geographical and social location, "créolité in the hood"—such is the playful, perhaps somewhat jarring phrase that has occurred to me as a suggestive formula for approaching some of the more striking cultural realities of the new, transnational diasporas. *Créolité* situates the reference in the Caribbean without affixing it to that unique space, adapts a long-standing cultural discourse to contemporary conditions, and centers the interpretive focus on culture and language (in the broad sense) and their insistence on particularity. Furthermore, because the creolizing process has traditionally had central reference to African cultural groundings and to the saliency of blackness, this guiding theoretical concept, more so than alternatives like transculturation, mestizaje or syncretism, lends due attention to the dimension of race and racial identity. The notion of *créolité* makes it clear that the universalizing tendency of hegemonic transnationalism "from above," whether in its Francophile or any other guise, is ultimately deeply racist and colonialist, the beneficiary as it were of the reigning asymmetries in the global cultural economy.

Adoption of the phrase "in the hood" also engages the racial aspect, especially insofar as the 1991 John Singleton film "Boyz in the Hood" from which it originated was eminently about the good times and hard knocks of young African American males in South Central Los Angeles. The usage "boyz" in that spelling suggests the Ebonics-inflected graffiti of the hip hop zone, while the masculine reference brings to the fore the salience of gender issues within the urban scene. Beyond that, "boyz" also signals youth as a central generational location for contemporary cultural creativity, and warfare. The phrase "in the hood" has been very widely proverbialized to refer to marginalized, poor, and working-class areas in the big cities, and to suggest a sense of specificity and familiarity to one's locale.

"Hood," of course, is a colloquial contraction of neighborhood, a concept weighed carefully but affirmatively by Arjun Appadurai in his essay "The Production of Locality" in *Modernity at Large*; his ruminations are germane to any discussion of cultural and diasporic place under globalization. "I view locality as primarily relational and contextual," Appadurai writes, "rather than as scalar or spatial. I see it as a complex phenomenological quality, constituted by a series of links between the sense of social immediacy, the technologies of interactivity, and the relativity of contexts . . . . In contrast, I use the term *neighborhood* to refer to the actually existing social forms in which locality, as a dimension of value, is variably realized. Neighborhoods, in this usage, are situated communities characterized by their actuality, whether spatial or virtual, and their potential for social reproduction."[25] In addition to its virtue in suggesting sociality and immediacy, Appadurai finds that "neighborhood" also "can accommodate images such as circuit and border zone, which have been argued to be preferable to such images as community and center-periphery, especially where transnational migration is involved [reference is here made to the work of Roger Rouse]."[26]

Of course the main connotation of the phrase "in the hood" surely refers to class, signaling as it does subalternity and a vernacular, grass-roots, "from below" perspective. As it intervenes in the discussion of globalization and transnationalism, "in the hood" evinces in a graphic way the local, the particular, the heterogeneous in the face of prevalent narratives of encompassing and dominant cultural change. In specific reference to culture, it is the popular (in the literal, original usage) over against the mainstream or "high" culture in both its elite and its commercially packaged significations. I mean popular culture in this sense of grassroots creativity, rather than its more common connotation as commodified and mediated consumer culture. In that sense it carries both a socioeconomic meaning in its reference to "the people" and a cultural one in its central place in discussions of social identity, such as national or ethnic identity. Structures of domination along the lines of gender and sexuality are also confronted from this vantage point. The "hood," in a word, is the site of new creolizations, the meeting point of multiple diasporas and the crossings and intersections of diasporas. In Glissant's term, it is the ultimate, modern-day "point of entanglement."

Re-grouping and In-Gathering

Even with all of these varied coordinates clearly in view, it is no doubt the qualitatively different kind and consequence of demographic spatial mobility, and intense migratory circulation, that most profoundly mark off the new from the "old," classical diaspora formations going back to ancient times. The momentous changes in communications and transportation technology in the past generation have made for a totally new "diasporic public sphere" (Appadurai) or "transnational space" (Sassen) characterized by bi- or multi-directional cultural flows unknown in earlier times. As Patterson puts it, "People, wealth, ideas, and cultural patterns move in both directions, influencing both the metropolitan center as well as the peripheral areas, although asymmetrically."[27] The accent on asymmetry is of course key, since the "flows" or "streams" are not actually those of culture per se, but notably of "cultural capital," culture as bearer of (real or imagined) social power and privilege.[28]

Thus the triadic relational field shared by diaspora, country of origin and host society, which is characteristic of all historical diasporas, has altered significantly. Now we witness the circulatory back-and-forth, and what Van Hear calls "re-grouping and in-gathering," eclipsing the from–to movement. The result is that diasporic peoples have assumed a far greater sense of agency in our times, and are leaving their imprint on both poles of the migratory orbit, in relation to both the broader civil society as well as the state. In a telling phrase, Robin Cohen entitles one of his articles "Diasporas and the Nation-State: From Victims to Challengers."[29] One thinks in this regard of Latino and other immigrants of color in the present-day United States, and of the North African and Antillean youth in their challenge to long-standing and obsolescent policies of "assimilation" in contemporary France.

Yet there is still another, final asymmetry that needs to be addressed. In this case it refers to the relative intellectual attention paid to one of the directions of these cultural flows as compared to the other. That is, while ample note and scrutiny have gone to the impact and impetus of diasporic presence in the metropoles, surprisingly little has been accorded the impact of return, going home, the role of cultural values and orientation accrued in the diaspora as they land in the site of origin. Remittances have overwhelmingly meant cash or money transfers or, at best, forms of political or civic participation, while cultural commentary and analysis has focused almost exclusively on the continuities and shifts of inherited national traditions and customs as they play out in the territory of exile. So let us now turn to the fascinating phenomenon of cultural remittances, the myth and reality of diasporic return to the native land.

Suitcase, Dominican Republic, 2007.

Photographer Walter Astrada. Permission
Walter Astrada.

2 OF REMIGRANTS AND REMITTANCES

Meanings of Return

"It wasn't until I came home that I understood why I left in the first place." Statements like this, common among those returning to their home countries after years of life away, make it clear that migration is a cyclical experience, not just a one-way uprooting but a process of departure and return. It's like the life-cycle itself: a person comes of age, leaves hearth and home behind to pursue life's fortunes, and eventually returns to pass the later years on the familiar pathways of childhood. One writer refers to return as "the natural completion of the migration cycle."[1]

The idea that out-migration implies re-migration, that what ventures off must come back, has been a truism in theoretical writing for many years. As early as 1885, the scholar Ernest George Ravenstein, Fellow of the Royal Geographic Society, delivered a historic paper entitled "The Laws of Migration," in which he asserted that migratory flows tend to generate significant compensating "counter-currents" or "counter-streams."[2] Subsequent studies from the intervening decades went on to substantiate Ravenstein's "fourth law" and provide numerous examples of European migratory return movements. Since the 1970s, a more specialized scholarly literature about re-migration has emerged, marked off by Frank Bovenkerk's monograph *The Sociology of Return Migration: A Bibliographic Essay* (1974), where many of the issues and angles of the return phenomenon are taken up and related to a range of quantitative and theoretical studies. As might be expected, scholarly and public interest has increased significantly with the advent of transnational demographic movements and widespread circular migratory patterns under globalization.[3] The drama of migratory "counter-streams" and the life-experience of migrants settling back into or paying visits to their countries of origin and ancestral homelands is endemic to the contemporary period, and promises to grow in frequency and intensity in the foreseeable future.

Nevertheless, despite this long-term and heightening attention, the idea of migration as a one-way, one-shot move remains prevalent and virtually unshakeable. A constant lament is that "return migration is the great unwritten chapter in the history of migration," that it has been "inadequately unraveled in the migration debate," and that "our understanding [of the subject] remains hazy."[4] It is also significant that the vast and complex theoretical work on diaspora contain little or no discussion of the experience of return; the two areas of thinking are thus far disconnected from one another. Rather, the "grand narrative" of the migration experience is still about push–pull factors generating life-changing transplantation from one geographical location to another. After the traumatic uprooting from the homeland there follows the mythic arrival of the "huddled masses" at the "golden door," and then the arduous but ultimately rewarding process of incorporation or assimilation into the new society. Of course this old-fashioned immigrants' tale has always been wishful at best, for even in its heyday the great wave of European immigration to the United States, to take the most familiar example, also witnessed a huge but generally unacknowledged countervailing flow of returnees to their native Italy, Germany and other homelands.[5] In times closer to our own, these trusty old paradigms have also tended to be supplanted by theories of transnational mobility and flexibility, with the very idea of migrants "going home" often written off as nostalgic and essentialist. To talk of "home" implies in this view a lapse into a purportedly superceded "national" frame of analysis.[6] For whichever reason, whether the continued sway of the one-way resettlement narrative or post-colonial fascination with a multidirectional, de-territorialized nomadism, there has been relatively little analytical focus on migratory "counter-currents" and their social and cultural consequences.

To take stock of what has been written, a first question raised in the literature is the reason for return, that is, whether the motivation to "go home" stems primarily from a failed or a successful experience "abroad." Do emigrants return to their home countries because their lives in the new society didn't work out, or because it was such a success that they were able to fulfill their wishes—sometimes referred to as a "calculated strategy"—and earn enough to go back and build their "little castle in the sky"? This line of inquiry often leads back to the motivations for leaving home in the first place, and the plans or intentions of emigrants as well as the economic and cultural capital they bring with them. While strong cases are made for either "failure" or "success" as primary causal explanations, there is no consensus nor does there promise to be any. The difficulty is that the range of possibilities seems boundless depending on a huge range of variables, and because the assigning of primary emphasis often depends more on the ideological agenda of the observer than on the social and personal reality at hand. To construe an explanation for return on whether an emigrant "made it" or not places the onus on the individual rather than on the society, or on the relation between home and host societies, which is where the main determinants actually lie. It is clear that a structural and contextual line of analysis is needed to do justice to the complex issue of how migrant peoples fare in the diaspora. It is also evident that political and cultural reasons for migratory motives and outcomes may in many cases override strictly economic ones.

As there is a multiplicity of reasons for return migration, there are also many different kinds of returnees. In his groundbreaking and influential research on return migration from the United States to Italy, Francesco Cerase offers a basic typology of the phenomenon by identifying four broad categories of returnees, the two most self-explanatory of which he calls "return of failure" and "return of retirement."[7] Because his approach is more critical and sensitive to structural determinations, Cesare attributes "failure" to the humiliations, prejudices, and stereotypes encountered in the new society rather than to the shortcomings of the individual migrant. As one version of a return of "success," Cesare then speaks of a third type, the "return of conservatism," by which he means that the returnee uses accumulated earnings and investments to gain a foothold in the home country at a higher status level than before departure, and because of this new-found privilege tends to reinforce (or "conserve") the prevailing value system.

Unsettling Innovations

Cerase's fourth type, the "return of innovation," is perhaps the most interesting, and certainly carries the greatest relevance for much contemporary, transnational analysis, including my own argument. For in this instance, also a story of "success" but in a different way, the return experience is portrayed as a highly dynamic process, involving the agency of returnees who view themselves as "carriers of social change." Here it is not so much money that is accumulated as new values and lessons acquired in the course of diasporic life. Upon getting back the returnee then seeks to apply these lessons, and uses them to help "resolve to a greater degree the problems that he and the group to which he belongs have to face."[8] Again, while the first three types in this influential schema do not diverge much from the success-versus-failure dichotomy, the "return of innovation" is itself an innovation in that it for the first time attributes agency and creativity to the return migrant, who brings back the ability and incentive to challenge and change the society to which he returns. Cerase's work contributes the key insight that the relation between host and home societies is a reciprocal one, and forms an integral part of diasporic experience.

Another central concern of return migration studies has to do with the returnees' adaptation to, or "reintegration" into, the society of origin. How do those returning "home" fit into the country from which they or their families had emigrated, and how are they viewed and treated by those who stayed behind? Much initial attention of course goes to finding a job and settling down in the new setting, but "coming home" is also about making friends, relating to family members or neighbors who never left or returned earlier, speaking the native language, getting used to a different pace of life, feeling like an outsider, and generally going through a strange and sometimes alienating kind of culture shock.[9] Needless to say, the collision between expectations and reality, this "journey of hope and despair" as it has been called, raises issues of race, gender, and class in dramatic and often painful and challenging ways. The range and variety of experiences is limitless, and difficult to generalize, which is why much of the most fruitful research on return migration has involved intense and extensive ethnographic work. Only in this way, by gathering and analyzing stories of life experience, is it possible both to capture the process at a close range and to identify patterns of adaptation and resistance.

The ideas of "innovation" and "re-integration" then raise the question as to the consequences return migration may bring to the home society. Beyond what the returnee encounters it is necessary to ask what the society encounters in the returnee, and what impact this presence has on the life of the country and place of origin. This final area of principal interest to return migration studies has gradually moved to the center of intellectual attention in recent years, and has extended from strictly economic to broader social and cultural dimensions of the transnational migration experience.

For the most part, and particularly in earlier work in the field, this reflection on the nature of returnee "innovation" and change tended to be posed in terms of modernization and progress. The main issue has been, and continues to be in policy-oriented studies, the link between return and "development" and the uses to which the economic and social capital brought by the remigrants is put.[10] A common image is that of return migrants accompanying and following up on their remittances. In this view, they typically arrive with suitcases full of money and practical skills, and consequently serve to give a boost to the often stagnant or slow-paced local economy in its move out of "underdevelopment." Corresponding to this uplift narrative is the idea of the returnees' modern, forward-looking ideology that comes to clash head-on with the vested interests and conservative value-system of the old society. On the strength of tradition and established authority, the entrenched home society is generally successful in thwarting this hope for social change, and the jilted remigrants are obliged to fit in, or leave. Just as the acquisition of entrepreneurial skills is generally regarded as the main lesson learned in the diaspora, so here too it is business acumen and the sound investment of time and money that constitute the most telling baggage returnees can use to exert an influence on their home societies. Because of the obstruction of these influences by traditional powerbrokers, the "innovations" and "social changes" hoped for by those returning agents of change generally turn out to be futile, and ultimately ineffectual.[11]

This bleak and pessimistic view of the potential impact of return migrants has been compounded in more recent, postcolonial writings from the 1990s. As mentioned, there the very notion of "home" under conditions of globalization is dismissed as essentialist and illusory nostalgia. The emphasis on nomadism, homelessness, and "migrancy" as a state of being, and a liminal "third space" as the transnational site of creativity and identity, undermines the dynamic polarity between host and home societies, between emigration and "return," and between moving and resettling which has been the analytical crux of thinking about diasporas and return migration.[12] With this collapse of any differentiation and tension between locations, going back to one's origins or ancestral country might be deeply meaningful for the individual migrant, but it can bear little or no effect on the social conditions or cultural reality there.

Rather than a challenge, then, the return phenomenon is for the most part treated as a "problem," one characterized by ambiguity at best, but more commonly by despair, alienation, and disillusionment. Even when analysis goes beyond the traditional focus on economic and civic "development" and business enterprise, most considerations of possible cultural or ideological influences arrive at similar negative conclusions. Any sense of social agency makes but a fleeting appearance, only to fade in the face of staunch ideological obstacles in the form of conservative traditionalism or entrepeneurial developmentalism.

Though these have been the prevalent lines of thinking regarding the impacts of diasporic return, there has been a thread of alternative analysis that is of special interest in the context of the present argument. As mentioned, in Cerase's circumspect analysis of Italian remigrants the *americani* (as they were called) generate among their re-encountered countrymen not only resentment and jealousy but also admiration and emulation for their acquired skills and forward-looking outlook.[13] Though this optimistic undercurrent is accompanied by the usual hymns of praise for the wonders of modernity and of the metropolitan site of diasporic life, it also includes strong instances of social criticism and activism learned in the labor movement and social struggles in the United States.

In addition to that of Cerase, some ethnographic research conducted in the Caribbean, such as that of Mary Chamberlain and George Gmelch among Barbadian returnees from England and the United States, has also identified positive and critical effects. It is observed, for example, that those who "bring back new ideas, work skills, and capital" may serve as "an important resource for the nation's development," which in this case means more than simple economic growth but a broader concept implying "an open-ended type of social change in which there is progress toward the establishment of a self-reliant society."[14] Of still greater interest in this regard, in an early study from the 1970s also based in Barbados, return migrants are seen to have a significant influence in awakening racial and political consciousness among those who had not left.[15] Unfortunately the authors do little to probe the potentially explosive implications of these insights, so that any positive and critical interventions into the "home culture" are more than offset by the sense of there being no impact at all. Once again, whatever effect there may be has to do not with externally acquired anti-racist or transformative ideas, but with increased economic and cultural capital accrued in the metropolis and the resultant incentive to "develop" and modernize.

More nuanced recent study of the cultural dimension of diaspora and trans-national relations, along with an initial reaction to extreme anti-essentialism and post-colonial nomadism, is allowing for new approaches to the homeland impact of return migration and of counter-currents to primary migratory flows. Re-evaluations of the concepts of home and homecoming are uncovering real or potentially transgressive effects of diasporic presence upon return, and over longer stretches of time. The very title of one collection of studies, *Homecomings: Unsettling Paths of Return* (2004), suggests that it is necessary to look beyond the development paradigms and limited ideological frames of previous analysis and probe the disjunctures and asymmetries underlying returnee–stayee relations with a more circumspect eye.[16] Containing contributions on a wide array of return migration experiences, from that of Hungarians and Japanese Brazilians, Israelis, Sudanese, and Armenians, the book makes a strong case for the complexity and novelty of contemporary "homecomings" and the need for new kinds and frames of analysis in light of today's globalizing realities and varied diasporic responses to them.

In his introduction to the volume, titled "Homecomings to the Future: From Diasporic Mythographies to Social Projects of Return," co-editor Anders H. Stefansson takes issue with a range of accepted truths, from the supposed "myth of return" to the notion that those returning have no bearing or positive role to play. Stefansson and the contributors give ample attention to the disenchantments and social distances, that "abyss of mutual misunder-standings" and the "mismatch between the imagined and experienced homecoming," that makes the drama of return so intrinsically ambivalent and at times jarring. But his refreshingly circumspect view also allows him to draw attention to other, largely neglected phenomena like the creation of new returnee identities and cultural enclaves, which he refers to as an emergent process of "rediasporization."[17] This intriguing idea of the "construction of new diasporas in the ethnic homeland" introduces a different understanding of returnees' efforts at building "future-oriented social projects," and to what is termed a "proactive approach" to the return experience. "The new skills learned and outlooks adopted abroad can make the home appear 'narrow and old-fashioned'," Stefansson points out, which may lead not only to frustration and disappointment, but also to an "empowering, 'liberating,' or 'progressive' potential."[18] Herein lies the perhaps deeper meaning of the book's subtitle, "unsettling paths of return." For the return experience turns out to be "unsettling" not just to the returnees themselves, but to the very society to which they return and its established values and exclusionary sense of national identity. Stefansson ends by citing Carol Stack in her memorable book *Call to Home,* about American Blacks returning to the South: "You can go home," one of her narrators says, "But you can't start from where you left. To fit in, you have to create another place in that place you left behind."[19]

Understanding Remittances

Migratory "counterstreams" are of course not limited to permanent home-comings, or even to the experience of personal and physical return. Intentionally or not, many returnees go back temporarily, sometimes for brief sojourns, summer vacations, visits to relatives, or for as long as they can stand the challenges and discomforts they may experience. They may decide to move on to another place, or return to the diaspora setting that they come to recognize as "home." They may be returning war refugees or political exiles or even subjects of repatriation. There are countless instances of second or third generation youth returning with their parents, and often undergoing severe rejection and humiliation by their peers. A remigrant group's ancestry may go back generations, like the Japanese Brazilians, or centuries, like those going "home" from the multiple sites in the Israeli diaspora. The return might also be an instance of "roots tourism," that is, "ancestral" or ethnic homecoming, where people "go back," often to places they have never been, in order to connect to real or imagined cultural roots.

Like *Homecoming,* many of the essay collections and ethnographic studies on the theme of migratory return encompass all or many of these varieties of experience, and go to illustrate in a range of ways some of the new, more nuanced understandings described above.[20] Factors such as generation, age, duration of time in the diaspora, geographic distance, along with differences in class, gender, racial identities and many other variables, play a key role in determining the kind of effect that the "counterstream" will have once it hits the return destination. The stories included and discussed in chapter 4 of the present book also illustrate some of this range of social experiences involved in the return migration experience.

But by far the most widely recognized and extensively studied "counter-stream" is of course not physical return at all, but the flow of remittances from diasporas to homelands. The practice is both long-standing and ubiquitous in today's international scene, and exerts a momentous influence on the lives and social experiences of millions of people worldwide. The literature on remittances is also voluminous, ranging from governmental and non-governmental reports and policy declarations to carefully documented ethnographic and econometric scholarship. Startling reports about remittance flows making up the preponderant part of entire national economies appear daily, drawing the lively attention of government and corporate observers.

Economic remittances are so thoroughly interwoven into the fabric of international trade and politics that by this point it is impossible to grasp the causes and implications of many contemporary events without taking them into central account. As of the mid-1980s, and coinciding with the neo-liberal thrust of international relations in recent decades, extensive accounts replete with elaborate graphs and charts and astounding data have been streaming out of governmental, banking, and NGO think tanks. While most of the writings about remittances are strictly financial, aimed at measuring cash and capital transfers in all their aspects and manifestations, there is also a sizable literature that goes beyond the economic to query what are termed "the political and social dimensions."[21] Here again, as in the return migration discussion, the main topic of interest is "development," and the role remittances issuing from diasporas play in promoting public services, opening and fostering local business and labor opportunities, and addressing needs not met within home regions and nations. Differences are drawn among kinds of remittances, especially between family and collective transfers, between those sent for wages or salary, and those constituting investments or saved capital. Account is also taken of relations among the mediating actors or institutions, and among the varied uses of remittances by those on the receiving end of the process.

More circumspect and less institutionally beholden analysts emphasize the complexity and wide variation of the phenomenon, as well as the need to understand remittances in their social and historical contexts.[22] Though the practice of remittances and the debates surrounding them go back far in the history of migratory movements, today's processes constitute an integral part of the "transnationalizing of social, cultural, economic and political life." They go beyond questions of finance to make for "the global stretching of [such aspects of contemporary life as] household decision-making, family life course and strategies, collective resources, social structure and cultural institutions and community activities and development."[23]

Aside from "extra-economic" dimensions and implications surrounding the remittance process, there are also non-economic remittances, that is, those values sent or transferred from diasporas to home countries that are not strictly economic or financial. One scholar of remittances, Luin Goldring, identifies technical or technological, social, and political variants, demonstrating in his analysis the close relation between remittances and return migration, and the virtual impossibility of separating the two.[24]

Two book-length studies that go far in elucidating what is meant by political and social remittances are Peggy Levitt's *The Transnational Villagers* (2001) and Robert C. Smith's *Mexican New York* (2005). Based on extensive and close-up trans-local ethnographies, both works bring to dramatic life the vibrant interaction, among Dominicans and Mexicans respectively, across national boundaries and cultures in many aspects of life, from family and religion to gender relations, economic planning, and civic participation. More than a formal issue, dual citizenship is here a lived practical reality and mutually enriching form of social action and identity. In each case, geographically separated localities are shown to be thoroughly interdependent, with remittances of all kinds from diasporic settings in the urban United States making for an omnipresent force in hometowns and regions, with some impact even at the national level. Smith's book is rapidly becoming the most widely cited work on Mexican transnational community since Roger Rouse's pioneering 1991 essay "Mexican Migration and the Social Space of Postmodernism." Levitt's study builds on previous research on Dominican transnationalism by such researchers as Sherry Grasmuck, Patricia Pessar, and Luis Guarnizo in tracking the back-and-forth currents of religious, gender, and family beliefs and practices between specific communities in the Boston and Santo Domingo areas.

While *Mexican New York* is the more insightful and original of these two studies of transnational life and the remittance process understood in an expansive, more-than-economic sense, Peggy Levitt's *The Transnational Villagers* includes an attempt to name and define the guiding concept in both books, what she calls "social remittances." Her book contains a chapter by that title, and prior to that publication she contributed a seminal article where she explicates her new term.[25] "Social remittances are the ideas, behaviors, identities, and social capital that flow from receiving- to sending-country communities." Levitt locates the concept in theories of transnational communities, arguing that such remittances give content to the public space between and among nations connected by significant migratory flows. From her subtitles, "Migration Driven Local-Level Forms of Cultural Diffusion" and "How Global Culture Is Created Locally," it is clear that she is talking about cultural transfers, which she specifies as "entrepeneurship, community and family formation and political integration." Levitt then elaborates on different aspects of social remittance, beginning with a characterization of how they emerge among immigrant communities out of the blending of background cultures and cultural experiences encountered in the new setting. She identifies a range of interaction patterns, from the more conservative "recipient observers" who have little interaction with the surrounding society and therefore exert less cultural influence from outside of the inherited culture, to "instrumental adapters," who learn and take on new skills "to be able to get along." She also speaks of "purposeful innovators," who deliberately expand and extend their cultural repertoire in order, not just to survive, but to "get ahead." In the case of the "innovators," the resulting "repertoire" is a highly hybridized cultural form that potentially has its strongest impact when brought to bear on the home culture. In similar definitional fashion, the author itemizes different types of social remittances, which she terms "normative structures" (meaning ideas, values, and beliefs), "systems of practice" (she names household labor, religious practices, and patterns of civil and political participation), and "social capital" (referring to prestige and status accrued in the diaspora). After describing the varied "mechanisms of transmission" of social remittances, Levitt ends by taking stock of their impact in the home country, and the "costs and benefits" they entail when they arrive and take hold.

Basing herself on a well-documented ethnography among Dominicans both in the diaspora and the home country, Levitt thus offers a useful conceptual mapping of this widespread contemporary phenomenon of transnational interaction. She is appropriately cautious in evaluating the many possible outcomes of the migratory counterstream and its role in societies heavily influenced by their huge diasporas. She acknowledges that while such remittances can in fact serve as catalysts for positive social change they can also introduce negative examples of class arrogance, egoism, and opportunism stemming from the asymmetries between home societies and diasporas.

This ambivalent impact is articulated by one of her informants: "Our lives are totally different now, and so much has to do with what we have learned from the United States. It's both good and bad. When Javier told us that he wouldn't stand being tricked by politicians anymore or having to wait on long lines at city hall because they are so disorganized there, these were good things that he taught us about his life in the United States. But when people come back saying they care more about themselves than about our community or that you can make a lot of money by selling drugs and that is okay, then we would rather not learn what the U.S. has to offer."[26] A similarly circumspect assessment, and basically the same conceptual framework, is evident in Robert C. Smith's *Mexican New York* as well as other recent studies of return migration and the impact of remittances, both economic and non-economic.

The shortcoming of this conceptualization—in my view and for the purposes of the present argument—is that it doesn't go far enough, and fails to draw out the deeper, more radical implications of the remittance experience. First off, there is the unchallenged identification of skills and "success" with entrepreneurial activity and upward mobility, and social progress with "development." Thus, while one of the central kinds of social remittance is identified as the will for social change, that change generally entails reforms and civic participation. Little or no room is given over to the lessons of radical social change that may have been learned in diaspora conditions and that would challenge the entire structure of colonial asymmetry responsible for the diaspora formation itself. Social remittances may also comprise the introduction of new understandings of the dependent, subordinate relation of diasporic migrants' home countries to the very metropolis where they learned their lessons. Improvement, while a welcome contribution, is not the same as change in a broader and more far-reaching sense. In Levitt's and other research, including Smith's *Mexican New York*, reference is occasionally made to the oppositional, contestatory quality of much youth culture learned in or from the diaspora, but there is no extended probing of this kind of remittance when it engages the realities of the home society.

Part of the problem is the frame of analysis: while much of the value of these studies lies in the local focus and human particularity of the ethnographies, the impact of remigrants and remittances at a national or hemispheric level is not part of the calculation. That is, the political activism and civic participation in the homeplaces under direct study surely have implications for the political life of the nation-state and the national culture, but those supra-local challenges go largely unexplored when discussing "local-level forms of cultural diffusion." Levitt's insistence that "the individual [is] the appropriate frame of analysis," while allowing for a focus on engaging individual and family life-stories, has the effect of ruling out, or at least minimizing, any account of the larger structural hierarchies and asymmetries at work in the diaspora and return migration experience. For that reason, the crucial differentiation between "from above" and "from below" perspectives in assessing diasporic conditions and changes falls largely from view.

In these and other recent studies, much is made of newly learned "ideas and values" as the content of social remittances, but what about ideological lessons, ideas, and values having to do with a different arrangement of social power so as to alter the situation lived by migrant populations in both settings? The same constriction of view concerns the frequently evoked notion of "identity," an aspect of social experience that also tends to undergo change in the diaspora: don't Dominicans and Mexicans (to stay with the two examples under consideration) often learn to understand what it means to be Dominican or Mexican in new and different ways when experienced in the light of "outside," exiled or emigrant life? And what about racial identities, which typically undergo such profound alterations within the new racial formation of diaspora society like the United States? Though this centrally important dimension of social remittances, that of racial ideologies and identities, does get some attention in Smith's book, Levitt finds surprisingly little room or occasion to treat the subject in her analysis of bi-national Dominican life, where the change in racial self-concept is turning out to be of transformative significance.

In still broader terms, the concept of culture itself is a tellingly limited one in both studies and others of their kind. A strictly anthropological and social scientific culture concept reigns supreme, with no evident interest in forms and practices of creative expression. Nor does this line of analysis address the powerful role of the media and cultural representation, which like artistic expression is an obvious and powerful conduit of non-economic diasporic "counter-streams." Rather, culture gets reduced to behavior, or at best, attitudes, with little room for "values" in a deeper, more philosophical sense. Even the treatment of religion, which does warrant ample attention in Levitt's study, is identified mainly with institutional affiliations and practices, as does politics in Smith's book on Mexicans in New York and Puebla. A more critical and robust guiding idea of culture is needed in order to draw out the full implications of this new way of thinking remittances and the diasporic counterstream.

Cultural Remittances

For these reasons, I propose the term "cultural remittances" to supplement the idea of "social remittances" because it seems to me a more accurate and challenging way of describing the content of the counterstreams that are catalyzing and accompanying change in many parts of the world.[27] By means of return and circulatory migration and multiple conduits of mediated and direct communications, cultural customs and practices, ideological orientations, forms of artistic expression, and ideas of group identity acquired in diaspora settings are remitted to homeland societies. The impact of these transfers is of course difficult to gauge in most cases, as is the question of their intentionality: it is unclear what effect they are having, and whether that effect was intended. But it is obvious to any participant or observer that, wittingly or not, challenges and changes do result.

Foregrounding the cultural dimension in this way need not mean a blunting of the social and political edge of transnational analysis. On the contrary, deploying a "thick," deep, and dynamic sense of cultural change may be a more effective way of dramatizing the challenges brought to bear by diasporic peoples on their homelands. Indeed, this idea of "cultural remittances" may help demonstrate that such challenges may go so far as to invoke a thorough revision of the histories of national cultures and identities as legitimated by the countries' traditional elites and state apparatus. Furthermore, explicitly centering the cultural within the idea of more-than-economic remittances allows for due attention to forms and practices of cultural expression as they are altered by the to-and-fro movements of contemporary migratory patterns. It is, after all, in language, music, literature, painting, and other expressive genres that the values and lifestyles remitted from diaspora to homeland become manifest in the most tangible and salient ways.

Who are "we," people in diasporas typically ask themselves. What does it mean to be Dominican, Puerto Rican, Mexican, Latin American or Caribbean? Can I be Mexican and speak more English than Spanish? Can I be Puerto Rican and prefer pizza to rice and beans? Am I American if both of my parents were from Haiti? Am I Haitian if I was born and raised and lived all my life in Philadelphia? Can I be both at once? These and similar questions swirl around the sensibilities of diaspora peoples today, and satisfactory responses (not to say answers) call for a robust, dynamic, and encompassing concept of the cultural. Perhaps the primary cultural consequence of transnational diaspora life is that it necessarily stretches the meaning of national belonging by disengaging it from its presumed territorial and linguistic imperative, and de-centering it in relation to any putative "core" values or marks of greater or lesser "authenticity."

Since those in the diaspora continue to claim a connection to their national or ancestral heritage (which is what makes them a diaspora and not simply an immigrant population), a typical diaspora stance is, "I am, even though . . . ." Or in other terms, "I may do, say, eat, prefer or hang out in this way, but I am still connected to that cultural place." It is a stance of insistence, even defiance, and sometimes a reaction to a perceived rejection or deprecation of one's background by the host society, which is often also the society into which one was born and where one has always lived. It is an anti-assimilationist position, albeit often articulated by those who assume a full range of the ways and attitudes of the host society, and a rightful stake in its political life.

The diasporan stance evinces complex, ambivalent, often extreme reactions from non-migrant nationals in the "home" country. "Los de afuera" (those from the outside) or "de allá" (from over there) are common ways of referring to the return diaspora, thereby qualifying, "othering," and generally dismissing the claim to belonging lodged by returnees, much to their pain and frustration. Yet at the same time, and often in the same breath, there is an embrace, a sense of pride that they are back in the fold, having chosen a connection to home and family over that strange and different other place. Intense emotions mingle: rejection and resentment alternate with acceptance and inclusion. In short, a place is made at the table, but not without lingering discomfort and suspicions. This highly charged affective encounter, so familiar in contemporary literature and in the lives of millions of transmigrants worldwide, lies at the heart of cultural remittances as a social experience.

Aside from such pressing questions of identity, authenticity, and group belonging, remittances may also have to do with issues of class, race, gender, and sexuality, often with sharp political and ideological implications. The perspective "from below" primarily concerns class position and cultural capital, even though other lines of social differentiation are also pertinent in this regard. Cultural remittances from below—the values and ideas emanating from poor, working-class, and colonial diaspora communities or sectors—come to clash head-on with elite and paternalistic versions of the national culture as purveyed by the guardians of established traditions and historical narratives.

An outstanding, historically expansive example of such an alternative vision of the national culture "from below," as it could only have been voiced from a diasporic location, is Bernardo Vega's memoir documenting the early history of the Puerto Rican community in New York. Since that remarkable book was published in the 1970s, thousands of working-class Puerto Rican families have returned to the Island from varied diaspora settings in the United States, seeking in vain their chapter in the conventional version of the country's history. Though few come bearing a trained political viewpoint like that of Bernardo Vega himself, many do have experience in working-class and community-based organizations, and their very presence in traditional Puerto Rican society is no doubt a critical and challenging one. Aside from their documentary value, Vega's *Memoirs* project a radically different understanding of the national culture and history, one in which the common people, and the diaspora itself as a collective social agent, play a leading and active role.

Cultural remittances having to do with gender roles and sexual orientation have caused a moral tremor in home societies, as has been documented and analyzed in the case of women's, gay, and lesbian experience in Latino and Caribbean diasporas. While the United States is hardly a haven from sexism and homophobia, it is appropriate to speak in relative terms of greater spaces and perspectives for movement and change. In the case of women's relative independence, social experience in the diaspora has made for an altered relation to work and educational opportunities, which has then had its ripple effect on domestic life and family roles. The examples of Latina gender experiences, both in the diaspora and in the home countries, has been the subject of much research and scholarly analysis, much of it demonstrating in graphic terms the unsettling impact of cultural remittances. Queer experience in diaspora settings, sometimes referred to as "sexile," has also had significant repercussions when remitted to deeply homophobic Latin American and Caribbean societies. Though there has been little scholarly analysis of the phenomenon as of yet, the documentary film "Brincando el charco" ("Jumping over the puddle") by Frances Negrón Muntaner provides a memorable glimpse at this experience in the Puerto Rican context.

Race Moves

Perhaps the most highly charged field for the play of cultural remittances, however, has involved the issue of race and racial identity, and most of all, questions of blackness. Although the legacy of denial and the age-old myths of "racial democracy" do persist in Latino and Caribbean diasporas, significant alterations in regard to African heritages and awareness of racism are evident, sometimes dramatically so—especially among diaspora youth and, of course, Afro-Latinos. Many Caribbean Latinos are racialized toward blackness, not only by the wider U.S. society but to some extent by their fellow Latinos as well. This process has been complemented, and complicated, by relations with African Americans and non-Hispanic Caribbeans, relations which have in some cases—most strongly, again, among young people —engendered an Afro- or Atlantic- diasporic consciousness and identity. Political activism and organized politics going back to the 1960s, and the more recent cultural phenomena related to hip hop and reggaetón, have fostered this eminently diasporic sensibility. A vibrant cultural hybridity and racial affirmation constitute powerful cultural remittances in our times. Youth in countries throughout Latin America, the Caribbean and in many parts of the world are asserting their specific and often combative sense of cultural identity in these expressive and philosophical terms. Indeed, the forceful new video documentary film "Estilo Hip Hop" by Chilean-American Vee Bravo, New York Dominican Loira Limbal and their associates includes stark portrayals of the highly politicized, revolutionary use of hip hop in Brazil, Chile, Mexico, and Cuba.

It is clear that growing up in urban diaspora communities has been a lesson in blackness for many Puerto Rican, Dominican, and other Latino and Caribbean young people. Racism in the form of profiling and police brutality has wielded the stick that imparts this bitter learning experience, which often turns out to be an enriching and affirming one if taken in the right direction. In addition, the emulation of African American culture has been a national and international pattern for many years, one that has by no means abated in recent times of transnational cultural diffusion. Whether it is Brazil, Belize, Trinidad and Tobago, Colombia, Mexico or El Salvador, not a country or region of the hemisphere has been without its imprint of African American stylistic influence. But it is in those national cultures with massive diasporas in the United States, and particularly those among them with sizable Afro-Latino populations such as the Dominican, Cuban, and Puerto Rican communities, that this diffusion has most conspicuously taken the form of a cultural remittance, with its usual explosive effects. In our time, the very foundations of Dominican, Puerto Rican, and even Cuban national ideologies are being shaken by the remittance of Afro-Dominican, Afro-Puerto Rican, and Afro-Cuban identities. These are borne in decidedly new ways by return migrants and their children as they resurface in home-country settings after a veritable apprenticeship in black consciousness acquired in working-class diaspora "hoods" in the United States. Can these transfers be written off as just another phase of Americanization, as globalization "from above," or are they rather a cogent example of what has variously been termed "vernacular cosmopolitanism" or "grassroots globalization," that is, cultural remittances from below?

It is only in practical terms, and in reference to particular instances of cultural transfer, that this line between above and below can be ascertained with any sense of certainty. Much of the hip hop that is emulated in local settings is of course nothing other than the thoroughly commercialized and ideologically offensive version that prevails in the media, a stereotyped version articulated at a distant remove from its original site of expression among marginalized and often rebellious urban youth. Indeed, the violently anti-social and drug-related gang culture remitted from inner-city neighborhoods in Los Angeles and other U.S. cities to countries like El Salvador and Belize are hardly compatible with agendas of inclusiveness and democracy. In fact, this phenomenon only bolsters the criminalization of many returning youth in the public mind, which is of course an experience all too familiar to Nuyoricans and Dominicanyorks when they venture back to the land of their parents and ancestors. Yet countless are the stories to the contrary, of working-class immigrants from Caribbean and Latin American countries spending formative years in diaspora communities, discovering and internal-izing new cultural identities and social roles, and facing walls of resistance from their non-migrant compatriots who seem to have a stake in upholding traditional ways and values, however backward and oppressive. Despite such resistance, though, it is heartening to know that change does gradually and reluctantly ensue.

A very memorable account of this process is that presented by Dominican writer and educator Chiqui Vicioso in her short memoir entitled, simply, "An Oral History."[28] Vicioso tells of going to New York in the late 1960s to study, getting caught up in the struggle for ethnic studies at Brooklyn College, and over the years coming to realize that she is a black woman, a Caribbean woman, an independent woman. She attests that these were revolutionary insights for her that changed her life, but they were self-discoveries that brought her constant and often bitter tribulations when she returned to live in the Dominican Republic. This kind of transformative process and the impact it has had in the Dominican Republic in recent decades is captured in sharp terms by Dominican historian Frank Moya Pons, who has written, "Racial and cultural denial worked for many years, but migration to the United States finally cracked down the ideological block of the traditional definition of Dominican national identity."[29]

The workings of cultural remittances thus suggest a radical re-charting of anti-imperialist cultural politics in the hemisphere. In the traditional view, the national territory is thought of as the fount of cultural perspectives that are alternative and oppositional to hegemonic metropolitan cultures of domination, and that resistance then informs the cultural and political agenda of the nation's diaspora within the metropolis. It is now becoming evident that this transnational flow may also travel in the opposite direction and that the colonial diaspora itself may well generate a culture of resistance to national elite domination and complicity. Cultural remittances—eminently transnational as a consequence of circular migration and the ubiquity of contemporary communications technology—implode in the national territory as something foreign, and yet in their local relevance not so foreign after all. When the focus is on popular culture (in the sense of grassroots community experience and working-class expression) and on youth culture, this multidirectional cultural movement and impact comes most clearly into view. What also becomes evident is the mutual articulation between cultural remittances from the outside and some of the oppositional cultural tendencies at work within the national territory.

Caribbean Latinos, diasporans stemming from the Hispanic Caribbean islands of Puerto Rico, the Dominican Republic, and Cuba, exemplify in especially cogent ways the patterns and impacts of return migration and contemporary cultural remittances, and are the main case under study in this book. In subsequent chapters we will explore how the cultural remittance process plays out in everyday life and finds articulation in diverse life-stories (chapter 4), and analyze the forms and practices of creative expression through which they are transmitted (chapters 5 and 6). Before that, though, in chapter 3, I will proceed to characterize the Caribbean Latino diaspora experience in historical and thematic terms, and to review the discussion of cultural counterstreams in that transnational geo-cultural location.

**Conjunto La Plata, Puerto Rico, 1947
(Davilita appears second from left).**

Photographer unknown. Permission
Gregorio Marcano.

3 *CARIBEÑO* COUNTERSTREAM

From Cuba to the Guyanas and across every inflection which language confers on the chosen tongue of each territory, this style of performance is evident and travels whenever this island people, and those islanded on the mainland, migrate without any loss of innocence to forge exotic and subversive enclaves in cities whose prestige once made them certain of their names. London, Paris, New York, Amsterdam. These are the Caribbean external frontiers.

George Lamming

Caribbean Diaspora and Return

Caribbean peoples are considered an "exemplary case of a cultural diaspora." In his overview of the history and typology of "global diasporas," Robin Cohen identifies the Caribbean and its scattered emigrant and exile populations as privileged sites for the study of contemporary diasporic life under globalization.[1] Culture and cultural change make up the dimension of collective experience that distinguishes modern-day Caribbean migratory processes from those primarily marked off by relations of trade, victimization, imperial, labor or religious relations between homelands and countries of destination. In this view, it is cultural dynamics that define the content of Caribbean diasporic life first of all because of the common African descent of its populations and Afro-Atlantic moorings of their cultural histories, that is, "being phenotypically African and being conscious of racism."[2]

The Caribbean region and its peoples are thus a site of diasporic formation throughout its history. Beyond that Afro-diasporic foundation, and thinking of the modern Caribbean and its new migrant communities in Europe and North America, the Caribbean is a quintessential "cultural diaspora" because of the ample evidence of "cultural retentions or affirmations of an African identity, ... a literal or symbolic interest in 'return,' ... cultural artifacts, products and expressions that show shared concerns and cross-influences between African, the Caribbean and the destination countries of Caribbean [people] and indications that ordinary Caribbean peoples abroad—in their attitudes, migration patterns and social conduct—behave in ways consistent with the idea of a cultural diaspora."[3] With all the immense diversity of the region and its long-standing and intricate history of migratory movements, the constituent markers of ancestral and historical unity among these varied experiences and demographic changes make it necessary to regard it as one group trajectory and social reality. Underlying the constant play of imperial power in the formation of the region and its multiple migrations—indeed, one could well add this common colonial and postcolonial history as a further unifying factor—it is the cultural dimension, the multiple layerings of creolization and re-creolization, that more than any other constitutes the Caribbean diaspora experience.

The Caribbean is also a privileged site for the study of return migration and the many forms that the diasporic "counterstream" assumes in present-day transnational relations. This history of return as desire and reality has involved, first of all, the longing for Africa as the primordial homeland, as manifest most dramatically in the twentieth century with the experience of Garveyism and the theoretical work of some of the region's leading intellectuals and political leaders, from Frantz Fanon and Aimé Césaire to Walter Rodney and Arturo Alfonso Schomburg. Indeed, Césaire's "Cahiers d'un rétour au pais natale" ("Return to my native land," 1956) ranks among the supreme poetic reflections on the return experience in world literature. As is evident in the diffusion of Caribbean artistic, literary, and especially musical forms, much of that "cultural diaspora" rooted in the Caribbean has made its way "back" to Africa, often in highly resonant ways. Furthermore, and more directly pertinent to the case of modern diasporic experiences, large numbers of Caribbean peoples have made their way home, through remittances and return migratory movements, from the many scattered sites of diaspora settlement where they have found themselves, from other Caribbean and Central American countries, and from urban centers and agricultural locations in Europe and North America.

What is more, many of these stories have been told, recorded, and analyzed. Going as far back as the early 1970s and beyond there has been a body of research and literary representation concerning Caribbean return migration and diaspora–homeland relations that probably outpaces in quantity and quality that about any other area of the world. As early as 1953 the Barbadian novelist George Lamming included the return home from England as a central part of his first novel, *In the Castle of My Skin*, considered a classical work of West Indian literature. Key and revealing quotes from Lamming appear in an early article (1975), "Migration and West Indian Racial and Ethnic Consciousness," which offers a valuable concise overview of migration and return between Barbados and both England and the United States.[4] The commentary there on the impact of diasporic life on Caribbean racial awareness and how that heightened sensitivity plays itself out upon return to Barbados is more insightful than much of what has surfaced on the subject in subsequent analysis. Related work by early scholars such as Roy Bryce-Laporte, Gordon Lewis, Nancie González, and Robert Manners set a solid foundation for the wide-ranging work on Caribbean migrations and their cultural significance, while Barbadian emigrant author Paule Marshall offered sensitive portrayals of diasporic life in her 1959 novel *Brown Girl, Brownstones*. More formal, though markedly less reflective, sociological research on the subject appeared in what appears to be the first book-length study, *Return Migration to Puerto Rico* by José Hernández Alvarez, first published in 1967.

In more recent times, and under conditions of more intense transnational relations, Caribbean migratory counterstreams have continued to attract the attention of scholars from many disciplines, locations, and perspectives. A representative and highly useful contribution is the collection *The Experience of Return Migration: Caribbean Perspectives* (2005), co-edited by Robert B. Potter, Dennis Conway, and Joan Phillips. As evident there and elsewhere, the English-speaking Caribbean is no doubt the favored location for work on return migration to the region, and of the Anglophone West Indies, even more than Jamaica it is Barbados that has proven to be the choice site for ethnographic and other scholarly research. Centering on the Barbadian diaspora in England and its return home, Mary Chamberlain's masterful book *Narratives of Exile and Return* (1997) demonstrates cogently how powerful the personal stories of migration, and especially homecoming, can be at a human and local level, and how much they can tell us about macro-processes of transnational cultural change. George Gmelch, known for his study of return migration to Ireland as well as more general theoretical reflections on the return experience,[5] makes another important contribution on Barbadian diaspora life and return home with *Double Passage: The Lives of Caribbean Migrants Abroad and Back Home* (1992). Based on the life-stories of thirteen Barbadian migrants in England and the United States and in many cases their dramatic return to their island homeland, *Double Passage* provides a vivid sense of the culture clash that so often characterizes that homecoming, and the meaning of the phrase "there's no place back home" that another commentator on West Indian return migration takes as the title of his article on the subject.[6] Of special interest in Gmelch's collection is the story of the Calypso musician The Mighty Gabby, who after gaining a political education over the course of decades working in Manhattan's garment district returns home a protest singer.

What surfaces from this ample literature on return migration to and within the Anglophone Caribbean is a range of unifying historical commonalities that make it meaningful to speak of one region despite all of the balkanizing divisions and discrepancies. It is, for one thing, a world area that has seen constant demographic movement throughout its history, beginning of course in pre-conquest times but taking on international proportions with the

European colonization and the African slave trade. The latter involuntary migration was of greatest consequence, as it was formative of the culture of the entire region and made of it a central component of the African diaspora, or the Black Atlantic. The constant scattering of Caribbean peoples throughout their history, and the resultant multiple layers of colonial and neocolonial rule, have made for extensions and reinventions of the African diaspora and at the same time new, nationally and regionally formed diasporas, primarily in Europe, North, Central and South America, and within the region itself.

This two-tier phenomenon of new diasporas spawned of a formative civilizational diaspora is unique to, or at least strongly characteristic of, the Caribbean, as is the passage from an extended epoch marked by European colonialism to a subsequent one under the dominion of the United States. Each of those colonial epochs generated major diasporic formations, especially in England until the end of World War II, and in the United States and Canada since the mid-twentieth century. The experience of intense racism in those metropolitan centers and the real and imagined "return" to Afro-Caribbean homelands make for the special content of the lived reality of that transnational imaginary. The complex, mutually enriching relations forged with other non-white diasporas in England, and with African Americans and fellow Caribbean peoples in the U.S. enclaves, become a significant component of the cultural remittances introduced into Caribbean life, especially in the period since formal independence. These latter ties, and the spanning of the Caribbean into Central and the northern rim of South America, are what lead Orlando Patterson to identify the Caribbean as the hub of what he calls the "emerging West Atlantic system."[7]

These qualities issuing from an analysis of the Anglophone countries are paradigmatic for the Caribbean as a whole, such that the "West Indies," the Antilles, and the Caribbean often appear virtually coterminous in the public mind and in much of the research on migration and "homecoming." There has been some important work on the Francophone Antilles transnational experience, notably that of Nina Glick-Schiller and Michel Laguerre on the Haitian diaspora and its links to homeland politics.[8] Generally, Haiti, Martinique, Guadalupe and other Francophone examples are treated as closely analogous to the Anglophone experience with its strong African presence and ongoing colonial and cultural links to the European metropolis.

It is the Hispanic Caribbean, "las Antillas," the second most studied instance of Caribbean cultural remittances after the English-speaking, which is most often seen as running askew of the more general regional paradigm. Representatively, in mapping his new "migration systems" Patterson separates the "Afro-Caribbean societies" (meaning the West Indies) from what he calls the "insular and south Caribbean Latin societies."[9] Similarly, in their important co-edited volume *Caribbean Life in New York City* (1987),

Constance R. Sutton and Elsa M. Chaney divide their case studies into two distinct sections, "Afro-Caribbean" and "Hispanic Caribbean." Similar cases abound and, aside from the differentiation in language culture, the issue is clearly about the designation "Afro-." For in the view of many Caribbeanists, and as articulated in cultural self-definitions as well, the Spanish-speaking Caribbean countries have more trouble with the African background, and with blackness, than the rest of the region. It is also clear that this real or perceived difference has its effect on the diasporic experience, and as regards the baggage and reception of cultural remittances on their re-entry into the home societies.

Before turning to the study of the cultural counterstream from Caribbean Latino diaspora enclaves back to the diverse island homelands, it is important to have a sense of the historical trajectory of Puerto Rican, Cuban, and Dominican life in the United States. Paralleling the intersections and divergences among the three national cultures and histories, the diaspora experiences of U.S. *caribeño* communities have witnessed both close bonds and sharp contrasts over the decades. At different historical periods one or the other of the groups has been of primary importance both in terms of its presence in and impact on the host society and its interaction with the home culture and politics. In broad terms, during the nineteenth and early twentieth centuries the Cuban community was the protagonist in that story; then for most of the twentieth century through the 1980s it was the Puerto Rican experience; and since the 1970s and into the new millennium Dominicans have come to take on an increasingly prominent place in U.S. Latino reality and its transnational relations. Taking a cue from the life of Davilita, a beloved Caribbean Latino musician from the early decades, let us trace some of the contours of that diaspora history. We can then return to consider the main lines of thinking about the longstanding "counterstream" that has accompanied that history, and especially its intense impact in our own times.

Islands and Enclaves in song

"Son tres" (The three sister islands)

La música de Borinquen, y la música cubana, y la quisqueyana,
[coro]: que sabe a ron, sabe a miel, sabe a caña
Que lindas son, que lindas son, las tres islitas hermanas,
Por eso yo, por eso yo, las adoro con el alma
Lo lei lo lai, lei lo lai [etc.]
Es el tabaco cubano el mejor del universo,
Y el café de Puerto Rico ni hablar mi hermano de eso
De Cuba es el son guajiro, de Puerto Rico la danza,
De Quisqueya es el merengue que a todo el mundo le encanta.

Fue en Cuba José Martí quien luchó su libertad,
Y Duarte fue por Quisqueya, y por Borinquen, ¿quién sera?
Son tres, son tres, las isles hermanas
Que las quiero ver, las quiero ver, las tres soberanas
Que no me quiero morir sin ver la union antillana.

The music of Puerto Rico, and from Cuba, and from the Dominican Republic / [chorus]: it tastes like rum, tastes like honey, tastes like sugar cane] / How beautiful they are, how beautiful, the three little sister islands / and that's why I, that's why I adore them with all my heart. / Cuban tobacco is the best in the whole universe, / and coffee from Puerto Rico, brother, let's not even talk about that. / [chorus]. / From Cuba the *son guajiro* and from Puerto Ricao *la danza*, and from Quisqueya the *merengue* that everyone loves. / [chorus] / In Cuba it was José Martí who fought for its freedom, and Duarte was for Quisqueya, and for Borniquen, who will it be? / [chorus] / And I want to see, want to see the three of them sovereign, / I don't want to die without seeing the Antillean union.

Davilita sings "las Antillas": "Son tres, las islas hermanas," the three islands— Cuba, Puerto Rico, and the Dominican Republic—are sisters, bound together in deep cultural and historical affinity. In his beautiful song of that title, the great Puerto Rican vocalist and composer Pedro Ortíz Dávila ("Davilita", 1912–1986) evokes the distinctive flavors and rhythms of his Spanish Caribbean, "el Caribe hispano," "las Antillas." He sings adoringly of their physical beauty, their seductive music, and their world-renowned cigars and coffee, all to the delicious flavor ("sabor") of rum, honey and sugar cane, whose praise he sings in the lilting refrain: "It tastes like rum, it tastes like honey, it tastes like sugarcane" ("sabe a ron, sabe a miel, sabe a caña"). Davilita also voices great pride in the three countries' struggles for freedom, and in national leaders of the stature of José Martí and Juan Pablo Duarte. But, as we shall see, it is here, when he turns to the historical experiences of the Island sisters, that the seams in that sibling kinship begin to show, and the great singer's adoration gives way to uncertainty, and the forceful proclamation of an unfulfilled political ideal.

Davilita was a Caribbean Latino, *un caribeño*. With all the heartfelt love he expresses for the islands, and though born in Puerto Rico, he spent nearly all of his adult life in El Barrio, New York, having arrived there at age 15 in 1927, and not returning to live in Puerto Rico until the 1950s. Through the 1930s and 1940s, the formative decades in the history of New York's early Latino community, he established himself, and was widely recognized, as the premier vocalist in Puerto Rican music. Over his long and illustrous musical career, he recorded over 3,000 songs.

Shortly after his arrival in 1929, Davilita joined up with none other than the legendary composer and bandleader Rafael Hernández, and was lead voice in Hernández's Trio Borinquen, renamed the Cuarteto Victoria, during the height of its immense international popularity. He also sang both chorus and lead with the variously named groups of Pedro Flores for many years, and was the first to record many of the historic compositions of both Rafael Hernández and Pedro Flores, two of the foremost composers in twentieth century Latin American music. His associations and achievements were boundless in the musical field of that period, and included collaboration with musicians of the magnitude and variety as Manuel Jiménez ("Canario"), Alberto Socorrás, Plácido Acevedo, Augusto Coén, Noro Morales and, after his return to Puerto Rico, Felipe Rodríguez ("La Voz"). Of exemplary note, his first recording, in 1930, was Rafael Hernández's "Lamento Borincano," and thanks to the prodding of Canario, Davilita entered history as the first to record that international anthem of the Latino migrant population, a composition that the author José Luis González considered the first protest song in the history of Latin American popular music. It was the voice of Davilita, a 19-year-old *boricua* from East 100th Street, that resounded from the record stores and tenement windows of El Barrio, and of many Latino working-class barrios, on the ominous eve of the Great Depression.

Musically, "Son Tres" is a *canción*. While it shows traces of Cuban *son montuno* and Puerto Rican *plena*, makes boastful mention of the Dominican *merengue*, and has a fade-out chorus of traditional *lei-lo-lai*, Davilita is careful to choose a more generic, hybrid song-form like the *canción* so as to encompass all three Caribbean traditions without privileging any one national style. He is intent, after all, to marvel at the symbiosis and cohesion of the three-part cultural family. And as long as he lingers on their shared sensorium —kindred tastes, smells, sights, and sounds—and expressive traditions, he is able to sustain that confident sense of delight and harmony. But when it comes to political history, the dissonance sets in or, more precisely, the sisters take divergent paths. For while Cuba and the Dominican Republic achieved national sovereignty, and can hail their founding leaders in Martí and Duarte, Davilita is made to ask, suggestively, of his own *patria*, "and for Puerto Rico, who will it be?" ("y por Borinquen ¿quién será?"). Of the three sisters, his Puerto Rico remains in direct colonial bondage, and thus stands apart from, despite their deeper affinities, the other sisters. As the song dates from around mid-century, and as Davilita was known for his strong affiliation with the Puerto Rican nationalist cause, one could surmise that the question "who will it be?" might well be posed in veiled reference to the supreme anti-imperialist leader Pedro Albizu Campos, who was then languishing in a federal penitentiary while his fellow combatants carried on the intense militant struggle for national independence. Or perhaps it is a sarcastic allusion to

Luis Muñoz Marín, the country's first locally elected governor who was in those years compromising away the very goals of sovereignty to which he had earlier dedicated himself.

Nevertheless, when Davilita contemplates the sorry political state of his homeland in the present, rather than sinking in defeat he is made to think of the future, and of the past. The song ends with an emphatic pronouncement of the singer's own longing for the sovereignty of all three sister islands, and for the realization, in his own life-time, of the historical ideal of the countries since their national formations in the nineteenth century, the ideal of "Antillean unity" ("la unión antillana"). With that final phrase, Martí, Hostos, Betances, Máximo Gómez, Sotero Figueroa, and countless other patriotic leaders come immediately to mind, as does the revolutionary poet Lola Rodríguez de Tió, who penned the axiomatic lines on Spanish Antillean unity, "Cuba y Puerto Rico, de un pájaro las dos alas" ("Cuban and Puerto Rico, two wings of the same bird"). In the same mellifluous tones, but with noticeably greater urgency, Davilita shows that his love for the cultural unity of his native region extends to the more disconcerting field of political struggle, and beyond the present to its rich and challenging historical legacy. In his warm embrace of the three sisters he does not shy away from the obstacles they face or the bifurcations in their political trajectories.

Of course Davilita might have been even more befuddled had his musical eye turned to "las islas hermanas" closer to our own time, after the Cuban Revolution and the Dominican Republic since the endless Trujillo nightmare. Beyond that, his concern over the divergent historical destinies of his three related peoples might have reached a crisis pitch were he to ponder the three emigrant enclaves which have taken such discrepant shape in the United States by century's end. As remote from each other as "las tres hermanas" now stand in the community of nations, the three diasporic "islands" of Caribbean Latinos offer up three radically diverse modalities of Latino presence in the new millennium. The familiar "sabor" is still there, of course, and most Dominicans, Puerto Ricans, and Cubans still enjoy that distinctive bond at a sensual, performative, and expressive level, especially when contrasted with the other major component of present-day Latino life, the Mexican American. It is necessary to retain a recognition of that family kinship alive, in the manner of Davilita, as the grounding of deep cultural solidarity. But as for their sociological placement and perspectives in contemporary U.S. society, the three Caribbean Latino enclaves may appear cousins, and distant ones at that, but hardly sisters-in-arms. On the other hand, because Hispanic Caribbean politics are today being played out so actively in the public field of U.S. culture, it could well be that, like a century ago, the diaspora setting will some day serve as the catalytic ground for a renewal, under new conditions, of the ongoing ideal of "la unión antillana."

Historical Dimensions

Thus the history of Caribbean Latino diaspora in the United States goes way back. The current media hype surrounding the "Latino explosion," like those in the past, lends the booming Latino presence and visibility an air of novelty, as though these throngs of new hyphenated Americans had just begun to land during the present generation. In the case of Caribbean Latinos in particular this sense of recency is pervasive, with the Cuban community supposedly dating from the years since 1959, the Dominicans since the mid-1960s at the earliest, and even the Puerto Rican enclave, while admittedly of older vintage, often being treated as a post-World War II phenomenon sparked by the industrialization of the Island economy in the 1940s and 1950s. U.S. Antillanos, like Caribbeans and Latin Americans in general, are usually portrayed as "new immigrants," part of the influx of peoples from the Third World issuing from the world-wide process of decolonization and the restructuring of global, regional, and local economies.

The reach of Caribbean Latino history is of course much longer than that, and actually predates and then coincides with the proverbial waves of European immigration of the later nineteenth and early twentieth centuries. Bernardo Vega, certainly the most substantive source for knowledge of that history, transports us as far back as the early nineteenth century. A case could even be made for extending the story to Alvar Núñez Cabeza de Vaca's expedition to *La Florida*, the only problem with that periodization being that it is hard to talk about the life of U.S. Latinos before there was a United States of America. Bernardo Vega, though, with his tale of interlocked autobiography and political history, gives ample reason for setting the conditions for a Caribbean Latino presence in the U.S. to the 1820s, when the completed independence of the continent from Spanish rule opened the door to the beginnings of U.S. regional hegemony as manifest in the Monroe Doctrine of 1823. Via the recollections of his long-lost uncle Antonio Vega, who had been in New York since 1857 and whom Bernardo met up with a few years after his own arrival in 1916, the socialist *tabaquero* is able to reconstruct his own family's genealogy. His great-great grandfather, it turns out, fled into exile from Spain to then take part in the lively smuggling trade that brought munitions and other aid to the independence wars raging in Venezuela and the other Latin American republics. Bernardo Vega establishes his own subversive pedigree in this way, while at the same time drawing the history of the Caribbean Latino diaspora into a broad and pivotal political context. For indeed, rather than the product of recent, late-twentieth century changes in the economic and political map, people from the Spanish Caribbean began gravitating toward the northern metropolis as soon as the United States assumed its regional hegemonic role and became a counter-pole to the stubbornly lingering foothold of Spanish empire.

What Vega fails to mention, though it would certainly sustain his case more convincingly than the doses of "myth" (as he calls them) that infuse his biographical version of events, is that already then, in the 1820s, the documentary and literary presence of Caribbean Latinos in New York had begun. In 1823, the 20-year-old Cuban poet and patriot José María de Heredia arrived to spend several years of exile in the American northeast, mostly New York City. Fleeing the Spanish and colonial authorities because of his avid clamor for the independence of his beloved homeland, Heredia founded and edited a newspaper, continued to write prolifically, and published his first book of poems, *Poesías*, in New York in 1825. Most memorably, he had occasion to visit Niagara Falls, to which he paid emotional and philosophical homage in his long poem "Niágara," one of the canonical texts of Cuban literature. It can also be considered, from today's vantage, one of the founding works of Caribbean Latino literature in the United States. Though it contains little by way of description of American society of the time, much less of any Cuban exile settlement, "Niágara" is nevertheless of cardinal importance in being such an early reflection by a Caribbean on the metaphysical significance of the U.S., written on North American soil, anticipating in this way the profound and prolific reflections of Martí, Hostos, and others later in the century.

Though "Niágara" stands as something of a curiosity item in the literary and historical annals, Heredia was not alone in his early exiled state, or the only one to give literary expression to that condition. In fact, another of his poems, "Himno del desterrado," became something of an anthem among exiled Cuban writers of the period, and served as the signature text in the first anthology of such writing, *Laúd del desterrado*, which was published in 1858.

New York shared the stage in this early period of Caribbean Latino history with Florida. As of the early years, as is also true in more recent times, "La Florida" took its distinctive place in the Latino imaginary. It was in Florida, not so much Miami as Tampa, Key West, and Ybor City, that the drama of Caribbean Latino life took on discernible shape during the middle half of the nineteenth century.[10] The tobacco industry played a central role in the formation of a Spanish and Cuban community and the racial and class divisions that unfolded in that context. Rather than the sporadic and numerically insignificant numbers of *antillano* exiles of the preceding decades, the Florida enclaves were the earliest evidence of a relatively dynamic and sizable population. Very little of this important pre-history finds its way into Bernardo Vega's account, which tends to leap over the mid-century period to arrive at the dramatic entrance of Hostos and Martí on the New York scene in the later decades of the century.

Vega acknowledges at several points the selective functioning of his aging uncle's memory, and comments on Tío Antonio's tendency to highlight and lend uncritical preference to Puerto Rican actors in the drama. Bernardo even justifies this *boricua*-centric bias by pointing to the subordinate role given to Puerto Ricans in international affairs. But with all of Tío Antonio's exhaltation of early Puerto Rican achievements, the nineteenth century is no doubt the Cuban chapter in the story of Caribbean Latino presence in the United States, from the earliest signs and articulations of an exile location to the tumultuous activism and vocal community presence in New York, Philadelphia, and Florida of the century's closing decades. As the principal Puerto Rican leaders and thinkers themselves recognized, it was the Cuban presence that comprised the bulk of the community in formation, and it was the Cuban struggle to which the Puerto Ricans remained integrally tied. If in Lola Rodríguez de Tió's vision Puerto Rico and Cuba were "two wings of a bird," then that bird was admittedly lopsided. The wings seemed as though they were not made for the same airborne creature. But in those heady times the ideal of Antillean unity was at the peak of its propagation, and such contrasts and contentions along national lines were not of overriding concern. The metaphoric bi-national bird, however awkward, will surely find its equilibrium, and soar to new heights of solidarity and sovereignty.

There is a wing missing, of course, from Lola's emblematic *antillano* mascot, the Dominican Republic, a further reflection of divergent historical experiences through the entire period. Of course some Dominicans did play a noteworthy role in the struggle against Spain—the towering revolutionary general Máximo Gómez was Dominican—and Santo Domingo itself was a significant location of exile activity—one thinks, above all, of the immense significance of Hostos in Dominican intellectual and educational history. But no sizable Dominican presence can be established in U.S. settings, much less any evidence of a distinctive Dominican enclave. Though much research remains to be done, the same can be said of the Dominican exile and emigrant experience through most of the twentieth century. Important exceptions like members of the illustrious Henríquez Ureña family and others have been identified, as have numerous individuals and *conjuntos* on the New York musical scene of the 1920s and 1930s. Bernardo Vega even mentions that a winner of the prestigious *Juegos Florales* literary prizes in 1919, according to him "the most outstanding event in the Spanish-speaking community in New York since the turn of the century," was a Dominican author, the esteemed Manuel Florentino Cestero.[11]

While a Dominican part in the building of the Latino community would wait until the final decades of the century, it would be mistaken to discount the ongoing Dominican role in the conceptualization of a pan-*antillano* ideal. One need only recall the dramatic opening lines of Pedro Mir's master-work, *Contracanto a Walt Whitman*, written in mid-century, to recognize the co-conspiracy of Dominicans in opposition to U.S. domination over the region and its cultures. Generally considered the country's national poet,

Mir begins his majestic "counter-song" by asserting his own personal full-scale pan-Spanish Caribbean identity, a "yo" which he then goes on to counterpose to that of the formidable Whitman: "Yo," he begins,

> I,
> a son of the Caribbean,
> Antillean to be exact.
> The raw product of a simple
> Puerto Rican girl
> and a Cuban worker,
> born precisely, and poor,
> on Quisqueyan soil.

Yo / un hijo del Caribe / precisamente antillano. / Producto / primitivo de una ingenua / criatura borinqueña / y un obrero cubano, / nacido justamente, y pobremente, / en suelo quisqueyano.[12]

Divergences and Convergences

Turning to the twentieth century, in the early years, along with the Cubans and Puerto Ricans, Spaniards figured prominently in that community. Whatever one thinks about the inclusion of Spanish immigrants and descendants in the present-day "Latino" configuration, there can be no doubt as to their presence and importance in the Florida and New York Latino settlements prior to World War I and beyond. This was particularly the case in the decades before and after the turn of the century, and most evidently in the world of tobacco and cigar production. Bernardo's entire account, from his first New York years and through the Spanish Civil War of the 1930s, makes constant mention of Spanish comrades and cultural activity, and he even counted the Sephardic Spaniard Jacobo Silvestre Bresman as one of his most faithful friends and influential intellectual and political mentors. The Spanish role in the anarchist and labor movements, including those in New York and Florida, is well-known and often told, a significant part of Latino history.

What often goes unmentioned in this necessary attention to Spanish immigrants in early Latino history, however, is the issue of class and racial differences in those multi-Latino interactions, where the seams of pan-ethnic enclave life showed through. As is described in the important memoir *Black Cuban, Black American* (2000) by Evelio Grillo, an Afro-Cuban who grew up in Florida in the 1920s and 1930s, Spaniards and white Cubans played an increasingly central role in the ownership and managerial operations of the cigar trade in later nineteenth-century Florida.[13] As a result, class and black–white divides took an ever greater toll on the earlier unity among the Spanish-speaking *tabaqueros*. An *Afro*-Cuban consciousness thus emerged early on among the black cigar workers, with the obvious implication that subsequent Caribbean Latino history needs to be studied, and told, with that crucial differentiation squarely in view. In her book on Puerto Rican musicians in New York through the 1940s, *My Music Is My Flag* (1997), Ruth Glasser offers further evidence of this racist dimension of Latino community formation, and especially the role of Spanish cultural presence in that kind of discrimination. On the basis of extensive interviews, Glasser tells of the exclusionary policies of the Asturian, Valencian, and Gallician clubs and cultural centers, which often drew the line on black Latinos.[14]

But with the experiences of the Depression and inter-war years, including the final decline of the tobacco industry, the Spanish role in the New York Latino community came to recede in both volume and significance, and the Cuban and Puerto Rican components of the multi-Latino diaspora assumed the central place, which they held in that history until recent decades. While Cubans continued to prevail in Florida and in pockets of the northeast, the Puerto Rican population came to far surpass all of the other groups, particularly after the decreeing of U.S. citizenship for Puerto Ricans in 1917. By 1930, New York Puerto Ricans were already twice as numerous as Spaniards, and as Cubans and Dominicans combined. During those decades, and through the 1950s, the latter two groups found themselves in similar positions as exiles from long-term dictatorial rule, a situation that was further complicated by the overt and covert complicity of U.S. imperial power, including direct military occupation. Puerto Ricans, meanwhile, as citizens and as mobile labor reserves resulting from the orchestrated industrialization of the Island, saw their numbers increase geometrically in the post-World War II years, a development that brought their presence to nearly a million by the 1960s and made them the second largest Latino group in the country after the Mexican Americans.

But prior to this divergence in their paths, marked off emphatically by the Cuban Revolution of 1959, Puerto Ricans and Cubans during the 1920s, 1930s, and 1940s constituted the core of the Caribbean Latino community in the United States. General social and cultural interaction can be documented, and is particularly conspicuous, for example, in popular music. Members of both nationalities proliferated and dominated in all the major bands and orchestras through those years, and shared musical repertoires and audiences. Styles were most commonly and preponderantly Cuban, which reflected the far greater visibility of things Cuban in the mass culture. It is sometimes recognized, as a telling example, that of the fifteen "Afro-Cubans" in Machito's unsurpassed orchestra of the 1940s, all but two were Puerto Ricans. It was the Cuban image that stood in as emblematic of the tropical, Spanish-speaking Caribbean, as evident in the proliferation of dance crazes and of course in the entry into the American livingroom during the 1950s of the ubiquitous figure of Desi Arnaz. The Cuban American critic Gustavo Pérez-Firmat has provided sensitive and lasting analysis of this phenomenon, which he calls "The Desi Chain," in his book *Life on the Hyphen*.[15]

But while the swelling Puerto Rican demographic presence was thus typically eclipsed by that of Cubans in the public sphere, the relation between the two cultures was one not of contention, but of remarkable creative symbiosis and confluence. Davilita's songs resound with these fusions and blendings: though his repertoire comprised mainly Cuban song traditions of the *son*, *bolero*, and *guaracha*, many of them were written by the major Puerto Rican composers Rafael Hernández, Pedro Flores, and Plácido Acevedo. As is evident in "Son Tres," there is a smooth flow of continuity between Puerto Rican and Cuban traditions. Both create and partake equally of "el sabor." What better evidence than the music that came to be called "salsa" through the last quarter of the twentieth century?

Afrodiaspora

The Cuban–Puerto Rican continuum, which has formed the crux of Caribbean Latino cultural history, is a field of blackness in the U.S. context. The shared African moorings of their national and popular cultures carry over strongly to the diasporic context, such that if they share language culture with other Spanish speakers, they at the same time share with fellow Caribbeans and other African-descendant peoples those deep cultural heritages, and of course deeply racialized social histories. *Afroantillanos* constitute by far the largest non-English-speaking black population in U.S. history, and Caribbean Latino history thus overlaps substantively with the history of Afro-Latinos in the U.S.

To a significant degree, in fact, what marks off *caribeños* within the Latino pan-ethnicity as a whole is precisely this interface with blackness and an Afro-Atlantic imaginary. As Afro-Latinos, they embody the compatibility of blackness with the notion of Latino identity in the United States. While in its dominant and consumer version Latino realities are often walled off from, or counterposed to, blackness and Afro-diasporic cultural experience, the *antillano* perspective instates the continuity and mutuality between them. This more porous border, of course, has made for a far more active reciprocity with African Americans. After a half century of close social interaction, Caribbean Latinos, and *afroantillanos* in particular, are the Latinos who most directly encountered anti-black racism in the U.S. setting, including from other Latinos. They are also those who have enjoyed the most productive sharing and exchange with American Blacks. Music history provides ample evidence of the latter dimension, while the figures of Afro-Puerto Ricans

Arturo Alfonso Schomburg and Jesús Colón illustrate, in different historical periods, the strong and complex attachments between the two populations at the intellectual and political level, and their unity in facing up to anti-black racism.[16]

This difference within the pan-Latino cultural configuration is not new to our times. The racial and color divide has been operative since early on, and has been evident over the long stretches of Caribbean Latino history in the twentieth century. The great Davilita is once again a key source on *caribeño* experience in this regard. The renowned black Puerto Rican emigrant of long standing once recalled the hierarchy he witnessed in the musical field, where Puerto Ricans and Cubans were typically paid less than other Spanish-language artists: "Victor never treated us like they did the Mexicans, the South Americans when it came to money . . . Venezuela, . . . and Argentina and all those countries charged a lot of money and [the company] paid them . . . . [Xavier] Cugat was Spanish, [he] charged as if he were an American, wherever he went. But the Puerto Ricans, no."[17] Predictably, Cubans and Puerto Ricans, inhabiting as they do the darker end of the Latino chromatic spectrum, are also most frequently situated at the bottom of the pan-Latino pecking order of privilege. And it would seem that Davilita's observations about the world of popular music would apply fittingly to all other areas of U.S. society, and to most any historical era.

But the implications of Davilita's comments run deeper still, and perhaps point to yet another distinction, this time within the *caribeño* diaspora experience itself. With his emphasis on the Puerto Ricans as those most devoid of any cultural preference or equal treatment, we are reminded again of the lines from "Son Tres," "and for Puerto Rico, who will it be?" ("y por Borinquen ¿quién será?"). All the other Latino groups, even the other *antillanos*, have their diplomatic representation, and their home countries are there to stand up for them, however feebly and selectively at times, in the U.S. context. The diasporas are an extension, as it were, of their native republics, as corrupt or tyrannical as those republics may be. Not so the Puerto Ricans, whose unique status as U.S. citizens has proved a mixed blessing at best, and whose U.S. residents are alone among the Latinos in their sense of disconnection from any governmental or institutional support from their home nation.

An editorial column of the same period makes a similar point about inter-Latino relations in New York; the Spanish-language weekly *Gráfico*, under the editorship of Bernardo Vega, included the following comment in an issue from 1927: "The most vulnerable group of those which comprise the large family of Ibero-Americans (in New York City) is the Puerto Rican. Truly it seems a paradox that being American citizens these should be the most defenseless. While the citizens of other countries have their consulates and diplomats to represent them, the children of *Borinquen* have no one."[18] This paradoxical and "exceptional" orphan state of the Puerto Ricans among the many Latino groups is directly attributable to its colonial condition and the ramification of that status in the diaspora in the form of internal colonialism. What is more, if the colonial relation drew visible lines of differentiation between Puerto Ricans and other Latinos, including *caribeños,* in earlier times, the same continues to be the case today. Class and racial subordination is compounded in the Puerto Rican case by the fact and rule of ongoing colonial dependence, a dimension of collective social experience that puts a challenging test to the inclusiveness of the prevailing Latino concept.

Within the *antillano* subset, the Puerto Rican presence is, in this sense, of a very different order than both the Cuban and the Dominican, as extremely divergent as those two also are from one another. Fidel Castro once referred to Puerto Rico as the "perfumed colony," and that it certainly seems to be with respect to relative degrees of economic misery and political authoritarianism. But in the U.S. setting, the community forged of a colonial labor migration stands in greater long-term disadvantage than that which has issued from political exile, or even the more recognizable Third World immigration as in the Dominican case. The sheer relative volume of the Puerto Rican emigration movement, where the diaspora stands nearly equal in size to that of the Island population, is but another blatant indication of this disparity. The "perfume," and the sugarcane legacy, have a bittersweet taste when it comes to the racialized, pathologized circumstance of the colonial minority citizen.

Interlocking Diasporas

On the other hand, Puerto Ricans are for related reasons the main U.S. *antillano* group who lived through and participated in the formative 1960s and 1970s period in U.S. history, though there was some Dominican and Cuban presence as well. The ethnic affirmation and political stridency of those years were of constitutive importance for the emergence of Latino identity in the context of U.S. minority struggles, and the emergence of a "Nuyorican" identity in those years came to pre-figure analogous developments among Dominicanyorks and some Cuban Americans in times closer to our own. These movements also demonstrated bonds of coalitional solidarity across national lines with African Americans, Native Americans, and Asian Americans, as well as the connection of these domestic social movements with political and cultural developments at an international level. In this respect, the social positioning and group history of Puerto Ricans would seem to approximate that of Mexican Americans more closely than that of the other Caribbean Latinos, whose cultural location and sense of group identity came to take shape subsequent to that dramatic and definitive stage. It is important to call attention to this differential political history and social placement of the diasporic groups, because many discussions of Latino pan-ethnicity, especially those which limit the focus to immigration, or to language background and other cultural commonalities, tend to leave such crucial considerations out of account.

In our times, the three Caribbean Latino enclaves exhibit as many disjunctures and discontinuities in the U.S. context as do their respective "sister islands" in the contemporary Caribbean regional and international settings. The anachronistic direct colony, the beleaguered neo-colony, and the foundering experiment in dependent socialism issue up markedly divergent diasporas, whose principal commonality corresponds to the degree to which their current configurations mirror and are defined by the status of their home countries in world affairs. Despite their obvious affinities within the full Latino composite, and the long-term historical congruencies and interconnections that underlie the persistent Antillean ideal, no facile assumption of intimate family loyalties or automatic political cohesion among U.S. Cubans, Dominicans, and Puerto Ricans would seem in order, at least for the foreseeable future.

Indeed, one recent analysis even proposes a useful typology of the three diasporas, referring to the Puerto Ricans as "colonial/racial subjects," the Dominicans as "colonial immigrants," and Cubans as "immigrants."[19] This contrastive schema is not merely descriptive, but also speaks of a process of racialization according to which diasporic Puerto Ricans become "African Americanized," Dominicans increasingly "Puerto Ricanized," and Cubans, specifically pre-1980s Cuban migrants, intent on disassociating themselves from the Dominican experience of approximating Puerto Ricans in their social status. This idea of a dynamic range of diasporic options is valuable in thus differentiating the situation of the groups based on their relation to structures of transnational power and ongoing dynamics of colonial and racial subordination. For the three main ethno-national groups comprising the Caribbean Latino diaspora do in fact cover the gamut of possibilities among contemporary transnational communities and within the pan-Latino continuum, from the least to the most privileged in terms of economic, political, and cultural capital. The tendency to vie and dis-identify among them would seem to outweigh any prospects of cross-group solidarity.

However, historical experience shows these relations and disparities to be in continual flux, and it is therefore important not to fix our analytical gaze too squarely on the immediate present. Just as the island nations themselves can well undermine and re-figure the familiar patterns of international demarcation, so too the three diaspora enclaves may recognize new grounds for rapprochement and cultural coalescence along the contentious ethnic queue. The present study, based on ethnographic testimony and critical interpretation of cultural expressions, would suggest that the signs of such a new development are already coming into view. Certainly the shared Afro-Latino background that tends most to distinguish them within the pan-Latino composite, and the attendant complementary relationship to blackness, promises to have unifying repercussions within the U.S. racial formation, where the significance of the color line seems to be in no way diminishing.

The socio-cultural location of Caribbean Latinos is thus defined by their relationship to non-Caribbean Latinos, on the one hand, and to non-Latino Caribbeans on the other. A key question for the future will be whether the prevailing Latino concept has the effect of perpetuating, in the enclave context, the Caribbean's long and tragic history of balkanization along the lines of language cultures, or whether alternatively it may help foster the kind of pan-Caribbean solidarity that shared life in the United States has engendered in earlier historical periods. It is clear that the transnational linkages and interrelations between diaspora and homeland politics are central to any prognostic view. As we shall see, the interactions among diasporic Puerto Ricans, Dominicans, and a new generation of Cubans reveal interesting convergences, and the impact of U.S. Caribbean Latinos could well end up changing the face of the Hispanic Caribbean.

Notes on the *Antillano* Counterstream

After spending formative years and the bulk of his adult life in the New York diaspora, Davilita returned to live in his native Puerto Rico in the 1950s. There he formed a duo with the immensely popular vocalist Felipe Rodríguez, known as "La Voz," and together recorded some of the best-selling and most widely admired albums of his career. In spite of this ascending success, Davilita did not find happiness in his long-lost homeland, and grieved about the discrimination he was forced to endure because of his militant anti-colonialist politics, his blackness, and his life-long residence in the diaspora. Lacking the overdue recognition of the country's cultural establishment, this towering figure of the national music died sickly and isolated in his hometown of Bayamón. The full story has yet to be told, but this sad ending to such an illustrious life can only be explained by understanding the phenomenon of circular migration and the cultural counterstream shared by all *caribeños* through the decades of diasporic community life.

Of the three island nations of the Hispanic Caribbean, it is the Dominican Republic that has generated the largest body of literature on the transnational and return migratory experience. Perhaps because the dramatic growth of a huge Dominican diaspora coincides with the emergence of transnational studies, the Dominican experience is sometimes referred to as a transnational community par excellence. A slew of major social scientific volumes, by Dominicanists Sherri Grasmuck, Patricia Pessar, Peggy Levitt, and Eugenia Georges, as well as important work by Luis Guarnizo, Jorge Duany, Silvio Torres Saillant, José Itzigsohn, and many others, all focusing on Dominican transnationalism, have appeared since 1990.[20] The massive out-migration after the end of the Trujillo era, concentrated in New York City and San Juan but fanning out to other U.S. settings, a range of European countries, other parts of the Americas, and elsewhere, has attracted broad scholarly, literary, and journalistic attention, and has made the Dominican case a central instance of transnational political and cultural life in the generation before and after the millennium.

Though diaspora-island relations have been of central interest in Puerto Rican cultural and political life for over a century by now, the phenomenon of return migration and remittances has generated far less focused attention than the much shorter-lived Dominican mass migration experience. José Hernández Alvarez' very early study mentioned above, *Return Migration to Puerto Rico* (1967), itself methodologically limited, has not been followed by significant subsequent interest in the subject, at least among scholars, though the theme has been treated in journalistic and literary work over the decades, especially since the return flow reached swollen proportions in the 1970s. The major contribution on Puerto Rican transnationalism thus far is no doubt Jorge Duany's 2002 book *The Puerto Rican Nation on the Move: Identities on the Island and in the United States.* It is indeed an important scholarly achievement, and contains a wealth of analysis of transnational cultural interactions. But even there, only one chapter deals directly with the sweeping experience of circular migration, and almost no mention is made of return movement and its cultural impact.

More directly on that subject is the excellent ethnographic study *Contested Belonging: Circular Migration and Puerto Rican Identity* (2000) by Dutch sociologist Erna Kerkhof. There the interesting life-stories and anecdotes gleaned from interviews in the west-coastal city of Mayagüez are accompanied by informed and sensitive critical analysis, the only drawback being that the author evidently did not have the opportunity to conduct complementary interviews in New York and other parts of the Puerto Rican diaspora itself. On the other hand, the book by Elizabeth M. Aranda, *Emotional Bridges to Puerto Rico* (2006) promises in the subtitle (*Migration, Return Migration, and the Struggles of Incorporation*) to address the return experience, but in fact most of its attention goes once again to problems of "incorporation" to the U.S. setting. "Emotional bridges" are of course an important part of the larger process of cultural flows, but this study unfortunately fails to address any of the other dimensions of that process. Further, the book's over-concentration on the "Puerto Rican middle class" tends to sideline the far more massive experience of the impoverished majority of the Puerto Rican diaspora and therefore makes the study of less interest to an analysis of cultural flows "from below."

Most directly in line with the present study is the book by Gina M. Pérez, *The Near Northwest Side Story: Migration, Displacement, and Puerto Rican Families* (2004), and especially the chapter "*Los de Afuera*, Transnationalism, and the Cultural Politics of Identity." On the basis of ethnographic work in Chicago and San Sebastián, Puerto Rico, where many "Chicago Rican" families come from, Pérez analyzes a range of cultural encounters by way of attitudes, changing values, and the stark and at times conflictive contrasts between the "outsiders" ("los de afuera") and those who stayed and have to deal with the influx of so many outsiders. The dramatic everyday clashes over language use, gender roles, valuations of family and education, what it means to be Puerto Rican, and racial identities are brought to dramatic life in this innovative work, which has been a frequent reference point for me in my own study. Pérez suggests that what the returnees bring to San Sebastián constitutes a challenge to accepted ways on many fronts, and one can assume that her own presence as a diasporic Puerto Rican woman contributed to that encounter. My goal here is to push this line of thinking further, by upping the stakes to include a collective challenge to the hegemony of an authoritarian and essentialist concept of national identity and history, and by expanding the idea of cultural practice to include the changes wrought in and by forms of artistic expression.

Finally, in the case of the Cuban diaspora, imaginings of the homeland are obviously more plentiful than actual returns, though cultural remittances may be even more consequential than for Dominicans or Puerto Ricans. In any case, with all the emotional charge attached to the topic, little scholarly work has been devoted to a Cuban cultural counterstream, though an important Spanish-language testimony, *Contra viento y marea* (1978), anticipates the historic visit of the Antonio Maceo Brigade, a group of sympathetic Cuban Americans during the opening of the dialogue in the 1970s. The personal memoir of one of that group, Román de la Campa, entitled *Cuba on My Mind: Journeys to a Severed Nation* (2000), offers an elegantly written reflection on the return, while the book by the more conservative Cuban-American critic Gustavo Pérez Firmat, *Life on the Hyphen: The Cuban-American Way* (1994), attests to the abrupt and at the same time long-term distancing between the diaspora and its embattled homeland. Nevertheless, mutually enriching cultural interaction, especially in the music field, continues under the radar screen, as is most dramatically evident in the worlds of Latin jazz and hip hop in our own times.

More general reflections on the Hispanic Caribbean as what might cautiously be called a cultural "sub-region" are surprisingly rare, particularly in view of the intense emotional and intellectual appeal of the "*antillano*" concept in the intertwined histories of the three islands. The extreme political trifurcation among the national narratives, especially since the second half of the twentieth century, do make generalizations difficult, though therein lies at the same time the challenge and fascination of comparative and contrastive analysis. Like the national political histories, the modern diasporas of the three countries have been radically divergent, even the Puerto Rican and Dominican ones which would appear to have so much in common. For the same reasons, the nature of return and cultural remittances and their impact also varies widely among them. On the other hand, there are also important convergences and congruencies that warrant attention and justify a unified approach, as exemplified engagingly in the book by Puerto Rican cultural critic Yolanda Martínez-San Miguel, *Caribe Two Ways: Cultura de la migración en el Caribe insular hispánico* (2003). For one thing, in addition to the looming Hispanophile ideological presence to this day, there is the afore-mentioned "trouble" with the African heritage present in differential ways in each national history, a factor that becomes perhaps even more salient in the diaspora context in the United States. Further, as *Caribe Two Ways* highlights so well, there has been an ongoing and intensifying migratory interaction among the countries all along, and the presence of mutually interlocking diasporas in each country, most visibly a prominent Cuban and a massive Dominican enclave in contemporary Puerto Rico. Of greatest importance for the present study, of course, each country has a huge diaspora community in the United States, each of them then implicated in the newly denominated "Latino" diaspora with its towering significance in the present-day culture wars. Indeed, it can be said that for reasons of political and colonial history the Hispanic Caribbean has been closer to and more directly enmeshed in twentieth-century U.S. social reality than any of the other Caribbean cultures, this in spite of the language difference not present or as significant in the case of West Indian diasporas.

There is thus ample fascination in focusing analytic attention on the impact of the Caribbean Latino diaspora(s) as they come home to roost in their troubled island nation homelands, unsettling their entrenched cultural presumptions, and perhaps pressuring them, however unwittingly, into more direct interaction than has been possible in the archipelago of origin. Here again, as is so often the case, it is from the "outside," from the transnational vantage of exile and diaspora, that the most penetrating vision of the national culture becomes possible.

But in order to gain a full understanding of the deep challenge represented by the migratory counterstream it is necessary to think the concept of diaspora, and of cultural remittances, in the most expansive manner possible. Issues of economic development, entrepreneurial achievement, or energetic civic participation are all significant, to be sure, which is why they have been so preponderant in much transnational analysis to date. But the role of the cultural, in the sense of "the work of the imagination" as expounded so incisively by Arjun Appadurai and Stuart Hall,[21] needs to be centered in this challenging interpretive project. The cultural, as in cultural remittances, means ideologies of racial and sexual identities as they intersect and collide with dominant national and class narratives. These aspects are perhaps best studied on the basis of personal testimony and lived social experience, so what follows, in chapter 4, will be a sampler of stories recounting cultural changes and challenges in this sense. But the cultural aspect also embraces the creative and expressive dimensions of social life as manifest in the poetry, musical styles, and visual iconography of group representations. The latter part of the book, chapters 5 and 6 and the Coda, will present some perspectives on the remittance of Caribbean Latino musical, poetic, and artistic styles and practices to the home countries, and their powerful, potentially transformative impact.

PART 2:

NARRATIVE GROUNDINGS

**"Nury" (on left) and a friend, La Romana,
Dominican Republic, 2007.**

Photographer Miriam Jiménez Román.
Permission Miriam Jiménez Román.

4 TALES OF LEARNING AND TURNING

Introducing the Tales

Since the main ideas for this book came from talking with people, I am aware that the best evidence I have for substantiating those ideas are the stories people tell me. My own experience has also been important, since I have lived and continue to live these transnational realities. But a lot of others live them in many different ways, sometimes more intensely than I myself. As time went by over the past ten years or so I went about identifying good stories, and good storytellers. Some of these tellers were, or have become, good friends, and others are friends, or acquaintances, of friends. For as people came to learn what I was interested in they would mention others they knew or heard of, and steer me toward them. I started to make lists of people I had to get back to, for clarifications or elaborations or more chapters in their life-stories. As my ideas took shape I knew I had to follow up, and to follow leads.

It's a far cry from a casual conversation to a formal interview, but there is a lot of gray area in between. On the one hand, as much as you would like to, you can never reproduce the casualness and spontaneity of a conversation. On the other hand you need a certain degree of formality if the goal is to develop evidence in support of an argument or line of analysis. Early on, as I got ready to start doing interviews a few years ago, I set my sights on that gray area, aiming for structured and thematically guided discussions that still retained an air of informality and affective interaction. A good laugh and trading notes about everyday experiences helps keep it light and encourages a probing of those nooks and crannies of life that often harbor the deeper, more revealing aspects of a social phenomenon. As is so often the case, the truth is in the details.

Many of the people knew that I am a writer and researcher, but few thought I would be interested in including their stories in my work. I would often let them know that I would be following up with them, so that my contact with them and request for an interview wouldn't seem as if it were coming from out of the blue. Though very few had ever been interviewed before, generally they knew what to expect when I sat down with them and my tape recorder. I know I put them at ease by leaving the location totally up to them. I met many in their homes, others in nearby or convenient stores or public places, a few in my office or home. Wherever was best for them. I let them know that it would take less than an hour, maybe even a half hour, though of course in many cases we went on for as much as two hours or more. In quite a few instances, we left it that there was lots more to say and that the conversation would go on, maybe for life. The topic itself has become a bond between us.

At the occasion of actually meeting up with people I would notice a touch of nervousness, as though they were expected to perform or give a speech or account for themselves. My instinct was to put them at ease with my own cheerfulness, bring up points of connection from earlier conversations, things we did together or people we know in common. Then I inch my way toward the theme at hand, reminding them that since we are talking about their lives and the meaning of what they have lived through, they are the experts, the ones with the valuable information. Then, finally, before putting on the recorder, I would in most cases give them a copy of my guiding questions. Not in all cases, because there were some people who I knew would likely be put off or intimidated by written words on a page. Those tended to be the ones with less formal education, though some of those same people actually seemed to place greater stock on the interview session when it had the appearance of being "official" or formal in some way. I would always assure them that the questions were a rough guide to what we would talk about, and that we would most likely be taking them up in other sequences than that listed, depending on the flow of the conversation. I always placed a premium on flow, on one thing leading to another, and the power of free association. That always seemed to make them feel more comfortable. More often than not I would go over the questions aloud with them in advance of actually turning on the recorder, the purpose being to give them a general sense of the scope and nature of the topics at hand, and a suggestion as to the sequence. I frequently adapted the questions somewhat in view of the specific interests and characteristics of each respondent. I of course had a version of the questions in English and one in Spanish, and conducted the interviews in whichever language the respondent felt most comfortable, which in many cases was a mix, Spanglish of some kind. My own bilingualism was a key asset, to the extent that I can't (and would not want to) think of doing this project without it. I think that my bilingualism being off balance also helped, that is, I speak a somewhat strange and hard-to-identify Spanish that is heavily tinged with Puerto Rican and Caribbean pronunciation and usages but also carries a complex accent combining gringo, Mexican, Colombian and a few other dialectal variants that I have picked up over the years. Thus, for the Spanish speakers, especially the Puerto Ricans, I give the impression of being both within and outside of their immediate cultural world, while in English I had little trouble coming across as a slightly off-beat but well-meaning and knowledgeable Nuyorican.

I would always mention, usually at the beginning when I asked them to identify themselves, that I planned to change the names of the respondents for publication, and otherwise remove some identifying facts and traces. I explained that, aside from my wanting to protect them from any possible misunderstanding, invasion of privacy or embarrassment, I am less involved in their specific, unique, and "named" reality than in larger patterns and experiences that many people have lived through and can identify with. While most of them simply nodded in concurrence, there were also those who objected mildly, insisting they are proud of their stories and have nothing to hide. Another few seemed relieved and wanted me to promise to stick to my intentions, as they didn't want others to know some of the things they would be saying or had already shared with me. In general, knowing that they would not be readily identifiable further reduced their anxieties, as did my explicit intention to share with them whatever I end up using of their testimony. I know that I have endeared myself further with each of them by systematically carrying through on that promise. Note that some of the respondents also figure in my analysis in the later chapters of the book, and I have therefore had to 'blow their cover' by revealing their identity. I made a point to secure their approval in all such cases.

The interviews themselves were, as they tend to be, idiosyncratic; I am amazed that even though time has elapsed by now, I still recall each of them lucidly and in great specificity. Despite the guiding template, each roamed in its own directions and established its own tempo and tenor. Though I wanted them to feel that nothing was out of bounds, at the same time I often reminded them that I was not after their full life-stories but certain themes and kinds of experience. The thematic focus helped to limit the time involved and to render manageable testimony for purposes of transcription and citation. I found myself maintaining that delicate balance between free-dom of flow and gentle prodding in the direction of the central subject of transnational lessons and challenges. In most cases I avoided words like transnational, diaspora, gender, race, even cultural or national or colonial, though the content of those terms was always palpably present in what they were saying. In listening back through them, and even during some of the sessions, I recognized a certain dramatic or narrative structure to each testimony, a building or cross-referencing that lent a kind of coherence to each ensemble of experience. I was pleased that so many of the respondents expressed warm appreciation at the end, once I had turned off the recorder. Some even volunteered, either on the spot or on a later occasion, that the interview was important to them, and that as formative as those issues and events were in their lives, they had never had occasion to talk about them, or even to think about them in any depth.

I found myself with three mini-disks filled with these twenty-some oral histories, all grippingly pertinent to my theme and strictly based on real-life experience. The question was, what do I do with them? How do I most effectively use them to ground my theoretical interventions, historical overviews, and critical interpretations of instances of creative expression? I choose the word "ground" carefully and in its most literal sense, because I see ethnographic testimony as the necessary mooring or foothold of both theoretical and interpretive work, the real-life, experiential correlate to the more conjectural language of social philosophy and hermeneutics. There is a school of twentieth-century philosophy called by the forbidding name of "hermeneutical phenomenology," most directly identified with the interesting French thinker Paul Ricoeur (1913–2005); I identify my relation to and use of the tales included here, and my idea of "ethnographic grounding," with that line of thinking.

In any case I saw three main possible ways of using the testimony I had gathered. I could transcribe them and simply publish the interviews as is, or at least cleaned up by editing out the um's and ah's. While such a use has the advantage of remaining faithful to the ethnographic moment and to the content and contours of the testimony in a literal sense, my own reading experience has been that the result is often tedious at best, and can be confusing and frustrating; I usually wind up resenting the interviewer, whose presence seems like something of an intrusion and whose questions like a violation, or at least interruption, of the life-story. Why that question or that line of questioning? Why not let the person tell his or her story, in his or her own terms?

Another option was of course the most common practice in social science ethnography, which is to use the interviews to glean quotes for the substantiation of the researcher's line of argument. Here at least there is a built-in practice of interpretation, based on the selection of specific quotes and their insertion into the scholarly text. The interviewing persona is in this case not just an intrusion, or in positive terms a guide, but reaps the harvest of the ethnographic database by demonstrating the direct value or relevance of specific statements to the thesis of the larger study. The problem with this usage is that it tends to discard the unity and coherence of the life-story in favor of these proof-values; the value of the narrative is trumped by the need to substantiate via citation.

After agonizing over it for some time, I found myself unhappy with either of these options. So I hit upon a third, rather unusual one. I knew that I wanted to preserve the entirety and cohesion of the life-story but not in that literal, Q&A-bound way characteristic of the transcribed rendering of raw interview data. I recognized that each of the interviews contained a story, or comprised the telling of a tale, but one which might not be apparent in the sequencing and structure of the interview itself. Further, I was interested not in everything that was said but in certain key themes that relate that life to the issues and arguments of the book. I liked the example of certain ethnography-based books (I think of the books by Robert C. Smith and George Gmelch referred to in my chapters 1 and 2), which contain vignettes of certain of the interviewed personages; those were stories that held my interest, were not intruded on by an interviewer, and not reduced to quotes dislodged from their narrative context. However, they tended to be in the third person, still mediated by that all-knowing scholar and told in other words. In addition, they also were burdened with a lot of extraneous information and sub-plots that only distract from the story itself and the main reason that it is being told. Worst of all, they often miss the punch-line or key, most instructive dramatic moment, the turning point. The fact is that many of the stories, if not jokes, are in most cases a kind of parable or allegorical exemplum of the theoretical or hermeneutic point I am trying to bring home.

The "Tales of Learning and Turning" are interviews re-written for the sake of narrative coherence and their inherent emblematic significance. All of the words and sentences are intact, exactly as spoken on tape. Nothing has been added or invented. What I have done is alter the sequence and immediate narrative context in which they were uttered, and structure the story in a range of ways to lend it greater dramatic impact and interest. I aimed to offer tales that would be as interesting and rich to a reader as the conversations themselves were to me, and whose tellers would take on as much human presence and character as they have for me in real life. Many times I was able to identify a key point, phrase or experiential moment that might draw the reader in, or serve as an effective climax or turning-point in the story. This "hook," as I might call it thinking of devices of many popular songs, also helps to cue the reader in to a specific aspect or angle of the social experience under study. I refer to the shoes in **Ester**'s story, or the military greens in **Toño**'s, or the round-trip ticket in **Nury**'s, or the admired dance step in **Marielena**'s. The whole story seems to be "turning" on that one detail, which also serves to signal the main "learning" experience embodied in that life.

As said, I have shared each of the stories with their respective tellers, and have gotten responses from most. I have received no substantive objections or corrections, but a slew of very affirmative, appreciative comments. I am not sure if they feel flattered by the way their lives had been synthesized, or grateful that I have taken their experiences at face value and only altered them by lending them a certain narrative poignancy. A few have commented that they see themselves as the narrator and main character in a short story or human interest reportage. Others have told me that they feel like I make them into a "good person." I assure them that they are, and that their own stories prove it.

In any case, I thus offer up "authorized versions" of so many rich and interesting lives lived between and across transnational borderlines. I invite you to read and enjoy them, preferably for the sake of the book in the order presented. I explain that order, and whatever else I glean from the stories, in my follow-up interpretive commentary, "Reading the Tales." Remember that I see the "Tales" as the fulcrum of the book, both the experiential grounding of the theoretical and historical contextualization of part 1 and the stage-setting for the cultural interpretations of part 3.

TALES OF
LEARNING AND
TURNING

"Ester" Telling Her Story, Hormigueros, Puerto Rico, 2007.
Photographer José Irizarry. Permission José Irizarry.

Andrés "And Now for Another Rum and Coke . . ."

Beatriz "My Own Person"

Carmen "An Embarrassing Moment"

David "Some Minor Points"

Ester "Shoes for Dinner"

Francisco "A Little Sex Education"

Gabriela "Like it Is . . ."

Hernán "Full Circle"

Isabel "A Fine Line"

Johnny "We had Pizzazz"

Lenny "A Common Ground"

Marielena "Show Me That Step"

Nury "My Round Trip Ticket"

Olga "Look How They Send Her Back"

Pedro "Rude Boy, *Friqui*, but Always Very Cuban"

Quique "They Didn't Get It"

Rodolfo "They Can't Believe Me!"

Samuel "Let's Face It"

Toño "We All Had Our *Verdes*"

Ursula "Another Way of Being (Dominican)"

Victoria "Keeping Up With the Jones Act"

Wanda "If My Parents Let Me . . ."

Andrés,
"And Now for Another Rum and Coke . . ."
(Y ahora, otra Cubita . . .)

You see that big old tree over there, across the street, the tamarindo? That's the same tree I used to sit under when I was a little kid, right here in the same neighborhood where I was born and grew up. See the shoreline over there in the distance, and the little store down at the bottom of the hill? It's all exactly the same, after all these years. Where I am standing right now was always my favorite spot to wait for my friends, or just stand around, 'cause of the breeze, you feel it? Here, on this spot, there's always a breeze, you can count on it.

I'm 68 now, just retired after 49 of those years living over there, almost 50 years, imagine, in New York City. That's most of my life, since I was 17, in 1956, when I left. Sure, I've come back, lots of times, but just for short visits during my vacations. But all of my working life was over there. In Brooklyn, the Bronx, but mostly in Manhattan, that was home to me. I did all kinds of work, and did my stint in the service. Most of the time, though, I worked in bodegas and especially restaurants. You know that place La Taza de Oro, on 8th Avenue just above 14th Street? Yeah, the Puerto Rican place that's always crowded, where the taxi drivers stop to pick up their rice and beans and *chuletas*? It's famous. Well, I was the counter man there, for 24 years! Actually, the owners of the place, since the beginning (it's been there forever), are from right around here, right up the road; they're family of mine, like just about all of the people who worked there. We grew up together here, in Barrio Guaniquilla de Cabo Rojo, and then wound up working and spending all our time together up there.

So I guess you could say that I became a man, a grown-up, there in Nueva York. That's where I met my wife, had family, saved up my social security, learned how to get around, talk English (it's still not very good, though, 'cause most of the time I was talking Spanish, at work, at home, just about everywhere). Sure, we played baseball here, and would go to see the local town teams around here when I was little, but there I went to Yankee games, it was a big deal.

I'm a black man. I think I always considered myself black, though no, actually I didn't think about it when I was a kid, before I went to the States. I'm black because when I joined the army, they put down, "race: black." But to tell you the truth, it doesn't really mean that much to me, 'cause for me racism, or races, they don't exist. I just don't agree with people when they say that to be black is lower, or less. I know there is racism over there, that there is, but I never felt discriminated against. Sometimes I used to feel for the American blacks, the way they were treated, but I was usually with family and other *boricuas*, where I felt comfortable. Yeah, I got held up in the street a couple of times, and I would hear comments, but my thing was just not to pay it no mind, just ignore it and keep walking. My parents would say, "Hacer bien, y no mirar a quien," you know, stick to what you're doing, do it well, and don't judge people, regardless of what they look like or say.

So, then a couple of years ago, in 2005, I reached retirement age and came back home to stay. That was the idea all along, of course: there was not a single moment, ever, when I wasn't planning to come home. It's been my hope and dream since the first time I left, and all through the years. And here I am now, at the same spot where I grew up as a kid. You see that building over there, the two-story house with the balcony? We used to play in the street right in front of it, and upstairs, that was the dance place. Tres Copas y un Amigo, it was famous all around here. On weekends it would be packed with people from the whole barrio and all around, who came to drink and socialize and dance to the music from the jukebox. It would blast all over the mountain, those old love songs, the wrist-slashers by Felipe Rodríguez, they used to call him "La Voz," "The Voice." Every other song was by him or the trios, you know, Trio Los Panchos, Trio Vegabajeño, and of course some jíbaro music, too, like Ramito and Chuito, they were real popular. I'll never forget it, it was like a party every week, from Friday afternoon to Sunday night, when things finally quieted down as people got ready to go back to work early Monday morning. There were times they had to take Monday off, just to recover!

But things are different now. That place closed down a few years ago, and now all we have is this little cantina, and the evangelical church down the road. Nothing like the fun and excitement of times gone by, but things are better in a way, too. Before we didn't even have roads or anything. See this paved road, and the other little roads up here in the hills? They were just dirt paths back then, people used to walk them, miles up and down these steep hills, even to go to the store, or to school, or to visit neighbors. Now we have cars, and trucks, and bicycles, and even some streetlights. And people have refrigerators, and running water, and indoor bathrooms, and wear shoes instead of going around barefoot. I love it, it's modern, there's been so much progress to make life a little easier. I got used to all that in New York, so it's easier for me to come and live here now. I learned to appreciate it, and to expect it as part of my life, and even though I miss the good old times, I wouldn't want to live that way any more.

One thing I like better about the way things are here is the way women are. There, the women go off to work, and they're more independent. Here, they're housewives, they depend on the man to bring home the habichuelas. Till this day, that's what women do here. And I like it better that way, I think women should mainly be housewives, take care of the home and the children. I don't like when they get too independent, and don't pay attention to the family or respect their man.

So all in all it wasn't very hard for me to come back, in fact it's been pretty easy. Everyone knew me and accepted me, no problem. Sometimes I challenge people, you know, the ones who never went up there and don't know about it, when they get narrow-minded and act stupid, like when they sound too much like they're against everything American, or on the other hand when they become so pro-American that they can't appreciate their own kind and country. That's one thing I have no patience for, when people deny who they are, and try to be Spanish, or American. We may be American citizens, but that doesn't mean that we're Americans. I may be Puerto Rican, through and through, but as I learned over there, I am also a black man, and proud of it.

And a working man, 'cause here I don't see that much racism, but there is a lot of abuse and prejudice against the working man, the poor people. I didn't live it myself, directly anyway, 'cause as I said, all of my working life was up there, except for when I helped in the fields as a little boy. Around here, in my barrio, everyone is pretty poor, and always has been, and the people with money, the ones who live over there (see those big houses over that way, on that hillside?), they couldn't care less about us. They live their lives as if we don't exist, except when they need us to clean their yards, or fix the leaks in their roof. It's like that in the States, too, of course, like the rich neighborhoods in the city, like the Upper East Side just below El Barrio, but not as sharp and deep as here. Or at least I don't feel it as strongly. Up there I got a sense that maybe it doesn't have to be quite as separate and exclusive as it is here, that maybe it doesn't have to be that way.

Now I'm going have another *Cubita* (you know, Cuba Libre, rum and coke), and sit down to play dominos with those guys over in the cantina. I am happy with my life, and always tell the young ones to be sure to travel, to get out of here for a while and see what it's like over there, wherever, so that when you come back you appreciate the place where you grew up.

Beatriz,
"My own Person"

The neighbors on both sides of us were there, and those two families across the way, them too. In fact I'd say we came back to a community where around eighty per cent, or more, spent years in the States, mostly in New York, and returned, just like us. So I always felt accepted, never rejected, I was never a "nuyorican" as they say nowadays. Everyone saved some money, and we all lived comfortably, not rich, but a lot better than when we left. I love being back, especially to live in my own house and not have to pay rent. In a way, it's like a dream come true, since all along, for all the years I was over there, I always intended to come back. There wasn't a day that I didn't dream of returning to my country.

And it was a long time. I left here back in 1952, when I was only twenty years old. I was a lucky one in my hometown, because unlike most of my friends I managed to go to high school. But the problem was, there was no work. As a young girl I used to do embroidery, piece work at home, you know, *en la aguja, el bordado*, like most poor women back in those times. We used to travel all the way to Mayagüez to pick up the work, that was a long way through the mountains back then. And the pay was miserable. So I got married and we moved to San Juan, where things were even worse. My husband went first, and then we followed, myself and my baby daughter, to try our luck in New York. And that's where I made my life. First I stayed home to raise my three daughters, and then when the youngest turned nine I took my first job, first in a garment factory, then in a department store, and finally in a hospital, where I worked for over seventeen years.

For thirty-five years I made El Barrio my home, in the projects alongside a lot of other poor Puerto Rican families in the same boat we were in, and Black Americans, and some Italians and other Americans, a lot of them immigrants, too. As time went by I learned to speak some English, never real well but enough to get along and relate to my neighbors and fellow workers on the job. There were a lot of different cultures there, which I liked. Our children grew up speaking Spanish with us in the home, but outside, in the playground and at school, it was all in English. After a while, when they were teenagers, we would talk to them in Spanish and they would answer in English, and talk English among themselves. It made it a little hard sometimes, and it hurt sometimes to see them losing their language, but we understood. In fact we even encouraged them to learn English well because that would help them get ahead.

We felt different from our non-Puerto Rican neighbors, though we always tried to get along and be friendly. I remember coming home with the kids and we were all put off by the nasty smell of cabbage cooking, or mutton, or whatever it was someone was making for dinner. Maybe they felt the same about the way our food smelled, but we never said anything to each other. The kids might have had their scuffles, but as families we always tried to get along and respect each other. And we'd turn to each other when there was trouble of some kind, or when we needed to borrow a cup of sugar or something. There would always be respect for the parents and older children when they went off to work early in the morning. We were all in the same boat. But with all that, we were different, and sometimes we were afraid, and I had to warn my kids who to play with and not to play with.

In Puerto Rico, back in the early years, Puerto Ricans weren't seen as black. I had no awareness about that before leaving for the States. But my perceptions changed because of being there. A lot of our neighbors were Black Americans, and once I could speak English a little we got along fine. I remember sitting on the benches with them, the parents of the Black kids, and feeling no fear at all and talking and laughing about a million things. I could see that even though I felt so different from them, out in the world beyond the projects we were looked at and treated pretty much the same way they were, as something less, as stupid and lacking in skills and education. That's how I learned the connection between poverty and racism, that the rich are usually white and the poor a lot of times are black, or dark. The same is true here in Puerto Rico, but if I hadn't lived there I may not have seen it so clearly. In fact, people here who never left often don't see things in those terms, even though it's obvious everywhere you look. But we almost never talk about that here, it's just not part of our conversation. All I know is that people who've lived and learned that over there arrive here more prepared to deal with that reality.

I've always been keenly aware of class differences, the rich and the poor, and that the poor are always under the thumb of the corporations, like slaves. It was in New York where I was in a union, and I took part in the affairs of the union. I learned from the strikes and the protests that that's the only way to get anywhere or anything. There, if I didn't have the union I would have had no one to fight for me. It helped me secure my rights, because I was paying my dues. Not that there are no unions and strikes here, there are. But here it's warfare, there things were more peaceful, and organized. I'm not involved in that any more here, because once I retired I was no longer in the labor force, so that it didn't interest me. The most important thing I learned, though, was that you can protest, and fight for what's yours, and appeal to the laws. But here, in Puerto Rico, I have no faith at all in the system of justice, since everything is so politicized. So much depends on what party you belong to, and who you know, and power and influence. Corruption is everywhere.

Even so, I still fight now and then. Like a few years ago, when the Pentecostal church up the block used to blast its services and music trying to attract converts and bothering the whole neighborhood with the deafening noise. So, I went around and talked with the neighbors, and we wrote up and signed a petition letter and took it to court. And we won, so that the church people had to show more respect and turn down the volume and close their door. I probably wouldn't have done all that if I hadn't seen how it's done in the unions and among the tenants in the projects in El Barrio.

And one thing I know for sure, if I hadn't spent those years living in New York I would be a different woman. I would have stayed in the olden days, and it's very different there. A woman is more independent there, you just feel freer and better when you can get out of the house and earn a living, and have an income of your own. The women who stayed here keep on being controlled by the man: he's the one in charge, who has an opinion and makes the decisions. I notice a lot of times that women who never left still don't take an active part in conversations when men are around, "no se miscuyen," they "don't get mixed up" in anything, they don't want to discuss or argue about things. Among ourselves, as women, of course, we do talk about those things, but the difference is there. So that was a very important lesson for me, and for all of the family. As soon as they were old enough all of my daughters got jobs and went out to work, mostly in fast food places, but they all have always worked, to this day. And I do think that things have changed here, in Puerto Rico, over the years. It's different than up there, but it has also progressed and is better that it used to be here.

So that, coming back, I felt so much better, I went right on being the way I was there. I'm the one who goes to buy what I want, and makes decisions about things on my own. I've stayed pretty much the same about a lot of other things, like my love for my country, my ideas about the United States, my distrust for the local politicians of all political stripes (though I am still against independence and in favor of statehood for Puerto Rico). And I even like a lot of the changes in my country since I was young, like the greater opportunity for work, the improved healthcare and transportation, everything's easier now, and better. And for me, thanks for a lot of that goes to the United States. In all those ways, and many others, I feel like I am the same person as ever, pretty consistent in my views and values. But as for being an independent woman, that's one thing I will never give up, and never go back to the old ways, never go back to my old self.

Carmen,
"An Embarrassing Moment"

I was embarrassed. Not so much anger, or blame, or shame in any deep way. Embarrassment is what I felt when they called me from the police station and told me that my daughter—my eldest—had been arrested for necking with her boyfriend in the town plaza. "Indecent behavior" they called it. She should have known better, that in the Dominican Republic you don't go around kissing or necking or anything like that in public. "Aquí no se hace eso," "That's not done around here." And then again, how was she supposed to know? She might have been born here, in Monte Cristo, our hometown, but she grew up her whole life in Nueva York, in the Bronx, and there you can kiss and make out and do what you want and nobody says anything. They wouldn't arrest you for it, that's for sure. "Son las diferencias," things are different, you know.

That was just last year, and I had only been back to Monte Cristo for a little over a year. My husband and I returned home after almost thirty years in the States, five in Miami and then the rest, more than twenty years, in New York. I've been a "costurera" nearly all my life, before I left home in 1976, and my whole time in New York I worked in a garment factory. I also raised four children, two born here in the Dominican Republic, and two over there, in the States. It has been a difficult life, a lot of hard work and sacrifice.

My main joy has been my family. Though I must say that, even though I love them with my life, my children have sometimes been hard to understand and very different culturally. My youngest daughter doesn't even understand Spanish, and all of them are leading lives very different than in my country. They've been successful—one even went to Harvard—, so I'm proud, but it's like worlds apart when it comes to anything but the deep affection we feel for each other.

As hard as it's been, though, I don't regret for a minute that we went to lead our lives there in New York, nor that my children have that as their home. My feeling is that anyone from my country who doesn't leave and go there, dies blind. Really, I feel like I learned to see there, in the U.S. Not that I think it's better than my country, no way. Through all the years, I have always loved my country, I longed for it every day. I knew I would be coming back and even set up my life in anticipation of my return. But it is only now that I can truly appreciate my country, and understand it somehow in a way that I never could have otherwise. I mean it, when I think what I would be like if I didn't live there, I feel like I'd be fast asleep, "dormida." Maybe it's just that I was fully an adult during those years, but it was in New York that I learned how important a sense of order is, how you can count on things, how you have certain rights and can defend them. I learned what it means to be independent as a woman, in fact my husband learned that there, too, because if he hadn't I wouldn't have stood for it. Not that I think that poor people have it good anywhere, but over there I could see a society with programs to help poor people out, unlike in my country, where it's "a capa y espada," fend for yourself, that's it. I even learned more about the relation between my country and Haiti, you know, the thorn in the side of Dominican politics. I became familiar with that history, which is especially important if you live along the border, like in my hometown Monte Cristo. Maybe I could have learned about that at home, but in New York there was no way I wasn't going to learn about it, not with my daughters around.

And now, I love being home again, even though I have been going through a lot of adjustments getting used to things again. In some ways it's like I never left, things are so familiar to me, and of course people are so warm and kind. Sometimes I detect a note of "desconfianza," a kind of distrust from them, but I attribute that to the cultural differences that have of course developed over all that time. I can understand it, of course; they have to have a chance to figure out who we are by now, and what we're like. The only thing about it that bothers me is when they assume we have lots of money, that we owe them gifts or something. I have to tell them, again and again, that we didn't have it easy over there, and that we worked our arms and legs off for lousy wages to pay high rents, and pay for all the kids, too. But things like that get worked out with time, and what I like most about life here is the slow pace. Things move more slowly here, more easygoing, without all that hustle and bustle and stress of the big monster city. Life is driven there, like always in development and progress and being modern and all that, which I like too, but I really prefer this pace, and the sense of family and community I have in my hometown. I just want to take the good with the bad, adapt again to this way of doing things without losing or forgetting the principles and values I learned in my other home, the Bronx. I think it's that with the much broader view I got living there I can now value and understand the close-up things more fully than ever.

Getting back to that night when I was embarrassed by what happened to my daughter, I myself agreed with the police officer who reprimanded them for acting that way, because I think there is such a thing as "indecent behavior" and agree with that and prefer my culture in that way. That's why I was embarrassed. But I also agree with my daughter that arresting them for that was too extreme. He could have just scolded her and sent her home, or told her parents about it. That would have been enough. Arresting them and making a criminal case out of it reminded me of that undemocratic, fascist thing that I hate about my culture. The thing that needs to change, to this day.

David,
"Some Minor Points"

When I go to Cuba, which I have been doing almost every year now since my first visit in 1978, I stay at the Hotel Nacional. I love that grand hotel, with all the charm of the olden days yet also the fresh stamp of the revolution. But two things have bothered me all along, since my first stay. One is that the hotel has no black people on the service staff. All you see are white and light-skinned porters, waiters, even the chambermaids, not to mention the receptionists and management. I once brought my concern up with some of the party militants and government officials I know: "Wasn't that the idea of the revolution in the first place?" But my objection fell on deaf ears, which meant to me that they think it's only natural somehow that wealthy and prestigious tourists and guests should not be attended to by black people.

My other beef is this. The Hotel Nacional is on the same block in Havana as the Department of Agriculture building, and when I go out for a walk I always pass by that stately edifice. But I notice to my displeasure that though the front yard of the building has the usual ornamental palm trees, the rest of the yard is barren and dry. The same is true of the front yards of the houses in the neighborhood I would walk through, and wherever I went. That's the other thing that most disappointed me about my beloved home country, the lack of vegetation and concern for the natural environment. They could even plant vegetables or fruit there, to add some needed nutritional value to their pretty unhealthy diets. So I took the occasion several times to discuss these matters with my influential friends, but again, they didn't seem to pay it much mind at all, and showed no signs of intending to do anything about it. All with a friendly, knowing smile of course.

I know that these are minor problems, perhaps rightfully overshadowed by the more pressing needs of the society, and in fact minor in my mind when compared with my love for my home country and delight at being able to pay it such regular and enjoyable visits. In fact, I remember vividly that on my first arrival, in 1978, I spent the whole night, all night till sun-up, sitting on the Malecón looking at the sea and savoring the sensation of being "home" after over forty years in exile.

I was almost 30 when I left in 1956, partly to escape the clutches of the Batista regime, which I forcefully opposed, and partly to pursue my medical career. From the moment I got to New York, at the time of the 26 de julio, I have followed the events of Cuba with avid interest. I was working in a hospital, and living on the Upper West Side, a dense Cuban enclave in those years that we commonly called Escambray, the way they call it Quisqueya Heights these days because of all the Dominicans. I quickly got to know a lot of Cubans, most of them liberals like myself, but my most numerous acquaintances were the Boricuas. I hung out with them, partied with them, I married a Puerto Rican woman, who's the mother of my son. In earlier years, before I left Cuba, I actually knew the great poet Julia de Burgos, who is finally today getting some of the appreciation she deserves, and my parents had a close acquaintance with the legendary Puerto Rican poet and anti-colonial militant, Lola de Rodríguez de Tió, when she lived in Santa Clara, my hometown, back in the later nineteenth century. In fact I'd say that my main entree into U.S. society was thanks to the Puerto Ricans. I was surprised at how many of them were supportive of the Cuban Revolution. When the revolutionary forces triumphed on January 1, 1959, I was at a New Year's Eve party in El Barrio. I'll never forget the exuberance when the events were announced, and Fidel and the rebels were shown on television marching into Havana. We were ecstatic, even though I myself was more of a reformist liberal than a guerilla fighter, in part because it seemed to cement the unity with Puerto Ricans so powerfully. I frequented in those and subsequent years a place called Casa de la Américas, located down on 14th Street, which was a long-standing meeting-place for leftist *cubanos* in New York and their sympathizers of many nationalities, including the Puerto Rican nationalists and socialists. In this way, and in my Escambray on the Upper West Side, I felt the constant presence of my home country in my life. I never felt too far away, and when the first contingent of the Brigada Antonio Maceo visited the Island in 1977, I took immediate interest. And then, after my own first trip in the following year, I have been part of the movement of Cubans building bridges with our country and the Cuban government.

Since that first visit, and every time since, I have been received by my countrymen with the greatest warmth and respect. They have shown me time and again the deep affection, which I likewise feel toward them. As a token of my appreciation and solidarity, for decades now I have made it my practice to send parcels of books to libraries in Havana; the Biblioteca Nacional, as well as the libraries of the Museo del Ron and the Museo del Tabaco, among other institutions. I send them all kinds of books, technical and literary, encyclopedias and biographies. Among them, often unbeknownst to me, are books that have been blacklisted, such as Reinaldo Arenas and Lydia Cabrera, important writers who were in exile from and opposed to the revolution. I have always objected to this practice of trying to erase *cubanos* who have left the Island from the record and deny them their public recognition. Look at Celia Cruz, a true national treasure, as though she never existed, it's a disgrace. It never really came to any direct confrontation, as they never pushed it when it had to do with my parcels of books, but that's another thing that tempers my enthusiasm for the "new Cuba." One time I stopped in on the acquisitions department of the Biblioteca Nacional to say hello, and ask about the reception of my donations. Noticeably embarrassed and apologetic, the librarian admitted to me that those parcels were still in the receiving area and were as yet unpacked and uncatalogued. When she noticed my disappointment she explained that they simply do not have enough staff to keep up to date on the unpacking of donated materials. I suggested that they might use some volunteers, to which she responded, still somewhat sheepish, "Aquí no hay voluntarismo." I was shocked, and am always perplexed when I notice the absence of that practice which I had seen so much of in my decades of work in hospitals and clinics in New York City. So that's another seed which I have been planting on my visits, along with the subtle suggestions about adding some greenery, and perhaps some fruit and vegetables, to the yards, and about ending the censorship of *cubanos* who left the country. To which I would add my constant harping on the need to add fish to the deprived diets of my compatriots, who are surrounded by the bountiful sea and served by an active fish industry but would rather go hungry than replace their demand for red meat, even if it's canned, with some tasty seafood.

Many of these constructive criticisms and friendly pieces of advice derive from all I have learned living in exile, in the Cuban diaspora in New York. Unlike many in the Miami community, I am friendly disposed toward many of the changes that have happened in my home country, though like most other exiles I am critical of some of the shortcomings and abuses I see there. But I guess that what I most bring "home" from life in my Escambray del Norte is a sense of tolerance. I am 80 years old now, and I have learned how to live with others, people of many nationalities and lifestyles. I have gained great pleasure and very valuable knowledge from those experiences. I know that values like those are needed in Cuba today, as they have been over the decades. And, as I send books to help in the education of my people, so I like to bring my ideas, my values and experiences to bear on the historical events that are shaping my country.

Ester,
"Shoes for Dinner"

When I came back to Puerto Rico in 1968 things were rough in my hometown of Hormigueros. I actually was from the neighborhood of Hormigueros around La Eureka, the huge sugar mill which was the main thing happening economically in the town, and where most of the poor people lived and worked. Almost like slaves for decades. We were referred to by some of the Hormigueros townfolk as "los negros de La Eureka," which implied something a good deal less than full citizens. Well, when I came home they were getting ready to close the mill down and leave the people without land or a place to live. So that a big struggle was in store for us, we would "invade" or take over the lands and squat, for lack of any choice, and we found ourselves up against an armed police force. Seeing the lurking danger, the authorities conceded and agreed to divide up some of the land and apportion out "parcelas," plots for a small house. But, as expected, the distribution of the lands turned out to be totally corrupt and unacceptable, so that we had to take it to the government.

So, no sooner did I get back home than I found myself in the midst of this intense community action. I played an active role, and before long I was identified by my friends and neighbors as a leader, and representative of their will and interests. A lot of them couldn't believe I would get so involved, so fast, and with such self-confidence. "Tú no eres la Ester que se fué," "Chica, qué cambiada te volviste!" ("You're not the same Ester who went away," "Girl, you sure have changed!"). I seemed more aggressive and more "liberal" than what they remembered me to be. I told them "son los golpes de la vida," I've been to the school of hard knocks. But I kept at it, providing more and more effective leadership to "los negros de La Eureka" in their righteous claim to just compensation and a right to the land. They called me "la abogada Ester," I became the people's lawyer by getting to know the law and finding out whom to turn to in order to make our demands heard. We even went in busloads to La Fortaleza, the Governor's Mansion in San Juan, where we took our case to the Statehood Governor Luis Ferré, who had just taken office that year.

I had gone to New York in 1958, at 21 years of age and with my two kids. I had worked as a seamstress in the years before leaving, and in New York I continued, though I also had a lot of obligations bringing up the kids and making sure they stayed out of trouble. We lived on the Lower East Side.

That's where I first got involved in community and labor activism. I worked among the women in the garment industry, and in my neighborhood with some of the long-term activist leaders. I learned English fast, and got along great with the many Black American women that I worked and lived with. I know I got a lot of my fiber and dedication from them. I sure learned to be proud of myself as a black woman, if I ever needed it. Racism was something I became very aware of over there, and I lash out whenever I see any sign of it here in Puerto Rico. One time, it must have been 1962–63, I remember we held a protest at City Hall, I think Lindsey was mayor back then, or he was running for office. We brought our appeals to him, and he gave us a hearing. But most of all I remember how I got involved in the Kennedy campaign, when he ran for president. I loved Kennedy, because he stood for so many things I believed in. Being Catholic may have had something to do with it, but not much. It was just the strong democratic hope he meant for so many working people, and for people of color like me. I got so involved that I was even invited to the home of Robert Kennedy, in Washington. And I went, of course. It was so exciting for me, and encouraged me even more to go on fighting for justice and equality.

I always remind myself, and anyone who shows interest, that my struggle, I mean my spirit of struggle and my determination, began at home, in New York City. I first had to set the record straight with my own husband. He had always seemed to me a good man, hardworking and dedicated. But he had a mean temper, and would tend to take his anger out on me. He used to beat me, and kept on threatening to get his way by hitting me. But then as I learned I started to say to him, "Don't you dare touch me, or I'll call the police. I'll have you arrested, rest assured of that, and you'll go to jail." Anyway, as is the custom, he used to be in charge of the money, for whatever the expense. I had to ask him for money when I needed it, and explain what for. So one day I asked him for money to buy shoes for the kids, all five of them. So he gave me $25, supposedly $5 for each pair of shoes for each kid. $25! Yes, things are much more expensive than they were then, but even so, that was hardly enough money for five pairs of shoes. Anyway, I did find shoes and bought them with the money I had at my disposal, one pair for each child. But here's what happened. When I got home to prepare dinner for the family, I had the kids stay in their rooms and proceeded to put one pair of shoes at each setting at the dinner table. When my husband came home expecting dinner, I told him that after buying the shoes I had nothing left to buy food for dinner, so that tonight we would be dining on shoes! Shoes for dinner!

So that's where my struggles started, and before long, that was the end of my marriage. We came back to Puerto Rico and got a divorce, and ever since I have been my own person. Out of all that, I learned how to be myself, "aprendí a ser yo." I am very humanitarian, you know, always helping people and standing up for them. Even here at the senior center where I live, here in Hormigueros, I spend a lot of my time driving people around—yes, I'm 70 and I drive—to doctors and clinics and to visit their families, and of course I have been elected the director of just about everything around here. I am kind and giving, but I have learned that there are laws and rights and that you have to fight for them, even if it means standing up to the people in charge, or the government. I've come to understand that our biggest obstacle is fear, even the fear to speak, and that we have to do all we can to proceed free of fear. It's true, I came back from my ten years on the Lower East Side changed, a different Ester, "con lengua y ánimo" as I like to say, with a booming voice and a hot spirit. And I will always be grateful for that.

Francisco,
"A Little Sex Education"

A lot of us began leaving the country when I left, 1965, right at the time of the revolution. Trujillo was gone, but the Marines came in to "restore order" after they got Juan Bosch off the scene. They were also "los años dorados," the "golden years" in the forming of a Dominican community in New York. Everything was new to us, not so much the language since most of us already spoke some English, but the whole incomparable scene, the overwhelming presence of the huge cosmopolis with all of the world's cultures, the bustling Latino presence. To this day I look back on those years, which extended through 1976 when I came back home to Santo Domingo, as the turning point in my life and world-view.

I went to New York to pursue my university studies, on my way to becoming a lawyer. In college I got involved in the student movement, against the war in Vietnam, and in the clamor for ethnic studies programs to address the educational and cultural needs of the African American and Latino students. Our focus was on Puerto Rican Studies, since that was closest to our own reality, and identity. But we were also active in giving shape to, and making sense out of, a specifically Dominican agenda in the diaspora; in fact, one of my closest friends and associates from back then was Francisco Rodríguez de León, "Paco" to us, who went on to write the book *El furioso merengue del Norte* (1998), the first history of the Dominican diaspora in New York. Our political attention was still riveted on the goings-on back home, but as the years passed we felt those bonds grow to our *compatriotas* living there, in Nueva York, and of course to a broader Latin American and Caribbean Latino community. Of special importance to us was the example and trailblazing presence of the *boricuas*, who had been there so long and seemed to know all the ropes.

Of course our tight-knit group of *quisqueyano* pioneers mostly came from the liberal middle class and even upper middle-class, with plenty of privilege to go around, though we became increasingly aware that most of the community back then was worse off than we were. I realize now that it was being outside the country, in a strange and sometimes hostile land, that made us so aware of these things. But it also made clear to us that we shared historical ties that connected us to all of our fellow countrymen, rich and poor. We sometimes found ourselves talking to and socializing with other *dominicanos* with whom we wouldn't have any relation back home, where those worlds are kept more strictly apart, disconnected, even at odds. At the same time we also bonded with other Latinos and Caribbean people who at home would just be considered "foreign," from outside. So our horizons got broader and our sense of identity changed a lot. We came to realize that there are other ways to be Dominican than what we thought, and what we'd been taught.

One of my strongest memories, and the cause of nagging embarrassment to me, is that when I left home for the United States, at age 18, I did not know that women had menstrual cycles: a "period," what's that? I just had never been taught, and had never had reason to be curious enough to find out. And in fact I still didn't know in the first year or so of life in New York. But then, to make some money to support my studies, I took a job in a drug store, up on Amsterdam Avenue in Harlem not far from where I went to school at Columbia University. And one day while on the job a woman came in and asked for sanitary napkins. I didn't know what she wanted, and had to ask my fellow attendant at the pharmacy, a *moreno* from the neighborhood. Once I saw the Kotex boxes I recognized the packaging, as I had unloaded cartons of them from the delivery trucks. But I was still left mystified as to what they were for and how they worked. Fortunately, my sister was staying in New York in those days, and I was able to find out from her. But not before I endured the utmost embarrassment when a few days later a group of Black American and Puerto Rican guys from the block came in and started making fun of me for my outrageous ignorance of the birds and the bees.

So, I came back home to Santo Domingo when I completed my studies, and when I got a girl pregnant and wasn't prepared to marry her. Another quick lesson in my faulty sexual education, this time driving me into forced return exile! After settling back home I then met this wonderful woman, Marcia here, with whom I have been happily married now for over twenty years and who is the mother of my three children. As you can see, we live in this nice, quiet neighborhood here in the city, and get along comfortably on my job with the government and Marcia's position in an agency for family planning. The irony is that she is in charge of sexual education, which as you can tell from my own story is a huge job here. Marcia can tell you about the resistance by the authorities, in the government and especially in the almighty Catholic Church, to any kind of modern-day sexual education in the schools.

And Marcia can also tell you the story of our neighbors here in this quiet middle-class part of town, who also returned home after years in the diaspora.

The reason for returning, they told us again and again, was explicitly to protect their children from the moral and sexual problems faced by teenagers in New York. In other words, they wanted to make sure their daughter didn't get pregnant. And, sure enough, before she turned eighteen Susana wound up getting pregnant by a local guy from her school. The funny thing is, Marcia and I can't help thinking that if the family had stayed in New York maybe she wouldn't have gotten pregnant. Maybe over there, where people talk about these things, maybe there the daughter, and the guy, would have known what they were doing.

Gabriela,
"Like It Is . . ."

I had to get tough with them. When some of the men saw my Afro and found out I had lived in New York, they assumed that I was a "porta-aviones," an "aircraft carrier" as the saying goes, that is, free and loose. It was like a green light for them to put a move on you. So I had to say, back off. When I first got back home for vacations it was assumed I would be staying with my family. But I knew right away that I wasn't going to be able to get along with them, and had no time for that kind of debate. So I moved to a friend's house, and when I think about it I realized that we must have been some of the first women to live alone, without a husband or family. My friend was part of a semi-clandestine movement against the dictatorship in its new, post-Trujillo stage. So she spent a lot of time meeting, planning, plotting with male comrades who came from all over the country. And one day I remember a woman from the building who never replied to my greetings came and knocked on our door. When asked how we could help her, she burst out with an apology because until then she had thought we were prostitutes. When two of the most well-known leftist widows visited us she realized that we were not sleeping with all those men and therefore she apologized by saying, "oh, I had thought you were prostitutes, but now I know that you're communists."

The idea was that when you leave the country, you get ruined, you're a lost cause. Once you go out there and enter the labor force you get off track, because here the only option is marriage. Emigration means a destruction of morals, because the most sacred of moral values is premarital virginity. How bitterly ironic in a country that has one of the highest rates of prostitution in the world, and where the whole economy rests on sex traffic and on women's bodies. Well, I guess if those old-fashioned Catholic ideas are what morals are about, then it's true, I am a moral deviant. And I guess that, yes, I did learn how and why to defy that kind of authority thanks to my years in New York.

I left my country in 1967, after finishing secondary school. I was going to be there for a year, sent by my mother, before entering a religious order. Getting there, I worked, first in factories (I recall a button factory, and then making hats), and then as a telephone operator. After learning enough English to get around I started taking night classes at college. It happened that in those years they were just setting up the first programs in Black Studies and Puerto Rican Studies, so that when I started at Brooklyn College I joined in those efforts. And before long it became clear to me that I would be staying longer than had been planned. I got involved with students from other cultures, Puerto Ricans, African Americans, students from other Caribbean islands. In fact it was there and then that I first became aware that I was Caribbean, and had a common history and cultural affinities with young people from Trinidad, Jamaica, and yes, Haiti! And of course our closest of kin, *los boricuas*. In the process we even got admission for more Dominican students, eight of them at the time, and that's where Dominican studies got its start at the university level. It was a time of great awakening and enlightenment for us.

And I also learned that I am a mulatto woman. Back home, in Santo Domingo, I was labeled "india clara," a fair-skinned Indian, which was the official classification of the government, and common usage among the people, for a person who looks like me. In other words, I was considered white. And for a woman who in this society is considered white to go around with her hair this way is a scandal. Like so much else, it's sexualized: like emigration itself, and spending time elsewhere, and taking a job outside the home, wearing an Afro means that I must be loose and easy. Obviously, the idea of sexual liberation has no positive implications whatsoever except for a man trying to get an easy lay.

Needless to say, in that kind of climate there was never any place for reading about race and the great thinkers of negritude and the Black tradition. Yes, some of us had heard of Fanon, but Garvey, C.L.R. James, Du Bois, they were totally unknown, and weren't even available in translation. So, while in Brooklyn College during the 1960s and 1970s, in those exciting times, I read avidly in the writings of those thinkers, and Walter Rodney, and of course, Marx, Che Guevara, Herbert Marcuse, Eric Fromm, Paulo Freire, Gunder Frank, Eric Williams, and the many other taboo subjects. And my whole view of the world changed dramatically, so that the idea of entering a religious order, and the plans laid out for me by my dear mother, faded from view. I traveled in Africa, in Latin America, and felt like part of a larger historical panorama than I had ever imagined. Eventually, I realized that I had to go back home, to the Dominican Republic, because it was there that I knew I would have to try to bring these ideas and visions to fruition.

That has been my struggle ever since, and I have been home, in Santo Domingo, for over twenty years now. I am encouraged by few things, as the society in general has been resistant to change its hard-set views about things. The youth today are showing some defiance, as they emulate their counterparts and break with some of the national traditions that sustain that conservative, xenophobic ideology. I remember one episode not long after my return that has stayed in my mind. For many years there has been a kind of carnival or festival, supposedly in acknowledgement of the African part of the national heritage, called "Octubre Mulato," "Mulatto October." There, in a minstrel-like kind of black-face celebration, people delighted in a praise of blackness that is intended to bring good spirits and a sense of light-hearted unity among the people, but in the United States I had learned that it was racist. I saw what was going on, I couldn't hold back: "This is racist!" I said to the people I was with, and I guess that, yes, I rained on their party. After all I had learned, I just couldn't go along, and was no longer that intent on "fitting in."

Hernán,
"Full Circle"

My daughter was really hurt, she was crying, and I was angry. I went to her school to talk about it with the principal. Graciela, my daughter, was about 13 then, and she had really frizzy hair, that stood up and looked kind of wild. So her classmates would call her "la hija de Don King" ("the daughter of Don King"), you know, the controversial African American boxing promoter with the big head of kinky hair. "Pareces la hija de Don King," "you look like Don King's daughter," and the overtones were clearly racist, since most of the other kids in her private school were light-skinned and middle class. So, myself a teacher at the university, I told the principal and the dean that they needed to educate the teachers and students about racism and respect for other people's feelings. I still have the letters I wrote them.

When I first came to live in Puerto Rico in 1980, I thought things were much better down here than they were in the States. I was born in Puerto Rico, but left when still a baby, and I grew up there, in different parts of the country 'cause my father was in the military. We spent years in Kansas, and then in New Jersey, where I came of age. In New Jersey most of my friends were white, so I tried to fit in by playing down my black ancestry. It was OK that I was Puerto Rican, as long as I seemed white enough. So I would have my hair straightened, and acted like the rest of my schoolmates and boyhood friends. I remember one of them saying, "you're the whitest nigger I know," and I was pretty happy with that because I felt acceptance. As I grew up, though, I began to realize that I did stand out after all, no matter what I did, and when we moved to New Jersey I started hearing the word "spic" and other derogatory comments, and it started to tick me off. That was one of the main reasons why I decided to leave and come to Puerto Rico, where things at that point seemed a lot more tolerant and I didn't have to worry about being a little darker and having a little Afro.

Not that I was made to feel like it was my home country, any more than the States was. No sooner did I get here than people started calling me "Nuyorican," which from their tone was obviously not meant as a term of endearment. I dreaded having to deal with the culture, which was supposedly "my own," and meet people my age, which seemed like it would take forever. I had no confidence at all in my Spanish, and tried as best I could not to use it, except among family. "Tú no eres de aquí" ("you're not from here"), they would say dismissively, as though there was no way I could understand anything. In other words, I was considered an outsider.

Of course I did stand out in many ways, including my views on things. My wife and kids would always say that I am more liberal, way too liberal on things like personal relationships, courtship, the role of men and women, that kind of thing. I listened to my own kind of music, didn't like to drink rum, and had a different attitude toward work and my supervisors at work. I had a much stronger work ethic than any of my peers, yet I also would talk to my superiors at the school, and didn't get passive and hold my aggression inside. So I guess I seemed very "American" to them, as much as I would have liked to fit in more easily. I even became something of a loner for a while, and still am.

In spite of all this, when I came to Puerto Rico I felt I was Puerto Rican, not black. It took a while for me to realize that being darker here does make a difference, and a big one. I had a student from when I first started teaching at the university, and we became friends and have been close ever since. He is black, darker than me, from Ponce, and I learned a lot from him. He would tell me about his experiences, and it all sounded like what happened to Puerto Ricans in the States. He found that girls would often back away from dating him, and when they would their parents would be unhappy once they saw what he looked like. When he was a sophomore in college he fell for a girl, who was white, and everything was going well. She obviously was attracted to him and felt for him as well, until he met her father. From then on, an uncle of hers would meet her after school every day, just so that my friend wouldn't have a chance to walk alone with her. He had lots of stories like that. I myself felt the sting, but from my own parents, when I started going out with Angela, my wife, who is a black woman from Mayagüez. My father, himself of black background, had always had a racist attitude, which I was exposed to but didn't really understand when I was younger living in the States. But he got worse when we got to Puerto Rico, so bad that he referred to my wife and kids as "negros," in very negative terms. He never forgave me for my choice of a partner, and both Angela and I suffered enormously from that.

Would I consider Puerto Rican society racist? Of course, but it's more subtle here, and often seems almost unnoticeable and "all in fun" and as though within the family. People don't like it when you make anything of it, and say, again, "tú no eres de aquí," implying that I wouldn't or couldn't understand. What I do know is that to this day, and I have been here for nearly 30 years now, a lot of people here are unforgiving of Nuyoricans, and are very prejudiced against those who grew up in the States. It's a kind of racism in its own right, especially since Nuyoricans are often cast as blacks, and as criminals. But I would say it is more a cultural thing, with roots in historical events, and colonialism. And as my own case shows, it's directed not just against those of us arriving from life over there, but even our children suffer the consequences in subtle kinds of ways.

The only thing I think I can do is work hard as an educator. I am 50 years old now, and teach minority American literatures in the university. I try to bring across the complexity of race and identity issues and the need for tolerance and a historical understanding. I noticed, especially in the early years, say fifteen years ago, that when we talked about questions of race and blackness, the black students would remain very quiet, while the others, the lighter-skinned ones, would talk actively about racial prejudice and how bad it was and how much discrimination there was against Puerto Ricans by the Americans. They didn't make the correlation and recognize that blacks here are often treated that same way by other Puerto Ricans. But, again, the black students wouldn't say a word, and appeared uncomfortable, except in their written papers, where some of the issues would get addressed in a different way. It was clear to me that something was going on here, by way of denial and taboos. And when I succeeded in opening up the discussion, and was able to engage the whole class in the subject, it was clear that they didn't have the language for it. It was a topic they just weren't used to ever talking about in a direct way.

By now, Graciela is in college, and has found her circle of friends with whom she seems to feel pretty comfortable and has a lot of fun. They're middle class and mostly of lighter complexion. Maybe times have changed, or maybe it's because she "fixes" her hair and is very conscious of what she looks like. But at least they don't call her "la hija de Don King" any more.

Isabel,
"A Fine Line"

For all of us, I have to say, it was the most emotional moment of our lives. When we saw the Island through the plane window, and then first set foot on Cuban soil, it was the return to our native land, the delirium about being "back." It was a strange feeling, because none of us had actually lived there. We were very young children, some of us babies, when we were taken away, and some of us were born after our parents had already moved to the States. But it was still a homecoming experience, and for me it was being back where I was born, after all the momentous events of the revolution and my folks' rush to get out from under, into exile. My family had no idea of the nostalgia that had been brewing inside me, for years, in this exile that has lasted my whole adult life and which I myself had not chosen.

We left Cuba in 1961, when I was 12. After a year and a half in Miami, we moved to the New York area, where I spent all of my high school years. My parents, who were upper class and very conservative, made sure to keep me in Catholic school and away from any "bad influences," which included not only boys and drugs, but any kind of liberal ideas about anything. Little did they know but even before finishing high school I was already getting "infected" with critical attitudes, about the war in Vietnam, the inferior status of women, social injustice of all kinds.

I moved to New York to go to college, in the late 1960s. I went to a conservative, all-girls Catholic college at the time. And, believe it or not, that's where I got really politicized. I became a student leader in the anti-war movement, took on a strong feminist consciousness, and started linking up with radical organizations. It was the time of the Young Lords Party, the revolutionary Puerto Rican organization, and the Cubans of about my age who were around started joining those protest movements and forming groups of our own. We formed the Latin Action Movement, which was active in Manhattan Valley on the West Side and in the South Bronx. Under the sway of that radical Latino movement, where Ché and Fidel were already big-time icons, we also started having different thoughts about Cuba, much to the horror of our parents (when we told them). We set up a study group, called Juventud Cubana Socialista (Socialist Cuban Youth), and then came the all-important group Diálogo, under the leadership of charismatic poet Lourdes Casals, which as the title indicates, actually set up initial dialogues with the Cuban leadership. Two magazines started coming out, one *Joven Cuba*, which lasted four or five years, and the other *Areíto*, which assumed great importance throughout the 1970s and beyond. Out of all of this activity there then emerged the Brigada Antonio Maceo, which set up the first visit to Cuba by Cubans living in exile. There were all of 55 on the first trip, in 1977, and hundreds on the second trip a year or so later. It was on this second brigade that I made my first return to my long-lost homeland.

My leftist politics of course made me disposed to be admiring and respect-ful of everything I heard and saw, and being Cuban myself that ideological solidarity combined with a kind of personal pride in all that "my people" were accomplishing. But like most of the others, I was not deferential either. My U.S.-bred radicalism made me outspoken, and impatient with hypocrisy and opportunism of all shades, so that it wasn't long before we started to butt up against the rules and the dogmatism. While we were wary about too much special treatment, for us the bureaucracy was stifling and filled with bad faith and double standards. The "choques" became more frequent, especially in reaction to the unsolicited advances of the so-called revolutionary male comrades, who seemed to feel vindicated in their flagrant sexism because of their revolutionary credentials. They were "aprovechando," taking advantage of the situation, and a lot of times they were successful at it. But most of us were pretty disgusted, and disappointed. The biggest disappointment, though, even though it was understandable in some ways, was that with all of our solidarity and self-sacrifice, and their own exaltation of our "heroism," I never felt that they actually trusted us.

The "diálogo," of course, has continued, and I am still involved in it to this day. Despite setbacks, like when the Cuban government closed off all visits by us for some years during the 1980s, there have been many subsequent encounters. During the 1990s, and through the so-called "special period," there were several major get-togethers, where the government met with representatives of those living outside Cuba. And, needless to say, throughout all this time there were recurrent threats of violence and intimidation by the anti-Castro community, in Miami and elsewhere, which scared us but also steeled our conviction that we needed to maintain that vital contact despite all of our own objections to things. Did we change anything in the process? I think we did, maybe even more than the reactionary exile community with all their noise and media bluster. Against the odds, our example, and some of our "dialogue," has managed to call the Fidelistas, at least some of them, on their revolutionary rhetoric, and reminded them of the principles they claim to stand for. Though they didn't fully trust us, and considered us, after all, Americans, they had little reason to question our sincerity. And with our emotional, nationalist feelings for our cherished homeland, they couldn't doubt that what we were saying had the interests of our lost *patria* at heart. I never thought when I first landed "back home" that I would come to play any kind of historic role. But I arrived there with radical political convictions, which I harbor to this day, nourished by my work with New York-based Puerto Ricans and African Americans and other groups that became part of my life. These lessons and lines of solidarity assured me all along that I wasn't there, in Cuba, as a tourist. I didn't want to just feel my country in a deep emotional way, but to be part of its history.

Johnny,
"We had Pizzazz"

The "nativos" had to get used to the way we played. That's what we used to call them, "los nativos," people from the island who had never been to the States. We didn't mean it in any negative way, just that they were so different. Especially, for us, in the way they thought basketball is played. They had never seen our style, the tough, aggressive, and at the same time graceful ball that we were used to playing back in New York, since we were kids.

Theirs was more the European style, you know, the fundamentals, by the book, according to the norms of what you are "supposed" to do. For us, they were slow, even lackadaisical. We had pizzazz. And I myself, I would kick their butt with my defense, my quickness and toughness. That's why I came to be known as "El Rayo," "Flash of Lightening". I was on the Puerto Rican national team for nine years.

I went down there in 1973, when I was 18 and a senior in high school. I was recruited to play for Ponce, one of the teams in the Puerto Rico league. I was born and grew up in Brooklyn, and had been playing in the schoolyards and on my school varsity teams all through my youth. I guess you could say I am from "the ghetto." I played in a place we used to call "The Hole" in Bedford-Stuyvesant, a court that was set down from street level and the stairs to get down to the court doubled as grandstands. A lot of neighborhood people of all ages would come and watch those games. They were hot, and very competitive. Of course there was a lot of showboating—though the era of the highlight reel hadn't set in yet—but most striking was the unbelievably athletic and creative game. That's where I cut my teeth, when I first became the defensive star I became known for by the public in Puerto Rico. I was tough, and fast as a whip, and nobody, I mean nobody, would get by me. The other guys knew that I never shied away from coming to blows, and I knew they didn't either, so the serious players reached a sort of unspoken peace treaty to play hard, but play fair and by our rules.

The scouts down there knew about us, thanks to the news service of people going back and forth between New York and the Island. They would come up and check us out, and pick out guys who stood out. They would concentrate on us, the Nuyoricans, I guess 'cause we were after all Boricuas and would fit in better down there. So in those years, the early to mid-1970s, a whole bunch of the best Rican ballplayers from the streets of the City, especially the Bronx, I might add, were imported into the Puerto Rican league, and recruited onto one of the rival teams there. There was Angelo Cruz and Georgie Torres, both great point guards from the Bronx, Neftalí García who played for Quebradillas, there was Charlie Bermúdez, who I played with in high school, there was the legendary Héctor Blondet, also from Brooklyn, who could be considered the Magic Johnson of our era. And there were of course the Dalmau brothers, Steve who excelled on defense, and most of all Raymond, the superstar of Puerto Rican basketball, one of the top five players in the league ever, hands down, and some would say the all-time greatest. They were from the Lower East Side.

And those are just the ones I remember as I talk, but there were dozens more. Together, we, the Nuyoricans, revolutionized the sport of basketball in Puerto Rico, and anyone who knows that history, and is open-minded, will tell you so. We put the country on the map, to the point that we stood up to the U.S. team in the Olympics. I remember the American players, some of them N.B.A. stars, saying "Puerto Rico got game!" You know, the way today they promote the women's teams in the W.N.B.A. I was so proud, both of my Puerto Rico, and at the same time of us, the Nuyorican kids from the mean streets of the Big Apple. And, I tell you, the game became so popular on the Island. In fact, we helped make it the number one sport in the country, beating out baseball, which it remains to this day. All-star games became major media events, and we were like celebrities. Wherever we went people would recognize us, like Menudo (at the time), or members of El Gran Combo. They'd call us by our first names, take pictures and ask for autographs. Sometimes all the attention would go to our heads, 'cause we just weren't used to it or ready for it. But for the most part we were just thrilled to be in our "home country," Puerto Rico, connecting to our culture, and able to actually contribute something to life there. A lot of us spent time giving clinics all over the Island, being kind and respectful toward everyone, except when on the court of course.

I got to say that I gained my Puerto Rican awareness when I went there, and during the thirteen years I spent there between 1973 and 1986. I learned what it's like to speak Spanish every day, and how people live and interact there, in the country I had heard so much about from my folks and other family and friends. If it wasn't for that fortunate experience, I wouldn't have a clue. But I also learned the tougher lesson of what it means to be Nuyorican. It was there, and not in New York, that I got to know what that's about. Many were the times that we were told, usually in a dismissive kind of way, "you're not Puerto Rican, you're Nuyorican." In so many words, and in so many ways, with all the excitement for our game, we were made to feel "different," like we don't really belong. Sometimes it even took an uglier form, like the times we were invited to "country clubs," where the upper class, mostly white folk, hang out. The racism you could cut with a knife, especially if we invited a friend or someone along who wasn't from the team, and happened to be darker or black. I'll never forget those uncomfortable, questioning looks, like "who's that?" and "what did you bring so-and-so for?" That would really sting, 'cause we didn't really make much of a distinction between ourselves and the Black Americans that we grew up with, and in fact learned our basketball skills from, those very skills that everyone was in awe of down there.

So there were differences like that, that sometimes would put a sour note on our golden years, and brought our own New York upbringing into focus. Like I remember when I brought my girlfriend of the time down with me for one season, and planned to stay with her in the same room and everything. Boy, did I find out quick what a no-no that is, or was back then at least. Premarital conjugal relations, forget it! Especially since we were so much in the public eye. But I stuck to my guns and made my intentions clear, since my thing was I'm not doing anything wrong. But there were other more general differences that I think had something to do with why we stood out so much as athletes. Not sure how to put this, but just starting from the basics, it was clear to all of us that we had more drive, more competitive edge, more hunger to win and excel than the players from there. Where did that come from? Hard to say for sure, but some of it is that in schoolyard or blacktop ball, if you lose you have to sit. And if you sit, you get cold. So you want to win to hold onto the court. Besides that, I think being poor and discriminated against means you have to be used to struggling, to beating the odds, to giving it your all just to survive and keep your dignity. That's what life had been like for us, and we just carried that commitment over to our game. It was about bringing the effort every day. For me, it was that you have to have quick hands, in life and at the hoops. In some way it just translated into a kind of work ethic, a sense of discipline and determination.

All in all, I think I managed to convey some of that to others there, and to change people's minds a bit, both on the court and outside, in the society. I know one thing for sure: I helped open a lot of parents' minds to sending their kids to college in the States. In doing the clinics, which I did a lot of for some years there, I convinced them to drop their fears and closed-mindedness and let go so that their kids could advance themselves and open new horizons. And, wow, were they ever grateful to us for that and the other ways we showed our respect and kindness toward them, in whatever way we could. I felt like it was all in the family in some way, in spite of the barbs I felt sometimes, and the mess-ups that I and some of the other New York players might have committed.

So "los nativos" did get used to the way we played, our dunking and behind-the-back passing and swarming defenses, but they also got used to some of the ways of thinking and living we brought with us as well. Though the official histories of *baloncesto* on the Island may not acknowledge it, it was us, the Nuyoricans, who opened up a whole world of athletics to our home culture, as we were ourselves connecting to that culture. And though the sport has gotten too commercialized over the years, and the mentality of the players has changed a lot too, to this day basketball is in the headlines and on the evening news every day of the season. That's the legacy we left. And on top of that, my son is playing for Aibonito as we speak.

Lenny,
"A Common Ground"

They used to tell me that they love my voice but that it's not a *bomba* voice or a *plena* voice. I got involved with the *bomba y plena* groups here in Mayagüez when I got back to Puerto Rico, and I'm now a fixture on that scene around here. But to this day it's been a long transition, and not always a smooth one. For a while there they didn't accept me at all and, frankly, I didn't even like *bomba* or *plena* that much. But they have always admired my voice, and I feel that if I belong anywhere it's with these folk, the ones who are playing and teaching *bomba y plena*, and upholding the traditions. So that, over time, we've made our adjustments, from both sides, and found a common ground.

The problem was that my own musical formation was in *rumba guaguancó*, as a drummer and singer, which I learned in Central Park, New York City, in the 1970s. I was born and spent my early years right here in Mayagüez, in the barrios Barcelona and Paris, the home of the *bomba y plena* de Mayagüez. Paris, in fact, is where the most famous native son is from, the legendary *plenero* Mon Rivera, and my family was close to his, going back generations. But then, when I was just 6 years old, I moved to New York, where I lived with my mother and sisters, first in Brooklyn and then, for most of the next twenty-five years of my life, in the Bronx. I did come back and forth a lot, 'cause my father was always getting in trouble with the law and I had to tend to that business. But for the most part, I became a New York *boricua*. As you can see, a very black one, so that a lot of my friends were African Americans and especially Cubanos. I came from a musical family, and my grandfather was a big influence on me, always pushing me to play and learn. But he wanted me to specialize in violin and piano, which he considered "real" instruments, and not drums, for which I had a strong inclination since my earliest years.

I am of course very strong-willed and stuck to my drums, from early on playing in Latin bands, sometimes pretty well-known ones. But I also had a drug problem for many years, and like my father wasted a lot of my best years ripping off, getting busted, and doing jail time. I guess the only good thing that came from all of that was that it gave me a lot of time to think, and to practice my music, so that I did figure things out and got into reading. What I see as the real turning point in my life is when I first heard the LP "Patato y Totico," where I got my first exposure to rumba as presented by the masters. I listened to it over and over, and decided, "I want to do that." That was in the early 1970s, just as the jams in Central Park were starting, and I got involved right away. I would hang there all day every Sunday, drumming, singing, learning all the ways of the *timbero*. It was really formative for me, especially when I was chosen to study with the great Puntilla (Orlando Ríos), maybe the greatest living practitioner of *guanguancó*. I joined the group led by Manuel Martínez called "Los Afortunados," singing alongside Abraham Rodríguez, the second voice to Puntilla. The rumba and salsa scenes kept me very busy, though I was on welfare the whole time, and selling drugs to support my habit. For about twelve years there I didn't come to Puerto Rico once.

Despite that full life in traditional and modern Latin dance music, I actually didn't know anything at all about Puerto Rican traditions; *bomba* and *plena* were totally foreign to me. I did not know those rhythms at all, nor as far as I know did many young *boricuas* at that time, especially those of us in New York. This was before Los Pleneros de la 21, you know, before the renaissance that has cropped up in more recent years. Our thing was *la rumba*, *batá* drums, invoking *los santos*, dancing, mastering those super-complex rhythms and, most of all for me, stretching my voice to reach those highs and lows of the rumba vocal lines. I simply loved it, as I still do to this day, and in all modesty I got pretty good at it. Other musicians welcomed me into their jams. Félix Arduén, the venerable father of *bomba y plena* from Mayagüez, was also in New York in those years, and one of the most respected *timberos* in the Central Park jams, and we got to know each other there.

By the later 1980s, 1987 to be exact, as I entered my thirties, time had come to return to Puerto Rico and get a life together here. I moved back to my old neighborhood, to the same house I grew up in as a kid. Though I was still strapped with my drug habit, love for the music was getting the upper hand, and eventually won out. I started playing with local musicians and, having my own stylistic preferences, started up my own group, "Lenny y Sus Rumberos," which soon gained some recognition in the area. It was mostly young guys, who knew some *plena* and loved salsa, and whom I starting teaching rumba drumming and singing. I could see that I had to leave room for *bomba* and *plena* in our repertoire, so that I started making adjustments, like adding *panderos* (hand drums typical of *plena*) into the instrumentation, and shortening the *coros* and speeding up the tempo of the vocal lines. As time went on, as we all got to know each other better, more and more accommodations and combinations came into play. Don Félix [Arduén] helped a lot in this transition, since he was revered by the whole musical community here in Puerto Rico and always admired my singing. So that my next group, which is still around to this day, is called "Rumbomplena," combining rumba, *bomba* and *plena*, both in terms of repertoire and in some cases within the texture of the same song. I guess you can call it a "fusion," but one that is very special to me and my people here in the Mayagüez area. It's not exactly a Puerto Rican–Cuban fusion, since rumba is the musical language I and a lot of other *boricuas* learned in New York, so it's more like a fusion of *boricuas*, here and there. Who knows if it will ever make it to a wider audience, that's not our point. Our point is to find, or invent, a common ground, where we can all feel good about making music together, as one family.

I have no doubt that my life-long love and practice of the music, and the way I have worked out a place for myself here, is what is responsible for me getting my life together. I now have a happy family life, I'm 100 percent dedicated to playing and teaching the tradition, and even have a little business making and selling barrel drums (*barriles*) for playing *bomba*. I know I have learned a lot in the process, and maybe I have even taught folk here some lessons as well. Lessons like, traditions are powerful, and have to be learned and deeply respected, but that without change, even the most beloved traditions will not survive. And my life has taught me that sometimes you might have to go away from your own culture, and get totally immersed in another one, before you can eventually feel at home in your own.

Marielena,
"Show Me That Step!"
("Enséname ese paso!")

I remember the day we first arrived in Puerto Rico. As I looked out the plane window and saw the green mountains and the bright blue sea with white waves and the sandy shoreline, I was crying, but crying from deep down inside. It was real, real emotional. I was finally in my homeland, now I'm going to find my roots. After all those years hearing about *la isla*, my enchanted island where I had never been in my life, those images warmed me inside, images of the delicious tropical scene, the flowers and fruits and palm trees, of *la familia*, the happy, friendly people full of hospitality. Little did I know!

It was 1965; I was 15. My father had gone to the States way back, when he was 17, and now that he turned 60 he wanted to go back and settle in the country where he grew up, near the town of Arroyo on the southeastern part of the Island. As a kid I was raised up in Nueva York, the South Bronx, where we lived with a lot of other *boricua* families, poor working-class people, and a lot of American Blacks. That was my neighborhood, I felt at home there, with no hang-ups about my identity or who I was or anything. Look at me, I'm *clara*, light-skinned, blond hair and blue eyes, but I related more to Blacks, and the other Puerto Ricans of course, than to any whites. In fact there hardly were any whites. We had our own style, I fit right in. The Black kids said, "you white on the outside but you black like us."

Then a few years later we moved to the North Bronx, where there was mostly *blanquitas*, white Americanas in my school and on my block, and there I started to have trouble. They be saying, "you don't look Porta Rican," and I say, "what does a Puerto Rican look like?" and they say, "Not like you." I try to explain what my parents had taught me, and other kids on my old block, that Puerto Ricans are a mixture of three races, that we come in all colors, like a rainbow and all that, that I have black cousins. But they didn't seem to hear me, they say, "but it couldn't be, you got that American look, that gringa look," and that triggered an identity crisis in me. My first one, but sad to say not my last.

Meanwhile, the whole time I keep hearing about *la isla*, my little warm paradise where all of this mess would go away, where everyone accepts you for what you are and hugs you, for being *boricua*. So when my folks decide to go to live in Puerto Rico, I say, "wow, back to my roots! I'm outta here!"

Truth is, though, what I found there was totally the opposite of what I expected. The pain of adjustment was heavy.

At home, my new "home" in the neighborhood where we settled, things were ok, among my cousins and their friends, though we were treated as different, "special" in some way. The problem was once school started. We wore the uniform, my sister and I, like everyone else, with the colors. I wore the colors, but in my own style. Let's call it Nuyorican style, 'cause that's how the other kids saw it. And when we first got there we were real pale, we didn't have as much sun, so I guess my whiteness seemed to stand out a lot, too. Anyway, we noticed a bunch of the other kids were screaming a lot, and I soon realized that they were screaming at us, my sister and me. "Mira, gringa, perra, pelotera," they would shout, "Lookie here, gringa, bitch, you look like a baseball player with those knee socks," and at first I didn't know what the hell they were talking about. But I did know it wasn't friendly, and that they were reacting to us, to my paleness, and to our different style. I felt so bad, I just wanted to go back home, to my house, or back to the Bronx. They, especially the guys, had prejudiced attitudes about Nuyorican girls. They thought we were loose, and they made passes at us, and kept bothering us. Nowadays we'd say they sexually harassed us. We shouted back, "Déjame quieta! Somos vírgenes!" ("Leave me alone! We're virgins!") But they didn't let up, and you know what, then the girls got jealous 'cause we were getting so much attention. They wanted to fight us. And when we tried going to the dean's office and the principal for help, they took their side, and blamed us. The other kids would just laugh at us, and pick on us, and make fun of the way we talked. The language barrier seemed like a brick wall.

And my parents were no help either, 'cause though they did have trouble at first finding a job, they were welcomed by family and had very little trouble fitting back into the society even though they had been away for a long time. So I never told them about our problems, and in fact I was never able to talk to anyone about this for a long time, till I got to the university, twenty years later.

Anyway, it was all real painful, the most painful experience in my whole life, and here I was with another identity crisis ten times worse than the first one. What am I? Am I really Puerto Rican, the way I always thought, if here there are Puerto Ricans laughing at me and calling me gringa and treating me like a slut? Am I Americana after all, when up there I was always treated "different," and where I was even proud to be different? I was deeply confused, and felt lost. It was so serious that many years later, when I started writing things down that happened to me, I wrote a poem about it all, which I called "Roots 1: Expectations and Roots 2: Reality." I never read that poem to anyone for many years, till when the writers from New York came down to present, that was the first time, and you know what, it got published in a magazine!

The only thing that was a little bit of a relief and made us feel better in those sad years was some of the other people in the town. Arroyo, and the town of Guayama where I went to high school, is a part of the Island where a lot of slaves were brought and so there are a lot of blacks, more than in some other parts of the Island. And, you know, I felt more comfortable with them and in their presence. I remember the times I'd be on the bus and looked around and saw a lot of black faces and it made me feel I was in New York. I missed that. I liked that. And there was even a time when some black kids there saw them picking on us and came to our defense. They said, "Hey, don't mess with my cousins." It was real interesting, and we felt good support from them.

Anyway, as time passed and we found our way around a little, they started to accept us, and give us a chance. In fact, after a while we even became popular. We still had our own unique style, that stood out, but they began to think it was cool, and admired it and imitated us. You know, the way we walked, jitterbuggin' and all, and our hair with the zig-zag cut and pony tails, and our music, rock and roll and Motown and Latin soul. And I was proud of all that, 'cause you know, I came to Puerto Rico at a rebellious age, they challenged us, but we challenged them back, too. I wasn't about to give up my diddly-bop for no one, I was proud of the blackness in me. So, they started to like our style, they wanted to learn about it and act that way, too. Like me and the other Nuyorican kids in the school and in our neighborhood. 'Cause as time went by there were more and more of us. And there was salsa, and there was Pedro Pietri and Nuyorican poetry that they started to hear about, partly from us. This is the stuff we brought with us.

So I remember one time during free hour when I was in high school, we were listening to music and practicing dance steps. And I was doing some moves to something, I think it was the Wobble or one of those crazes of those years, or maybe it was some Joe Cuba record, some boogaloo, and I remember the same kids that used to bring us such grief coming over and saying, "*Oye, enséñame ese paso!*" "Hey, show me how to do that step." I'll never forget it, how the tables turned, "*Enséñame ese paso!*"

And now, looking back over forty years of life here, now that I am an English teacher here in Mayagüez, where I have been living for many years, now I realize that by standing up for what I was, and still am, by not giving in to the peer pressure to conform, I have learned a lot, and I have also taught a lot. Because of my experience, and the same experience that a lot of other New York *boricuas* have lived through here, the new generation of people here are more tolerant. We have taught them, by example and from what we have said, to accept people as they are, to be less narrow-minded, and to know racism and prejudice when they see it, just as we learned it on the streets of Nueva York.

Nury,
"My Round-Trip Ticket"

"I have my round-trip ticket." That's what I say to myself when I go back home to La Romana, my hometown in the Dominican Republic, and someone says something really ugly or offensive to me. "I'm leaving and you're staying," and I think, wow, being able to get away, that's definitely an advantage that the Dominicanyork, or any diaspora person, has over those who stay. It's an advantage, and implies a certain kind of privilege. It's another way to cope with the situation, but to me it has a more important meaning than that. As a Black woman walking down the street and subjected to potential or real verbal abuse, I come with a certain kind of information, let's say, I experience that situation with the assurance that the whole world is not that place. The world is bigger than that, and there are lots of other people who think the way I do about justice, race, class, and gender. Just knowing that the world is bigger makes you think differently, it gives you a certain humility, and rids you of some of the arrogance of nationalism, your ethnocentrism. It makes things relative, and limits things. It takes some of the edge off of the hurts you might suffer at the hands of your own people.

And I have always gone back a lot, especially since my mother moved back, sometimes three or four times a year. I've never lost touch with life there, even though I've lived all of my adult life here, in New York City. I spent the first twelve years of my life, till 1972 when I moved to New York, in La Romana, the youngest of ten children. We were a huge, working-class family, and after my father died when I was one, my mother took care of it all: a job, keeping up the household, and dealing with ten kids going through all kinds of changes. We lived on the West Side, in what's called Manhattan Valley, around Central Park West below 110th Street. It was early on in the Dominican migration, before the mushrooming of Washington Heights and other neighborhoods, though there were already quite a few Dominican families living in that area. But most of our neighbors were African American, or Puerto Rican, and other nationalities, too, but all poor and working class. I've always kept that point of view, the perspective of working-class people, and think that a lot of these issues of identity, and race, and gender, can best be understood by factoring in class.

I came so long ago, and so much has happened since, that I really don't remember much by way of first impressions on arrival, nor of the differences between La Romana and New York. At that age you just live. A place is just a real place because your family is there. But one thing that did stick in my mind is that here you can smoke in the street. I don't mean tobacco, cigarettes or cigars, or anything else like that. I mean that when it's cold—we arrived in November—your breath makes steam and it looks like you're smoking. I couldn't believe it, and my first thought was that I want to bring that back to show my friends in La Romana, they'll be amazed. And then, on second thought, no, I don't want to bring that back, smoking in the street as I call it is from here, it's this place and context, and I realized for the first time and still believe today, that it's important to keep the two places apart to some extent and not always be comparing and contrasting. Here's here, and there's there, and I can play in both places. Here is where the cold is, there is where other things are that are from there, and in some way belong there. There's a relation, sure, but that relation is me, my sensibility, and my artistic sense.

Yes, I am an artist, or as I prefer to say, an artisan. I work at literature, theater, performance. I started writing early, when I was only 7, little stories about my teachers that made my friends laugh. Some were pretty nasty, too. Seems like I was always a rebel. I still write, poetry, scripts, stories, in English, Spanish, mostly I would say in Spanglish. My national origin as a Dominican is always there, in the background and in my head, because that's me, but my work is still unknown in the Dominican Republic. In fact, my work is not well known in general. But wherever it is known, I have experienced a dialogue that has a continuous life.

People there think it's crazy that I identify as a Dominicanyork. The term carries such negative connotations, all the stereotypes of drug dealing, crime, violence, loose morals, associated with people "de allá," why would anyone want to embrace that word? To me it's, again, a class thing. Dominicanyork doesn't only refer to national background but to one's class position within the diaspora, whether you're of the working-class majority or among the privileged set who can accommodate to the people who decide what's good, and what's "literature." I like the word, partly because it carries so much of me in it, including not only Dominican, but also working class, and the "receiving" place, too. And besides, for a poet, Dominicanyork is like Nuyorican, it's poetic, and has its own beautiful rhythm. The word "Dominicanyork" was first used by a sportscaster or someone in the basketball world to refer to the Dominican player from New York who went to play in the Dominican Republic in the 1970s. You see, even it's origin is active, sweaty.

So I love spending time in La Romana, and not just to visit family. It's also because in spite of all the sharp differences I feel, and that I have to console myself continually with the thought of my round-trip ticket, I still feel part of that town. I know the streets and the people and all the ways and byways, and in some way I do belong there. Everyone knows my family, as we know them. We were born and raised together. So there is a special kind of affection, a concrete bond. It is a small town.

We are often referred to as "Los Prietos," the Black Ones, not that we are blacker than others but that's just how they identify us, inoffensively. We don't take offense at all, but consider it, if anything, a term of endearment.

One time recently I was "home" and some of the local people, politicians and writers and other "important" figures, wanted to pay me tribute at some kind of official occasion. I think they did it 'cause I must have caught them off-guard when I happened to show up at the event to meet with some friends from out of town who were in attendance. Anyway, they ushered me to the stage and, after some perfunctory account of my supposed achievements, had me say a few words. I started by thanking them, and then introduced myself with the words, "Soy la menos Romanense de los Romanenses, y la más prieta de los prietos," "I am the least Romanan of the Romanans, and the blackest of the Blacks." There I was, in my oversized tee-shirt emblazoned (by myself) with the words "La Romana Republic," my nappy hair in Bantu/Zulu knots all over my head, my dark eyes sparkling and mischievous from behind my dark-rimmed glasses, my black face peeping out from behind the imposing lectern, and everyone present understood exactly what I was talking about. (Or did they?) I went on for a few minutes, surprising and gently challenging the befuddled crowd, all the while thinking of my round-trip ticket, my perennial visa to keep going.

Olga,
"Look How They Send Her Back"
("Mira Como la Devuelven")

My family doesn't understand me any more. "What happened to you?" "Look how they send her back!" ("Mira como la devuelven!") When I left Puerto Rico in 1982, at age 17, I was a white, upper middle class, closeted lesbian who was for statehood. When I came back 17 years later, in 1999, I had become a woman of color, *independentista*, openly gay, and in favor of economic and environmental justice. Yeah, of course I was still Puerto Rican, but I was Puerto Rican in a different way. I was so turned off that when I left I thought it was for good, that I'd never come back. I came back because I didn't want to live more of my life away from, than in my home country. But I also knew that I didn't want to return to what I had left, the racial prejudice and the homophobia and machismo, and all the hypocrisy and denial, that I felt all around me and had to get away from.

My partner, Susana, is different. She's from a poor background, she was not in the closet (though not openly "out," either), she was for independence, and she was older, 25 years old, when she left for the States in 1987, five years after I did. And her plan all along was to come back after a few years of going through graduate school. She knew that she'd have to come back with some savings, and a diversified education, so as to be best prepared to move into the academic world here on the Island. But she, too, will tell you that she came back a changed person, with a different relation to her home country, than before her twelve years spent living in the States. The society had changed in the interim, she herself had changed, but most of all, like myself, she had come to see Puerto Rico with different eyes.

I remember before I left my worst fear was that my parents would find out that I was queer, that I would disappoint them by not turning out the way they had planned: a nice, comfortable middle-class wife and mother, married to a successful professional, a lawyer or doctor or architect, and settled down in a safe, clean suburb, an *urbanización*, somewhere, and spend my life taxiing my kids around and going to the beauty parlor at the mall. So I used to go out with guys, gay guys, so as to make them think I was dating a new boyfriend. They would cover for me, and I would cover for them, both of us dreading more than anything in the world what people would say. I even have friends who got married so that no one would know. I know that if I had stayed living here in Puerto Rico I would still be that way.

Now my attitude is, who cares what they say? Now I can affirm myself, and live my life proud of who I am, thanks to living away, in a different social scene, and thanks to Susana for helping to show me the way. In fact, she herself is now much more affirmative about her own sexual orientation and less cautious and reticent about it. In her professional life (she teaches at the university) she's a double threat to the male power structure, being a strong woman and a lesbian, but she lives a rich and happy life according to the values she believes in. She's an activist for Puerto Rican independence, for a range of environmental causes, for women's rights, and stands up with the gay community to prevent any acts of discrimination or violence. She is quick to point out the inconsistency of people who think they are progressive because they are for independence, but who behave in an anti-environmental, racist or sexist way, or keep on talking pejoratively about gay people as though that were cool.

From the time we first got back here we have found ourselves constantly challenging what we find around us. We have some new friends, but not too many, because we can't put up with values that we took for granted before we left. We won't just take the easy road and go along with it, but have to say something a lot of times. We won't dress or act the way women here are supposed to, just to fit in. I was raised in the upper middle class, and am still relatively comfortable, but I don't want any part of the privileges I supposedly inherited, nor the attitudes that seem to go along with them. I remember we went to an activity a few weeks ago where everyone stood up for an invocation. You know, like a religious prayer to Jesus, and we shocked people because we wouldn't stand up with the others. Again, "what's with her? What got into those two?" I felt like an extraterrestrial or something. But after having lived so long in a multicultural context, among people, including friends, from a lot of different backgrounds, I couldn't see paying tribute to just one faith, or just assuming out of hand that we are all Christians. I guess I'm just outside the box. And we don't care too much if we make others unhappy by our actions and statements, because if we don't do something then we're the ones who are unhappy.

Of course we know that much of what sets us apart nowadays is because of what we learned during our years in the States. Yes, there were people here in Puerto Rico fighting for gay rights, for instance, before and all the time we were away. But Susana always reminds me that the very words for the different sexual identities, gay, bi-sexual, trans-gender, all of those English-language codes, are used here and were imported from the gay liberation movement in the States. And the same is true of the environmental movement, and the anti-racist struggle. The language comes from there, and we feel more than free to continue using it, even though the conservative nationalists from here will go on saying, "eso es de allá," "that's from over there," implying that it is part of imperialist ideology, or just "foreign." We know that's just a subterfuge, a way of shutting us up and making us feel like traitors so that we'll drop our cause.

Susana and I have talked about all of this a lot, because we are sometimes wary that what we are saying and believing can sound like a song of praise for "American culture," and the superiority of "American values." Both of us, though, are staunchly opposed to U.S. politics and arrogance, and do not want to be identified with the dominant culture of the dominant world power that in our opinion is holding so many people down around the world. We don't want to feel that we are in any way reinforcing or abetting that kind of imperialist power in our own country, which is a colony of the United States. No, that's not what it is about. What we learned there is not the beauty of American culture, but the culture of resistance that exists there, the culture and politics of opposition to the dominance of that culture. It seems that in that big rich country there is space (maybe it's a luxury of that inequality) for resisting and standing up to the powers that be. Of course it also has room for some people to assume that culture uncritically, and even to benefit from it and get rich by going along with it and taking part. In fact, that's probably the main way it happens, and we are more the exception than the rule. But there are a lot like us, too, who learn the moral value of fighting against inequality and injustice while there and then stick to those values wherever we go, including home.

Susana's story has been so important to me, partly because it's just like my own, partly because it is so different. She always tells me that before she left she never considered herself a person of color, or a "minority." But after getting there, she became all of those things, or rather, they gave her all of those labels that she had never used. It was difficult for her to assume them because she felt they were being imposed by the gringos, and she was anti-U.S. in so many ways. But as time passed she came to take them on, understand them, affirm them, and fight for respect. She'd say, just because you don't use those terms doesn't mean people don't see and treat you that way. "To see myself as minority," she says, "changes my perception of everything. And when I came back to Puerto Rico, where these categories don't have as strong a hold, I gained a better way of seeing how we, as a majority in this country, can hold down those that we consider a minority. So you go from being a minority there, and stepped on, to being in the majority here, as a Puerto Rican, and stepping on those considered minorities, such as the Dominicans, or the Nuyoricans, or the Jews. So I learned how an identity can be oppressed in one context and oppressive in another. So which of my own identities am I going to fight for, and which ones do I need to modify because in this situation it may be oppressive, or exclusionary?

So here we are, generally quiet, calm, peaceful people, with our machetes drawn, never knowing when we need to defend ourselves against elements of a culture that we embrace as our own but which needs to be changed so that we, and others, and our environment, can feel safe and protected. It's a real challenge for us to live here, when we could have stayed in the cozy safe haven of a New England college town. But we are *puertorriqueñas* and always will be and want to be. We feel that we can best show our love for our country by challenging it, by questioning instead of just accepting what are supposed to be our "unique" values when a lot of those values are really only those of the people in positions of power and privilege. That's what "happened to me"; that's how "they sent me back," a changed person, a different kind of *boricua*.

Pedro,
"Rude Boy, *Friqui*, but Always Very Cuban"

As I first set foot on Cuban soil, my first thought was, "I'm coming home!" My second thought, a few weeks into my ten-month stay, was, "Home is suffocating!" People were friendly, reminding each other that "they speak our language." Only to add, still meaning well, ". . . sort of." That was in 2002, when I was in my early 30s, and I was off to do research for my doctoral dissertation. I was hot on the trail of roots, Cuban and African, and would have to look the other way when I'd hear comments like, "Cuál es la talla de este tipo?"—roughly, what's up with this dude? Or what's this guy about?

I was born in New York, two years after my parents left Cuba in 1968. We lived in Washington Heights, and then, when I was around seven, moved across the river to Union City, New Jersey. I grew up among other working-class Cuban American kids, along with some Italians, Irish, Jews, and a few African American families, all working class and lower middle class. But for me, the Black American and Puerto Rican and even Dominican cultures were not very strongly present. I wasn't into salsa, or hip hop. I guess we were closer to white American culture when I was in my teens, or actually, as for musical tastes, British post-punk and New Wave. Seemed like a comfortable fit. My Italian friend Vinny, his parents spoke to him in Italian, they were like us, you know, "port of entry" immigrants. But for me, personally, I've always been an "other" in that mostly white Cuban context because, look at me, I am very black, and big. And I've always been the kid into books. Now I know the terms, I was an auto-didact, an organic intellectual.

It was when I got to college that I "became Cuban." By that I mean when I became conscious and self-conscious about it, especially as I had more contact with non-Cubans, other Hispanics, like Puerto Ricans. One of my first mentors, if I can call him that, was Raúl, the Puerto Rican (or actually, Nuyorican) student leader who was off into nationalism and anti-imperialism and all. That's when I first recognized that true education is transformative, still my guiding principle today, as a high school teacher. I started to challenge my parents when they referred to Fidel as "el loco," and engaged them on a lot of issues. In college I moved further left than them, even though, ironically, they had been sympathetic to syndicalist ideas and remained hostile toward the privileged and super-rich. And actually, I don't like Fidel that much, either; I guess you could call me a "leftist anti-Castroist." Even on the race issue, my father would tell of how as a boy he was refused participation in a spelling bee because of his color, and my mother was more rooted in Afro-Cuban culture than any of my other relatives.

To African Americans, I was weird. They couldn't figure me out, black as I was and yet different, don't talk the talk somehow, nor walk the walk. I remember my Black American friend Jay from college, he had a flat-top, and how he'd look at me and ask, "What's up with you? You look like a rude boy or something." As I said, always the "other." Funny, but at times when in college I felt like a kind of ambassador, between the black, the white and the Hispanic. But always very Cuban. Going to graduate school—we're in the early to mid-1990s—opened up my world even more, and now it was that the African American came into full view. My first close friends among the brothers, my first relations with Black women, my growing admiration for the culture and intellectual traditions; I read Richard Wright, Ellison, Fanon was part of those discoveries as well. I never have felt close to the vernacular, street, nor even the revolutionary Black Power end of things, but I did come to feel pretty comfortable in that easier-going and inclusive "boho" culture. There was some place there for me.

Which is a little like the way I found the right fit in Cuba as well, some years later. No matter how hard I tried to fit right in, we from the States just looked different, we were fatter, our clothes, we were different, the men wear cologne. I thought of myself as a "ghetto Cuban," not actually from a ghetto, but in the sense of marginalized. In other words, I was very affirmative of my Cubanness but at many removes from the authority, helpless and irrelevant to the Cuban state. I was called everything in the book: it was "el negrón" at a debate on lo Afro-Cubano, it was "el gusa" (for "gusano," what my Cuban wife sometimes calls me nowadays, in partial jest), "un yuma," one guy even made up "el CUSA," as in Cuba USA. But where I finally landed, in a cultural space that I could feel comfortable in, was among "los friquis." Yes, I found a home in Cuban "friqui culture," a non-traditionalist, anti-conformist counterculture often sporting dreads and other cultural markers. And while we still speak of the U.S. as "la brutal," the *friquis* hold their highest disdain for the "cheos," the tacky traditional Cubanos of whatever stripe but especially those of the bureaucracy. The *friqui* attitude is a mix of idealism and playful sarcasm, their countercultural impulse having more affinity with Europe than the U.S. With all my Cuban nationalism and ancestral Africanism there was still room for something of the rude boy. Whatever else you want to say about them, the friquis are about change, and are definitely a challenge to Cuban society, but from within.

And that's what I am about in my own life, in Union City today. For us, the present-day leadership in Havana and Miami may not be the same, but they are from the same social class, and have a lot in common: both seem bent on a uniform and homogenized sense of what it means to be Cuban, to "belong to the Cuban family." With all the changes I've gone through, I still gravitate toward the working class, and I still consider the island of Cuba "home." But in New Jersey, along with other like-minded Cubans here (and you'd be surprised how many there are of us), we are trying to build a Cuban cultural space outside of the Island that is not "Cuban–American" in the convential sense. And, I might add, a space that is not-for-profit. And when the orthodox, Island-born Cubanos, of all ideological persuasions, try to make their claims to be the true-blue authentic ones, I tell them "Mira, soy más cubano que tú porque lo elegí," "Look, I'm more Cuban than you are because I chose to be one."

Quique,
"They Didn't Get It"

I guess I'm the right guy for the job. I work in the public schools, here in Mayagüez, teaching and counseling among the ninth-grade students, you know, 15-year-olds. A lot of them are like me, raised up there, mostly in New York City, or Chicago or Philly, and now living here. You can imagine how many, since they say there's an influx of 150–200 returnees a month, and it's been that way in the Mayagüez area for years. So there's a lot of them, Nuyorican kids, with the language problem, and the *reggaetón* air about them, rejected right away by teachers, parents, even some of the other kids, the ones that don't gravitate toward them and hang with them. The music's about the same, though gangsta rap is not too big for the ones from here, but hip hop's the thing, and *reggaetón*, Don Omar, stuff like that. And the dancing is the same. So they actually have a lot in common, in spite of the differences, and the parents and most of the teachers freaking out.

It was different back when I came to live here, in 1977, though that was the decade that the big wave of return migration was happening. I was 30 then, my life till then spent in the Bronx, in Puerto Rican and Black neighborhoods. Actually, I went to school with a bunch of the guys who became well-known Latin musicians. Willie Colon was in my class, and we knew each other. When his first records came out, in the late 1960s, we went wild, that was our kind of music, big time. My music coming up was doo-wop, and rhythm 'n' blues, like the Drifters, the Platters. We harmonized in the hallways and the subway tunnels, wherever the echo chamber was good, though at home it was the old music, you know, *música jíbara*, and the Trios. When boogaloo hit the scene, that was us, so we loved Joe Cuba's band, the Latin soul ballads, "To Be With You," all that stuff. So when I land in Puerto Rico and hear what they were listening to here, you know, all that pop stuff, I felt like I was the elite. Remember that song, "Yo traigo la salsa"? That was me, I was bringing on the salsa. There was no comparison, our sounds were so much badder, and a lot of folk here knew it, and wanted more. They especially liked the way we danced; they couldn't believe our steps. I was married, but a lot of the other women my age, the teachers, neighbors and parents, would be, "Quiero bailar con Quique." I used to bring my 8-tracks and my LPs to parties I went to, and a lot of people would tell me to put them on.

I was sporting a big Afro in those days, I still have some pictures, you wouldn't believe it, but I did stand out. Look how light I am, but I was black, and they felt it. No doubt but that I gravitated toward the darker *boricuas* of my age and hung with them. They liked me and respected me more, especially as I was a good English teacher and knew what I was doing. But when I would start talking about the shit we had to put up with in the States as Puerto Ricans, along with the Blacks, some people would want to dismiss what I was saying by claiming, "Ah, pero tú eres anti-yanqui," "Oh, you're just anti-American." The statehooders especially would come out with that, but I found that a lot of people here of other political stripes would also act like I was making it up, or exaggerating. Or, alternatively, they'd take the other tack, and be like, "oh, yeah, that stuff happens up there, isn't it great that we don't have any of that here?" They didn't get it either.

I knew Spanish OK, and could get along, but actually being English-speaking stood me in good stead: they really needed English teachers in the schools, 'cause the ones they had, all from the Island, hardly knew English, actually, and weren't very good teachers. I realized early on that the strong presence in the classroom and the schools of Nuyorican culture, which was in English, could be used to our educational advantage, as long as it was treated with understanding and respect. So I started using Piri Thomas and Pedro Pietri and other writings like that, and got the students to write stories and letters and all. And it worked, so that with time I had developed a method of teaching English, and reading and writing, that other teachers started using as well. Not all of them, 'cause there was, and is, still a lot of prejudice, and ignorance. But to this day, I have been working effectively in that way, and educating among the other educators.

Nowadays, it's *reggaetón*, which is even in Spanish, so it's closer to the hearts of the local kids even more directly than hip hop of a decade ago. I take the *reggaetón* tracks and we compose lyrics to them, about language, about what's happening in the school, whatever, but play down the foul and macho stuff. Yeah, we clean it up for educational purposes. But it's a bridge, the kind we need to be looking for, between the kids from here and there, and the generations, and all kinds of other divisions that are out there. In fact, some of the Nuyorican kids are gay, and out of the closet totally. Back in my generation, even though when I returned I was older than these kids, being out would have been unheard of. Forget it. But now, with a lot of the straight kids shaving their eyebrows and wearing earrings and a lot of other markers, even the way they dress sometimes, well, there's not the heavy macho homophobia there used to be. And then too, some of those outted Nuyorican kids, boys and girls, can be pretty tough, and don't take shit, and stand up to some of the anti-gay slurs and disses. So they command respect.

So, the public education system is a good place to do this kind of cross-cultural bridging. I can see that there is a huge need for systematic cultural sensitivity training here in Puerto Rico, and some kind of transitioning for the newly arriving Ricans from the States. It's one of the biggest challenges facing our education here, not just for those kids themselves, but for the whole educational environment. And the Nuyorican stories themselves, the stories of the return migrants and their families, are proving to be an invaluable tool. Just yesterday I was at Inter-American University in San Germán, invited by an organization called The National Project, to give a kind of workshop for thirty-seven teachers on ways of teaching and writing English. I handed out a few short readings for us to look at and discuss, one of them being Piri Thomas' story "The Konk," about the painful process of hair-straightening practiced by, or actually *on*, kids with "bad hair." I was pleasantly surprised how receptive and interested they all were, except for the guy who was in charge of the program, who was noticeably uncomfortable.

Many of them even recognized that such anti-black practices are not limited to the racist U.S. but are alive and kicking here in Puerto Rico and other Latin American countries, and that they can be fatally damaging to young people and their self-esteem. So, I do see things changing, and I have hope, though we sure have a long way to go.

Rodolfo,
"They Can't Believe Me!"

"**W**ow, tú lo haces igualito," "you do it just like him," my friends would say when they saw me doing the Michael Jackson moonwalk. Ever since I first saw a Michael Jackson video, back in my hometown Vanes, in the Holguín province of Cuba, it changed my life. That was in 1989, when I was about 16, and I started collecting every Michael Jackson video and recording I could get my hands on. I never stopped practicing and imitating his moves and steps, and before long everyone wanted to see me do it. I started break-dancing just at the time that hip hop was becoming popular in Cuba. I became an "aficionado" dancer with the local government-run Casa de Cultura, and started traveling around the country doing shows with a troupe. I got paid something for my work, but not enough to live on, so I worked as a mailman for a while, and then in tourism, as a cook. But my heart was in dancing— cumbia, salsa, merengue, rumba, but most of all breaking, and my favorite of all, Michael Jackson.

My dream was to become a professional dancer, but I found myself frustrated at every turn. Not only was it impossible to "break in" and start earning enough to be able to focus on that, but the bureaucracy just seemed to stand in the way of advancing in that field. I decided to try "el bombo," the draft lottery that allows for people to leave the country and go to the United States, or wherever. And believe it or not, I won, my name came up! So on that fateful day of April 21, 1997, I left for Miami, and in fifty short minutes, everything changed. I was lured by the idea that everything in the States is "modern," and that everything "modern" is "lindo." It didn't take long before I realized how wrong I was.

My relatives in Miami met me at the airport. They took me to their neighborhood and welcomed me into their house. Right away they started to shower me with congratulations for having gotten out from under hell on earth, the "dictadura," and for my good fortune in joining them in paradise. By the next day, after hours of tirades and exaltation, I knew for sure that they were not my kind of people. I began to regret having given in to my youthful impatience, and the nostalgia set in. Yes, I missed my hometown, my friends and immediate family, the parties and dance practices, and even the hard work and sense of social commitment. Things I had taken for granted, 'cause I had never known a Cuba other than the embattled revolutionary society I grew up in. I walked around so sad for a while there that people used to call me "el gorrión," a little bird that was proverbial for someone who is always moping and down and out. The upshot, as I see it now, is that I have wound up learning more about Cuba being here in the U.S. than I ever would have learned if I had never left.

So I left Miami quick, and moved to another Cuban enclave here, Union City, New Jersey, where I felt better. My father had settled here, and though his views of Cuba are much more negative than mine, at least I could admire him for being a hard-working guy. I got a regular job, went to college for a few years, and got involved with dance groups. Mostly salsa. I was with Puerto Ricans, Dominicans and a few other Cubanos, and did shows in the New Jersey area. That's how I met my wife, a Dominicana, with whom I am very happy and have a baby boy. I must say that just about everything I have experienced has awakened my interest in and sympathies for my home country. I became thirsty to read and learn all I could about history, politics and culture, and moved further and further to the left. A lot of my friends and associates were Puerto Rican and Dominican radicals, many of them friendly disposed toward the Cuban Revolution.

Though most of the people I hung out with were Latinos, and Spanish-speaking, I also befriended some African Americans and took an active interest in the issue of racism. I came to understand that though I myself am pretty light-skinned I have always considered myself black, that is, of African cultural heritage. I realized that nearly all of the members of my various dance groups, both in Cuba and here, were black, as were the dance traditions we embraced. In retrospect I now know that even my love of Michael Jackson and attraction to North American culture was invariably about African American culture. Even in my most frustrated days in Cuba before leaving, I had no great love for "American culture" as such, but had a huge admiration for Black American music, dance, and political culture, and wanted to emulate it.

And so, after being here for five years, in 2002 I started making visits to my family in Vanes. I have been back three times by now, and plan to go as frequently as I can. Every time I enter the country the guards can't figure me out, a light-skinned Cubano with long hair, a Black Dominican wife, and wearing my Che Guevara necklace. It blows their mind, they can't believe me. In Cuba a lot of times they think my wife must be a Cuban prostitute and I a European sex tourist. The things I have learned in my years in the U.S. never cease to turn heads and shake up things among people there, though that's not at all my intention. One of those things that surprises them is that I don't go around bragging about how much money I make and how great everything is over here. I show them pictures of myself on the job, mopping floors in IKEA, and they are really impressed. "Estás detrás del umpire," "they got you standing behind the umpire," they say, in a colorful phrase that basically means you're a nobody. I know they're a little disappointed at first, but then they tell me that they really respect me for not putting on airs and acting all self-important. And for showing them that for most of us in the U.S. we have to work our asses off to make ends meet.

I'll never forget the first time I arrived back in my hometown, how emotional it was for me to see the little houses and narrow streets with very few cars but teeming with people walking, running, talking energetically. My old buddies greeted me with the same old affection and camaraderie, as though nothing had changed, but my mother would say, with loving tears in her eyes, "cambiaste," "you changed." Not that she had any trouble welcoming my black, non-Cuban wife; I don't remember having witnessed racism during my youth, and don't recall it in that way, though now I realize where my grandfather was coming from with his obsessive comments about blacks. What must have struck my mother and other relatives and friends was my Ché necklace, and my rebellious looks, and the way I talked about politics. Growing up I had been neither a faithful "Communist youth" nor a die-hard *disidente*; I had my grievances, for sure, but generally I worked hard and made my contribution. Without making a lot of waves. And like most other kids my age, I looked north, to the huge, dynamic United States, for the latest cultural innovation. Now that I had gotten so much more familiar with American ways, I had become really opposed to what I regarded as the cultural and political arrogance of the U.S., including in its relations with my home country. I had become an anti-American Cuban American, a strange combination for folks in my little Cuban hometown.

One thing that I understand much better now is that my deep and enduring—and semi-underground—love for Michael Jackson's dance moves was itself a challenge to Cuban society at the time. And it was (and is) a challenge not so much because my collection of the videos and recordings was done without official sanction, nor because it represented black, African American culture. No, the challenge was about sexuality, or rather, homosexuality. Michael's body, his moves and looks, his cultivated androgeny, the wearing of earrings and the make-up we used for our dance performances, were all testing the homophobia line, pushing and bending the boundary of effeminateness that holds such sway in Cuban culture. I'm not sure where that rebelliousness on my part came from, as I was unconscious of such things, and even shared in the homophobic machista world of young Cuban males (and females) of my early years. I certainly wasn't acting in any kind of conscious solidarity with gays. But by now, after my years living over here, and hanging out with progressive, rebellious friends, I am now aware that it was an issue, and that with all the admiration of my dance virtuosity there were those thinking there was something "off" about me. As genuinely fond as my hometown loved ones are of me, and I of them, we all know that I don't really fit in any more.

Samuel,
"Let's Face It"

That happened when I was 14, in Río Piedras near where I grew up as a kid. When I was playing I ran into an electric post and got a wooden splinter lodged in my head. They thought I was going to die. I was in the operating room for eight hours. And it was when I came out of that scary situation that I started to write, like that splinter awakened my artistic side, which I never even knew was there. I wrote so much, stories, poems, that my grades suffered in school.

It's funny, but my other life-changing event came just a year later. When I was 15, in 1989, I spent a year living in New York City, and I "discovered" the Puerto Rican poets in New York. I go to readings, to the Nuyorican Poets Café, I meet some of the young poets, like Mariposa, Willie Perdomo, the Welfare Poets, and a few years later (around 1993–94), when I meet my master, Pedro Pietri, it just blew me away. "Me cautivó," it captivated me, and I said to myself, "Diablo, qué es esto?" I loved the power and genuineness of this writing, that comes from the heart without any fancy professionalism or pretences. I realized there was another way of being Puerto Rican, and of writing poetry, more like the way I am and want to write.

Ever since then I have been writing in this vein, looking at social problems and issues here on la Isla, but with the tools and tone of my mentors in Nueva York, the Nuyorican poets. I looked around for poets here doing the same kind of thing, and didn't find any. Everything here was so slow and boring, it didn't have that force and freshness at all. I also liked the bilingualism, and the freedom, of those voices from La Manzana. Even the angry poets from the 1960s and 1970s here, I don't know, but to me whatever fire they may have had back then seemed to have gone cold, and they've had no successors. Yes, I can identify, I myself, with a poet like Hugo Margenat, who died young and had his own voice. And, going back further, with Julia de Burgos, and with Angelamaría Dávila and Mayra Santos from closer to my own generation. But nowhere, in none of them, do I find the appeal and innovation and relevance of the Nuyoricans.

I think it has something to do with the existence here of a cultural elite, an academy with its institutes and societies and all that. Everyone has to pass through some kind of test of "standards" and correctness. It's all sort of "high class," with its levels and prizes. Over there, for the Nuyorican poets, there is none of that, and no formal training. The writers are regular people, from the street and from poor families with no education. Like myself. Even the writers there who came from here, like Victor Fragoso and Manuel Ramos Otero and Nestor Barreto, I liked better than the ones who stayed confined to the Island situation. For me, in my own writing, there was a perfect parallel: with my base and awareness of New York, I talk about the Puerto Rican experience from here, from this side, but with the technique used by the Nuyoricans.

So, they baptized me "El Nuyorican," and the literary public came to accept and even admire me, but with an obvious distance. There was a mix of fear, 'cause I am from the streets, and dismissal, 'cause I have no credentials. Though some of the young professors and graduate students and academic poets play up to me sometimes, it is clear that I have no real place in any Puerto Rican literary tradition or anything. I am usually referred to as "un poeta maldito" or "poeta de la calle," the guy who's never around and lives in his own world. So, my role turns out to be that of the "poete maudit," like Rimbaud or something. Maybe the name fits.

Things are changing here, though, and we even have our own Nuyorican Café, spelled that way, in San Juan. On Sunday evenings we have open mic, and I am the MC. There I don't feel alone, and I love the vibe there. It's more low-key and slow than the Cafe in Loisaida, but there is something happening, no doubt. There you get the feeling that there is some kind of a movement going on among the young writers, I mean younger than me, I'm 33 by now. I read from my own work, too, and some of them are obviously learning from my writing and working in a similar style. And for all of them, as for myself, New York is the compass, and those poets are the masters. And needless to say, hip hop is the context for everything that goes on. Let's not forget that Vico C, who was our first outstanding rapper from here in Puerto Rico, goes to New York and brings back that sound with him. And hooks up with Nuyoricans living over here. That's how it got started for real here, let's face it.

But, as I see it, hip hop never really took root here in Puerto Rico the way *reggaetón* has in the last few years. Rap remained pretty much underground, especially the real, non-commercialized stuff. But as Tego Calderón showed us, if you want to get to that larger audience, and make some income, you have to turn to *reggaetón* and try to do something with that. So, a couple of years ago I decided to do just that, and now have a *reggaetón* CD, "Teatro del Barrio," which came out this year. And my third book of poetry, after *Barrunto* and *Residente de Lupus,* will be out very soon; I titled it *The Fucking Map.* I am real happy these days to get the feeling that things are changing, and new channels of expression are opening up, among the young people, and even including some with little formal education. And of course, women writers and performers as well. It kind of shocks me that, while all kinds of other social themes come up, there are so few gay and lesbian poets, at least who make it to the stage, and bring out that perspective. But as it looks now, I feel confident in observing that the strongest tendencies within what is called Puerto Rican culture, whether musical, literary or in art, come from New York. In my view, that is the reality, one that I have been aware of ever since my life-changing experiences of over twenty years ago.

Toño,
"We All Had Our *Verdes*"

It was great, all we had to do was recycle *los verdes*, our military greens, and we fit right in. In 1998, when Black August brought down the revolutionary rappers to the 4th annual Cuban Rap Festival, we got to meet Talib Kweli, Dead Prez, Mos Def and a bunch of other politically conscious rappers for the first time, and we were delighted to see that they were wearing camouflage and military garb, and not the usual hip hop get-up of the special jeans and sneakers and hats and of course the bling, which we couldn't afford or even find anywhere around Havana or anywhere. But we all had our *verdes*, from our days in the revolutionary youth brigades, and now we could throw them on and look just like our new-found idols, Black and Puerto Rican street rappers with a social conscience.

In a weird way it was a kind of boomerang, 'cause Black August was started by the Malcolm X Grassroots Organization, which is based in Brooklyn and has a Black Power/Black Panther kind of ideology. You know, claiming to be strongly influenced by the Cuban Revolution and especially the guerilla image with its military fatigues and all. So here was that iconography coming back to Cuba, recycled through the Black revolutionary movement in the U.S. and, of course, hip hop in its subversive, socially conscious incarnation. So we had a chance to really dialogue with those folk, and hang out big-time with people we thought of as our counterparts. For us, hip hop in Cuba was a subversive movement, the only form of popular music at the time that talked about real-life social conditions and that involved the disaffected youth during the so-called "special period." We were pissed off, because we felt the revolution was deliberately marginalizing us, and was everywhere betraying its own ideals, which we still wanted to believe in. I myself was raised in a revolutionary household, my parents were party militants, even my grand-parents were revolutionaries, and my father is head of the CDR on our block. I and my friends, from my neighborhood and from school, were anti-capitalist, nationalist, anti-imperialist, everything the revolution supposedly stood for; in fact, when I was a teenager they called me "El Rojo." But we were getting angry, and then cynical, when we saw all the opportunism and hypocrisy everywhere. So rap became a vehicle for us to express our rebellious spirit and talk openly about what was going on in our society. And our heroes were not so much Ché and Fidel but Malcolm X, and the Black American and boricua youth in the States, or at least our glorified version of them as we witnessed them on TV and through the music.

When I was a kid, entering my teenage years in the late 1980s (I was born in 1976), soul music was all the rage. The long-term Cuban fascination with Black American music reached cult status, and far surpassed Cuban music in popularity among the working-class sector that I was part of. I set up my own system to pick up on the radio stations from Miami, like 99 Jams and others, that brought us Motown, James Brown and all that great stuff from back then, and that was the immediate precursor to the hip hop boom of the later 1990s. We even watched Soul Train whenever we could, and went around trying to look like the artists and dancers that seemed so cool to us. And of course it was forbidden fruit, which made it all the more appealing. Even the merchant marines and the traveling sports and music stars helped by bringing back LPs and 8-track beta cam videos.

This musical love first got connected to an explicitly political agenda when rapper Paris came down to Havana for a concert in 1989, really early; I was only 13 at the time and missed it. But in the early 1990s a lot of us were listening to whatever rap we could get our hands on, which didn't usually include explicitly political stuff like KRS-1 or Public Enemy, but we still loved it. We were especially enamored of rap in Spanish, like El General, Vico C from Puerto Rico (he'd even be on Cuban TV, since it was in Spanish and had no obscenities), and most of all—'cause he's cubano and raps in Spanish over Afro-Cuban rhythms—Mellow Man Ace (remember "El Mentiroso," the mega-hit from 1994?). Not that he ever came down to Cuba (he hated the revolution, being a Marielito), or even rhymed anything political. But maybe 'cause his machismo and braggadocio were definitely Cuban-style, we really could relate to him, like in his song that goes, "Yo soy el más pingón" ("I'm the guy with the biggest one"). But even the English-language Black American rappers that we could see on TV and music videos, we were always commenting and goofing around about how this or the other of them looked just like one of us, the same features and all, and we imitated everything about them, their gestures and attitude, the way they walked and moved their arms and hands, the facial expressions, the whole show.

So we were like a "lost generation" back in those later years of the 1990s, and rap served us to vent and give expression to our fury as working-class adolescents who had something to say. Other socially conscious genres like Nueva Trova were old hat by then, and hopelessly co-opted, and the salsa boom with groups like Los Van Van had gone international and an integral part of the tourist industry, with little to say about social problems in Cuba itself. Not to mention the biggest music hype of the time, the Buena Vista Social Club, which was for us—though we might have loved the music itself—

nothing but a nostalgic throwback totally created by international capital. So, aside from the highly alluring style of the music and broader cultural movement, hip hop provided a vibrant public space for putting forward a working-class and above all a Black identity and perspective. We were drawn to the strident voice of Black pride and power that we saw in this musical culture, and found that though we were all Black there was no space for that in official Cuban culture, or if so, it was just treated like quaint folklore with no critical bearing on what was going on in our own lives. I myself come from a mixed background, my father light-skinned and my mother black, but the interesting thing is that the white side was the more humble root whereas the black side of my family was in the lineage of the black bourgeoisie. But I identify as black and affirm that side of my background. Why? Because I feel that's the side of me that I need to fight for.

For some years, beginning already in the later 1990s, I had been feeling there was no future for me, nor for my closest friends, in Cuba, and started thinking about leaving. The excitement of the Black August days subsided when after four years of participation in the Cuban Rap Festival that project decided to expand and go elsewhere. We started noticing that some of our favorites among the big-time rappers were going commercial, and selling out. In 2001 I came to the States on a visit with some Cuban rappers, and it was clear that I could have a role here. Then in 2002 the Cuban rapper Papá Humbertico came out with his album "Denuncia Social," where he spoke out against problems of police brutality (never at the same level as in the United States, but still abusive), prostitution and the stigma against prison inmates. The international press, including CNN, picked up on it and announced that "Cuban Youth Rebel Against Castro," and even though we considered ourselves on the left, and were not directing our attack against Fidel in particular, the state finally began to get a whiff of the potential force of our resistance movement. So what did they do? They set up the "Agencia Cubana del Rap," a strictly bureaucratic entity whose real goal was not to foster but to control rap and bring it under the wing of the government. Of course they tried to incorporate me into their plan, but I refused because I couldn't identify with that and felt it ran directly counter to what we had been trying to do.

So, in 2004 I made my way out of Cuba and made New York City my new home and base of operations. I continue with my journalism and public presentations at hip hop events and cultural centers in a range of different locations. I feel comfortable with the hip hop community, especially the progressive wing of it, though I sometimes find myself having to take issue with the glowing romanticism of some of the uncritical, pro-Cuba rhetoric of some. To this day I feel that I was raised on African American culture, or African diaspora culture, as transmitted to my generation across the blockade and language barrier. It wasn't other *cubanos* who brought it to us, and certainly not the reactionary community in Miami, with whom I have no relation and don't want any. But still, I feel that the cultural expressions that we embraced and carried forward were part of a big diaspora of color based in the U.S. and which includes a lot of other Latinos, and even some Cuban Americans. To me, being a revolutionary means not being stifled by anything, and not being blocked off from the cultural creativity and identity that is you, and that you embrace as your own. Whether here or there, I am still a rap guerilla. My military *verdes* prove it.

Ursula,
"Another Way of Being (Dominican)"

As a kid, and into my teenage years, going back to the Dominican Republic was like paradise. Imagine, from the hot and dirty New York streets I'd be in the country, outside all the time with a bunch of other kids my age, mostly my cousins and their friends. The fresh air, the games and adventures, the fun we would have seemed so free and without any dangers or hassles. We could just play and run around to our heart's content.

But then, as you grow up, you start to notice things and form your own opinions and views about things. Like you'd notice that the women tended to be uneducated, and that they're not supposed to be fully developed as individuals. They basically had to hold the home front and not ask any questions. That was very clear to me 'cause my family wasn't even that conservative, and was mostly run by women, working women. I would wear dreads when I was down there, which was "un escándalo," a total outrage. When I tried to explain, it would be "What, you black!? You have such nice light brown skin, and your hair is curly but not really 'bad.'"

You got to understand, I grew up in Harlem. I was born in Bayamón, Puerto Rico, to Dominican parents, in 1979. After my earliest years down there we moved to New York in 1983. We moved around a lot, but always in Black neighborhoods and schools. Latinoness hadn't kicked in yet, and being Dominican wasn't as cool as it is now. Where I grew up, you were either Black or Puerto Rican, and I gravitated toward the African Americans. Looking at me, most people figured I was a light-skinned Black American. So I guess, culturally, I am closest to African American, and felt the sting of racism directed toward me on many occasions. I fit in pretty well with African Americans, though when asked I always did identify as Dominican. I felt like I had to affirm that about myself, especially when I realized my African American friends would get a little suspicious of me because I spoke Spanish. That happened a lot. And that's when I would sometimes feel closer to my other friends, who weren't stuck in that narrow idea of who's "black" and who isn't. Because the clique I used to hang with always included others, like Caribbeans and kids from Ghana, and even a few Dominicans. Eventually one of my very best friends was a Black Honduran girl, you know a Garifuna, who was into rasta and all, and I found that real liberating. That's how I learned to be black in a more international kind of way.

So I remember how, when I was on into my teens and getting more and more hip to the heavy racism and narrow-mindedness that I came across in the Dominican Republic, I remember how an uncle of mine that I always liked pulled me aside. I guess he checked out my dreads and heard the way I was talking about being black and proud and all. But he pulled me aside and showed me his collection of Bob Marley records. He was kind of private about it, like he didn't share this with other people, and like I would understand, and I did. For me it was like a little oasis in that desert of racism and prejudice that I met up with on my vacations at home, including from my own cousins and aunts and uncles. I began to realize that those trips were more and more of a culture shock for me, with everything that I was learning growing up among Blacks and Puerto Ricans in New York clashing head-on with some of the ideas and values that seemed to prevail in la República. I questioned to myself, what made me Dominican, and sometimes would feel like maybe it's just because my life had been a life of many migrations, and that's typically Dominican if anything is.

So, yes, I guess I am Dominicanyork, even though I don't use the term that much. When in the Dominican Republic, my being from New York was my main quality. I dressed and walked and talked and laughed and did everything my way, and a lot of times people there found that different, and funny, or weird, or whatever. But for the kids there, that I played with, I was the "cool" cousin from New York. The level of curiosity, and yes, admiration, was intense, and I know a lot of times they wanted to be like me. In the little world that was my family's neighborhood, and among the young people, I know I was having a positive effect, and opening up some minds even though that's not what I was trying to do or anything. And I also know that I wasn't the only one. So many Dominican kids in New York would go back, and still do go back, for summers and holidays, that it probably adds up. And the influence is not mainly through the media, I think, but because of hip hop, and all the kids going back. It's coming through family, not the media.

Of course everyone down there is influenced by U.S. culture, since it's everywhere, and saturates everything. Even the people spouting a heavy patriotic rhetoric and swearing they'll never go live in the States, they all have this love–hate relation with American mainstream culture. But there's a generational thing here. Among a lot of the young people, my cousins and friends that I hung out with there, it's also about being different, and not going by the norms of the grown-ups. Call it a culture of resistance? Whatever, but at some point all these things collide. I know from my work as a DJ that there are hip hop groups in Santo Domingo that are explicitly and outspokenly "black," and make that a major message of their music and performance. Conservative Dominicans, trying to hold on to the old norms, like to dismiss it as just trying to be American, 'cause that's the dominant, imperialist culture. But for me, what my counterparts in the Dominican Republic are seeing and saying, is that there is another way of being Dominican, and that you don't have to deny being black and hate Haitians to be Dominican.

Victoria,
"Keeping Up With the Jones Act"

I've been here in San Juan all this year, 2006–07, taking college classes toward my Master's degree and getting to know what it's like to live here. I couldn't believe it, but on the last day of class they had a little party, with music, and when they saw me dancing they said, "Mira, ve, la Nuyorican sabe bailar salsa," "Check out the Nuyorican, she knows how to dance salsa." I had said it a few times during the semester, that salsa is *from* New York, but it just didn't seem to sink in. I've learned so much this year, about what Puerto Ricans are like over here, and how little they know, or want to know, about what we are like over there. They hardly ever want to admit that they might have something to learn from us, too.

Not that it's the first time I'm here. I used to come over every summer when I was a little kid, 7, 8 years old, and then again in my teenage years. I'd go stay in the summers in the town of Isabela, with my grandfather, and used to hang out with my little cousins, who always made fun of me for the way I spoke Spanish. Or, as they and my aunts would say, how I would "kill the language." That's the word they used. I know they were only teasing, but it would really hurt and I would feel so stupid and out of it. It made me shut up and not want to talk. My aunts were Nuyoricans themselves, and now I am aware that they didn't speak Spanish very well either, but they would join in and joke about "la gringa" and that I wasn't Puerto Rican. Maybe it was a generational thing, who knows? But the distance between us was big, even though we had a lot of fun together.

I think one reason that I get so hurt is that when I was in high school in the Bronx I was so into Puerto Rican culture that I used to be known as Miss Puerto Rico. I wrote papers, did class presentations and reports, and was always talking about it, Puerto Rico, my pet theme. I couldn't seem to know enough about it. In fact I learned so much, then and later in college, that when I got here I often found that I knew more about the history and the culture than a lot of people who live here and went to school here. And yet, because of the way I dress and carry myself, but especially because of my accent in Spanish, I wasn't considered a "real" Puerto Rican. A lot of times it seemed like they were listening to my accent and not what I have to say.

I grew up in the South Bronx, from a poor working-class Puerto Rican family, where I was the most well-spoken, and had the lightest complexion. So my brothers and sisters teased me by calling me the "white girl." But I hung out with other kids from my kind of background, and grew up on hip hop and the whole urban youth culture of the 1990s. I did so well in school that I was accepted into the elite college, Sarah Lawrence, where I also felt totally out of place. There I was the Puerto Rican, the only one among a bunch of upper-class white girls. I was so uncomfortable that I left after my first year and transferred to Hunter College, of the public university, CUNY, where I finally felt at home among my own kind, and able to take classes that were interesting and inspiring to me. I learned a lot about class and race relations, and what colonialism is about. All the time studying subjects relevant to Puerto Rico and the Caribbean, and Latinos in the U.S. And when I graduated I figured, now is the time to live there and see what it is really like.

So I took a course in Puerto Rican literature, all in Spanish, and I was the only student from over there. The professor was trying to be nice, of course, but when she would point my way and say to the class, "And here we have a Nuyorican!" I would feel like a rare specimen of some kind, and that her tone was patronizing, at best. At first I was petrified because of my deficient Spanish, but after a while I started to speak up about things. Time and again, mention would be made of "la diáspora," but with what seemed to me a combination of guilt and condescension, and startling ignorance even though the teacher and some of my classmates acted as though they knew something about it. Here they had a Nuyorican right in their face and didn't know what to do about it. Like when they were puzzled that "la Nuyorican" had trouble speaking Spanish and yet listened and danced to salsa. When they said the word salsa it was like they owned it or something, that it's theirs not mine, and didn't seem to know or care that salsa is a New York, a Nuyorican creation. The only readings by Nuyorican writers were for the very last class, and it wasn't even on the final. They liked the way I read Tato Laviera's poem "nuyorican," but didn't want to talk about what it said.

What they often said, or implied, was that the way I talked and the music I like is "Negro Americano" and not Puerto Rican. Many times I heard, "why do you wanna be black?" or "Nuyoricans are just copying the African Americans." Of course I told them how we share the same social spaces, neighborhoods, schools, and that our cultures feed off one another, but that didn't carry any weight with them at all. "But why do they act black? They behave like blacks, they think they're blacks." To which I also answered, "well, some of them are," but to no avail. They insist on this clean and total separation. And I read the report that some 85 percent of Puerto Ricans identify as white, and said to myself, "ah ha!"

"Mira la nuyorican, mira la cocola," would be what I hear now and then. After my brothers called me the "white girl" when I was younger, to hear these people calling me "cocola," the black girl, was the height of irony for me. It has been even heavier now that I got a job in a hotel in Isla Verde. There the management wanted someone who speaks perfect English, so I got the job. And I started seeing all these upper-class, bourgie Puerto Ricans, and laughed when I realized that it was the first time I ever saw Puerto Ricans who are rich, and like I never knew they existed. So some of my wannabe fellow receptionists in the hotel ask me if I want to go to the Bon Jovi concert, and I say to them, "I don't listen to Bon Jovi." They were taken aback, and asked me why I listen to soul music and heavy New York salsa, and of course so much hip hop, the real hard stuff. And I would be like, "what do you want me to listen to, opera? or rock?" Another twist for me: they are more "American" than I am. I would tell them: I don't like mainstream American culture, the commercial, pop version of it, because it's plastic and tacky to me. So here I am "la gringa," telling my more-Puerto Rican-than-thou colleagues that American culture, white American culture, is garbage to me. And that's what they seem to aspire to in so many ways, in the millions of fast food places, in the malls, on MTV, all the stuff I avoid and have always found sickening.

So here I am, the light-skinned "cocola," the "gringa" who hates "la cultura gringa," who never stops telling them, you know what, it's not so great over there, not so pretty. And, for a lot of them, that breaks their bubble, 'cause I can't help feeling that—what's the phrase?—they are just trying to keep up with the Joneses. Now I giggle when I hear about the Jones Act that made Puerto Ricans into U.S. citizens back in 1917. I want to write an essay some day, "Keeping Up with the Jones Act."

But I think what's been disappointing me most is that they don't seem to want to see the connections between here and there, how similar life is, especially for the poor, working-class Puerto Ricans. This came up in my literature class, when we read the book *El entierro de Cortijo*, the one that's set in the projects down here in Santurce when Cortijo died. I loved that book, and commented how that scene could easily be in the Bronx, near where I grew up. My boyfriend, Luis, who's from here on the Island, saw my point, when he thought about the time he went to visit "la casita" in the Bronx, when the people were all hanging out and listening to bomba y plena and all. How similar it was, how much that book about Cortijo's funeral resonates when you know what down-home Nuyorican life is like. But my friends and classmates here didn't want to hear about it, they said that can't be and scenes like that are "typically" Puerto Rican, meaning, from here on the Island. Again, it's not so much the ignorance, but the indifference, and lack of any sign of real curiosity. That's what bothers me, and what I am trying to deal with. I know, it takes time, and I am learning new things all the time. And, with all my frustrations and impatience, it's not like I'm not having fun in the meantime, no way!

Wanda,
"If My Parents Let Me . . ."

My parents don't want me to go, even for a visit. They say it's too dangerous, especially for a single woman. And I gotta admit, I'm a bit ambivalent about it myself, based on my last visit. Don't get me wrong, I am dying to go spend some time in my home country. 'Cause yes, for me it is home, even though I have never lived there and hardly know it except for what my family and friends have told me, and what I've read, which is a lot.

But I have mixed feelings since the last time I was there, a few years ago, when I had a lot of negative impressions, I must say. We were on a cruise, my parents and I, and we docked at La Romana. It's the first time in twelve years I had been there, back in 1992, when I was only 7 years old. So, the first time as a grown-up, since I had gotten to learn a lot about the country. When we landed at the pier and set foot on land, I was crying, it was so emotional for me. The marina at La Romana is beautiful like a resort, with gift shops and restaurants and all, for the tourists. But when we started riding in the tour bus toward Santo Domingo I got a better glimpse of reality. We drove through a few towns, and *bateyes* where the cane workers live, and if there was ever any doubt in my mind about the conditions Haitians live in, they were quickly dispelled at the sight of those shocking scenes. I mean, squalor, miseria. And everywhere I looked, the garbage everywhere, I was shocked: "Get me out of here, take me back to the Bahamas." We passed a rotunda at one point, with a famous monument of Duarte. My mother told me that it used to be covered with a huge wall, which people called "La pared de la vergüenza," because the wall was there to hide the hideous sight of the shantytown behind it and in view of the monument. And all along the way, in all the towns we passed through, all I saw was black people, I mean real black, which struck me big-time after all I had been told that Dominicans aren't really black. And I said it loud, "I see nothing but black people here," so that the tour guide could hear me.

And then, at the hotel in the capital city, it was all for tourists. The food had nothing at all Dominican about it; in fact, it reminded me of the Portuguese and Spanish food we used to eat when we went out to eat back in Newark where I grew up. You know, Iberian food. I spend twelve years not coming to the Dominican Republic and I can't even have a fuckin' platano! The only thing Dominican I had was a Presidente beer, and that's 'cause I was so shocked I needed some alcohol. And then, as we were about to leave and head back to the cruise ship, I'd notice the little boys rubbing their stomachs and begging for money or something to eat. I was disgusted, and outraged, what with all the talk about how beautiful and warm and human everything was "back home."

And yet, my feelings were mixed, very confused. Because in a strange way, it did feel like home. I am home there, even though I carry hand sanitizers around with me, as a kind of self-defense. But when I see my relatives there, in Santo Domingo, it is very different than when I am with them here: there they really feel like family, I feel a stronger bond with them, and more cohesion as a family. Also, I was able to notice certain changes for the better, not from having been there before but from observing from back in New York. I am obsessed with the little dolls, *las muñecas*, traditional porcelain figurines usually called *la mujer sin cara*, woman without a face because they try to make them look like they could be anyone, without any specific definition. Anyway, I have been collecting them for years, relatives and friends bring them back for me from over there, 'cause you can't buy them in the States since they're too fragile to mail. Well, when I went to the gift shop just before leaving I checked out the *muñecas* and noticed that they come in all shades now, they even had some that looked like me, very dark brown, and even a really pitch black one. I couldn't believe it, and right away bought some to bring back with me to share with my friends in college. My mother was surprised, too, and when I got back and showed them to my aunts in Newark, they were also very surprised and had never seen anything like it.

So I had a lot of heavy impressions of my home country, and got back realizing that I have to go back and spend more time, to deepen my knowledge and really engage the society in some way. But I have to convince my parents that it'll be OK, so that they don't get too nervous. One thing I realized is that my view of the Dominican Republic is fully conditioned by my experiences in the States over the years, living in Brooklyn, Washington Heights, and then Newark for most of my adolescence, and then going to Barnard as a young Black Latina. Since there weren't a lot of Dominicans in Newark in those years, most of my friends were African American and especially Puerto Rican, and I hung out with them in and out of school throughout my growing up years. I was taken for an African American all the time, until they'd hear me speaking Spanish, and then they would have me be Celia Cruz in the school shows, with the wig and big dangle earrings, you know, the whole outfit. 'Cause I was the Latina that was "*la más prieta*," the blackest. My mother hated it, me being cast in that stereotype role, and I didn't like to be singled out and to be "different," in that I was both black and foreign. 'Cause we were a very Dominican family, we ate Dominican food, listened to a lot of *merengue* and *bachata*, were obsessed with our hair, the whole deal. And I myself was always very proud of my Dominican identity, and never tried to conceal it or diminish it in any way. But outside, I was closest to African Americans, and of course *boricuas*, who also spoke Spanish and were closer to us culturally, and most of them were black as well. My closest girlfriend in high school was half African American, half Puerto Rican, and I remember how we used to talk with each other about how racist our parents were.

The interesting thing is that my parents, who have been the major influence on me to this day, were really ambivalent. On the one hand, they were fully into the old Dominican thing about denying their blackness, using phrases like *"pelo bueno y pelo malo"* ("good hair and bad hair") and "improve the race," and casting aspersion on the Haitians and blaming them for all our ills. On the other hand, they got vocally furious when they sensed any racial slight or profiling, which is something that happened to us now and again. My mother even used to complain to me about how racist the Puerto Ricans and especially the Cubans can be toward Dominicans, because we're supposedly "blacker." In fact, when they first moved to the States in the 1980s my folks were living in Crown Heights, Brooklyn, among a lot of West Indians, and had no problem with a Caribbean identity. And my father lived in Santurce, Puerto Rico, before coming to New York, in a strongly Afro-Boricua neighborhood, and always loved Ismael Rivera, you know, Maelo. He had all that good music from back then, that I listened to and loved, especially Maelo's song "Las Caras Lindas (de Mi Gente Negra)", and Joseito Mateo's version of the old merengue "El Negrito del Batey," both of which I loved because of the black themes, even though my father didn't really talk to me about that. And I remember him wearing his hair natural, in an Afro, and dashikis that were popular symbols of African roots in those days.

But still, I came to understand as time went by that they really harbor racial biases in a lot of ways, some subtle, some less so. And I have had an ongoing debate or dialogue with them about those issues.

What's interesting is that with time, as I've gotten further in my education and they realize that a lot of times what I am saying makes sense, without them admitting it they are changing. Like sometimes I hear my mom using the same arguments I use with her when she is taking issue with things her friends or cousins come out with. As I learn cultural history I bring out to them how strong the Haitian influence has been throughout the Spanish Caribbean, and they can't deny it. By now it is easy for me to point out the illogic of what they say, and how much it contradicts the good values they themselves have taught me about being fair and tolerant to all people, and standing up against prejudice and injustice when we see it. How can we do the same racist things to others that so often happen to us as soon as we leave our country and live in San Juan, or New York? The immigrant experience is making all the difference for a lot of Dominicans. They come to this country and see that we're the Haitians here. They see things from the perspective of the outsider, and that's when labels like "Afro-Latino" come to take on more meaning. I know it's a slow process, and sometimes a painful one, but it's making a difference, I have no doubt about that.

So now I'm 23 years old, just graduated with a degree in public health, and am getting ready for the next stage of my life. I feel confident about my Dominicanness, yet I also gravitate toward a broader Afro-Latina connection, which ties me through a common identity to my Boricua, African American, Caribbean, and other sisters and brothers. I recognize that the main cultural influences on me have been African American, Puerto Rican, Haitian and Afro-Cuban, and that without those the Dominican in the US would not be what he or she is. But I am dying to go to the Dominican Republic, my home country, to really get to know it on its own terms, and from within. I just want to listen and learn, but there's no way I can leave all I have learned and experienced behind. I need to put the two realities alongside each other, and in each other's face, and see what I come up with. That way I will come to know my country better, and myself better. And I do believe in change. Let's hope I can convince my folks that it's alright.

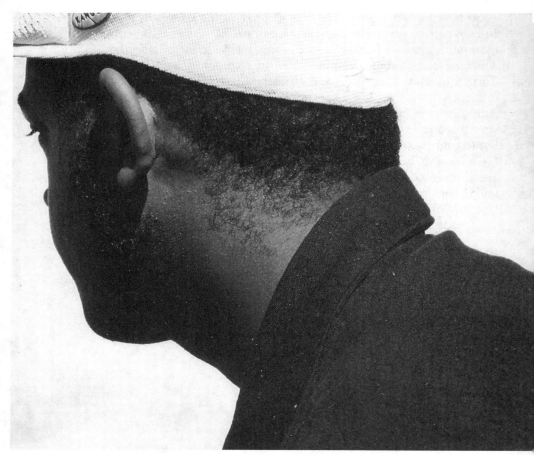

"Pedro" Sitting by the Malecón, Havana, Cuba, 2002.

Permission Yesenia Fernández Selier.

Reading
the Tales

The tales provide a rich fabric of human experience, lived transnational action and interaction as remembered and retold by Puerto Ricans, Dominicans, and Cubans whose lives straddle diasporas and homelands. I call them tales of "learning and turning" because, partly in response to my prompts and nudges, the tellers have trained their memories on those dramas of insight and understanding, those moments of contact and change that characterize so much of transnational life in our times. I like to think of them as one intricate patchwork with infinite possibilities of extension or re-configuration, a narrative collage with as many potential inserts and insets as there are individual and group engagements with trans-local cultural movement and transformation.

The experiential arc of emigration, diaspora life, and return figures centrally in the structuring of each life-story, though that triadic set of locations assumes a wide range of shapes and sequences in the process of recalling and re-enactment. The emphasis is always on intersections, sometimes of a conciliatory form by way of re-cognitions and re-connections, but often these cultural crossings can be jarring, and involve collisions and clashes of the most telling kind. My guiding and probing during the interviews, and my re-working and shaping of the texts, aims to draw special attention to those revelatory instances when such cultural intersections, most notably the discordant ones, have the effect, however subtly and what would appear inconsequentially, of unsettling and challenging the assumptions of the inherited national cultures. Most directly, to what extent does diasporic life prepare some returnees, and the remitted values, tastes, and visions generated in the diaspora, to serve as agents or catalysts of social and cultural change?

The tales can be read in any or no particular order, and can also be grouped in any number of ways, such as by nationality, gender, theme, or generation. They are perhaps best read in the sequence presented in order to follow my line of interpretation in the pages following the tales. I have chosen to sequence them chronologically (and to arrange the tellers' names in alphabetical order to facilitate access and cross-referencing). By chronological I mean, in very broad terms, from the older to the younger tellers, and according to the historical period when each experienced the most intense cultural contact and change. Thus the first five tellers are at least 60 at the time of telling, and mostly over 70, and their diaspora and return experiences generally reach back to the 1950s or early 1960s. The next ten or so (**Francisco** through **Quique**) are now in their forties and fifties, and had their most pronounced cultural experiences from the later 1960s through the 1980s, though all of them, especially the last few, are still engaged very actively in contemporary cultural challenges. And then the last six are now in their twenties or thirties and were formed culturally since around 1990. Thus my chronological arrangement of the tales means to suggest a periodization of the experience along generational lines, which can be appreciated by reading them in that order. There is a distinct tenor to each period or generation, the first characterized by the relatively slow process of adaptation in both settings and the sheer reach of autobiographical recall, the second by the impact of the dramatic political and cultural changes of the 1960s and 1970s in both diaspora and homelands, and the third by the transcending impact and diffusion of hip hop under the thoroughly transnational circumstances of cultural relations in the present generation.

There is of course good reason to separate the testimonies by nationality, since the Puerto Rican, Dominican, and Cuban experiences have been so different, and drastically so in the Cuban case. My decision to scramble them together, with some regularity of alternation, is a bit risky, as it could well lead to confusion and ignoring of those differences. What struck me, though, as I conversed with the tellers and pondered their fascinating life-stories, is that there are very important parallels among them above and beyond those differences. I realized that the process and outcomes of cultural remittances may well be so widespread, and so determined by the increasingly transnational conditions, that those parallels at a human and everyday-life level may be even more telling than the contrasts that derive from clashing ideologies and diplomatic systems. Maybe detecting the specifics of each national case by alternating among them can allow for a more fine-grained sense of those contrasts and an appreciation of the continuities and common-alities at a phenomenological level that may result from or reflect the disjunctures between political and cultural determinations.

What is more, the nationally circumscribed diasporas intersect and overlap to such a degree that what is brought or sent back to the home countries is often more a composite than any ethnically discrete cultural ensemble. As all of the Cuban tellers make clear, what they bring "home" from their locations of exile is infused with their exposure to Puerto Rican and even Dominican influences and examples, some of which draw them into a discordant relationship with prevalent ideological and cultural values in both Havana and Miami. As for the Dominican diaspora and return experience, these testimonies demonstrate clearly how closely they seem to follow the path set by the Puerto Rican community that preceded them, while also bringing into relief the particulars of each process, often an expression of differing relations and structures of power and of the discrepant class composition and profiles of the two diasporas.

It is along the lines of gender and sexuality that some of the sharpest fissures become manifest. As of the early generation, stories like those of **Andrés** and **Beatriz**, or **David** and **Ester**, point up the difference between a woman's and a man's account of otherwise compatible trajectories. Then from subsequent periods there's, say, **Olga** and **Francisco**, or **Victoria** and **Toño**, and it is striking how otherwise parallel life-courses can diverge so noticeably around issues of gender and sexual preference. Not that any of the tellers would be considered the worst sexists or homophobes, but the perspectives can be nearly diametrically opposed, and memories and retrospective narrations seem to have differing points of emphasis. It is clear, too, as much of the gender-focused research on transnational migration has evidenced, that the diasporic context generally involves a greater sense of independence for women and greater public space for lesbians, gays, and people of diverse sexual orientations. It is interesting that the tales assembled here would appear to indicate that men and straight people may even undergo something of a switch on these matters as well, as for example is the case with **Quique** and with **Rodolfo**. Who can forget **Quique**'s report on the response of Nuyorican gays in the high school where he teaches in Mayagüez, or **Rodolfo**'s insight into the sexual valence placed in Cuba on his emulation of the body movements of Michael Jackson? Or the powerful stories of **Olga** or **Carmen** about their return "home" with thoroughly transformed ideas about their sexual and gender rights? None are clear or particularly sanguine as to what difference their new views and behavior might make on the larger scheme of things, though their comments are often followed by observations about how "those things are changing."

Despite the differences in gender and sexual perspectives, then, the same general pattern seems to hold in that the remitted or transmitted cultural values tend to run askew of and to challenge prevailing patriarchal and homophobic traditions, and that the experiential and philosophical "shifts" that occur in these regards, both in the diaspora and upon return, are generally of a democratic, liberatory tenor. This is why, as is most consistently true in the Dominican case, women tend to be less interested in returning to their home countries, or are at least wary of regressing to a prior, more vulnerable condition, and why they have such conflicted, off-putting experiences when they do. It also explains why the state of "sexile," the formation of diasporic gay communities and proliferation of gay presence, is such a widespread phenomenon in current transnational realities, as it has been for some time. What is new is that remitted diasporic values and practices are joining forces for change within the respective homelands to generate a vocal and sometimes defiant public presence, and in some instances new social movements and new communities.

Similar and equally dramatic changes are afoot in the area of race relations and racial identities, especially, in the Caribbean case, as concerns the recognition and affirmation of blackness. Once again, the tellers speak of the diaspora as a more open and public, though no less racist, space for addressing racial realities, and many tell of being drawn into, or coming under the sway of, civil rights and anti-racist political and cultural activism. The transmission of such perspectives, and especially black identification, to the "home" cultures can be explosive, as is most evident among Dominicanyorks in relation to traditional Dominican negrophobia and anti-Haitianism; the lives of all the Dominican tellers present here attest to this clash, more so the closer we come to the present generation. But, as stories like those of **Marielena** and **Pedro** attest, the diasporic challenges to traditional Puerto Rican and Cuban racial cultures can also be sharp and meaningful, in both cases serving to uncover the deep-seated complacency and denials that have been taken for granted for so long. Entrenched ideologies of the "national family" and racial democracy, and in the Cuban case of the presumed achievements of the revolution, are now being tested by "external" cultural influences which it is that much harder to dismiss because they are being introduced by "one's own," people of the same ethno-national background. The diasporans would be the first to admit that they were strongly influenced by the civil rights and Black Power movements in the U.S., but would at no point deny their national origins nor concede to be written off as gringos. Indeed, many of them, certainly among those telling these stories, are decidedly anti-gringo, both culturally and politically, and yet are generally as patriotic as those who never left and may object to or resent their intrusion, or perhaps more so.

Indeed, one of the more striking points of "learning and turning" in the return diaspora cycle has to do with national identity, not so much its loss but the insight into a new or different way of being of that nationality. Of course the most common way of thinking about this process has to do with assimilation, that is, the shedding of inherited national characteristics and attachments and the assumption of a new and different national identity, at first with the hyphen to indicate continued ethnic difference, and then full incorporation into the "receiving" or "host" culture. The other extreme way of conceptualizing this debated process, generally propagated in paternalistic tones by nervous nationalists from the home countries, would have it that Puerto Ricans, Dominicans, Cubans remain such wherever they are, "hasta en la luna" ("even on the moon"), as the saying goes. Because of such pressure to remain "authentic," many diasporans feel the need to compensate, or even overcompensate, by demonstrating an even more fervent patriotic allegiance and preservation instinct than is true of "los nativos," as **Johnny** refers to those who never left the home country. For this reason, when they return, or in their contact with the home culture, many diasporans are seen to bring an infusion of that old-style patriotism that can appear very salutary though a bit quaint when perceived from the social context of the home territory.

What the tales reveal, and many grassroots movements in diasporic communities indicate, is that there is a strong and widespread urge to retain national ties and identities, but that the very idea and content of the respective nationality are different when perceived and embraced in the context of the diaspora. Listen, for example, to **Samuel** discovering a different way of being and writing Puerto Rican in the example of the Nuyorican poets, or **Gabriela** bringing back her altered Dominicanness from her years in New York, or **David** being Cuban in a different way when he visits "home" after decades in exile.

Or, to depart from the tales a bit, look at the alterations made on the "traditional" casitas when they incorporate elements from life in the Bronx or El Barrio, or the re-doing of Dominican cultural patrimony at the Centro Afro-Quisqueyano in Washington Heights, or the meaning of "keeping it Boricua" when fighting for the future of El Museo del Barrio. Aside from important stylistic variations, there is in many such instances of diasporic patriotism a strong infusion of class and racial content attesting to the kinds of social struggles those communities have taken up in the home away from home. Yes, people continue to feel Cuban, Dominican, and Puerto Rican, but they are so in a different way than as articulated in the territorially based and traditional nationalist rhetoric. Affirming their nationality often implies fighting poverty, discrimination, racial prejudice, and other forms of social injustice and marginalization that are constitutive of diasporic reality. Such struggles, of course, inevitably involved joining forces with other nationalities in alliances of solidarity and converging interests. As the example of **Ester** illustrates so emblematically, when that revamped form of patriotism strikes home, the returning diasporan may assume an important leadership role in analogous struggles in the country of origin. Or, as **Olga**'s testimony suggests, when those values learned in the diaspora take on life in the home culture, new spaces of expression and lifestyle can open up and thus shift in perceptible ways the public discourse on (in this case) gender roles and sexual orientation. All in the name, for **Ester** and **Olga**, of being better Puerto Ricans.

These shifts in understanding of gender, racial, class, and national relations and identities carry obvious political and moral valences, and indicate contending values and ideological persuasions. They are changes and challenges that transpire within a larger, philosophical field, which in the tales and the pertinent scholarly work have much to do with the inevitable exposure of diasporic national groups to other cultural realities and perspectives. The guiding terms in this regard are "multiculturalism" and "hybridity," and in a broader, even more controversial register, "enlightenment" and "tolerance." I will choose not to linger on the first set of terms, in part because I view them as overused and potentially misleading, and partly because they are foreign to the mindsets of most of the tellers. They might think and talk about multicultural realities and hybridized cultures, but not in those terms. Many of the tellers, on the other hand, either speak of "enlightenment" and "tolerance" in those very words, or use metaphors or refer to practices and attitudes that are directly about that. They speak of how their eyes were opened, how they became more accepting of new and different communities and customs, in **Carmen**'s case, for instance, of how she learned to see and think critically by spending part of her life away from her Dominican hometown. Or **Andrés**, who is back in the very haunts of his rural childhood but now sees the neighborhood with new eyes. The examples proliferate.

One can notice, too, that there is a chronological progression, or variation, of these philosophical alterations according to the different periods or generations over the years. For the first, earlier and older generation, the accent is on the discourse of modernity and progress, and how the returning diasporans favor the sense of order and development of the metropolitan setting over what they perceive as the lack of reliable services and progress of their homelands. In some cases, the tellers say that they themselves have changed in that direction, and have now come to expect those kinds of social facilities wherever they live. The reason that such talk of "enlightenment" can be controversial is most obvious in this immediate post-World War II stage, which is the one most studied in the return migration literature, especially with a view toward the English-speaking Caribbean. George Gmelch, for instance, in his admirable study of Barbadian migration (*Double Passage*, (1993)), argues directly that return migrants can indeed be "agents of social change," and attributes their progressive ideas to the exposure to "Western culture." It is clear that he leaves out of consideration the extent to which these lessons of change might just as well be anti-Western in their deeper impulse. The testimony contained in the tales demonstrates well that much of the interest in change voiced by many of the tellers is identifiable as anti-American (thus, anti-Western) more than as the simple importation of "American values." The second generation, whose diasporic formation coincided with the social movements of the 1960s and 1970s, offers important support for this interpretation. Here the touchstone of enlightenment and tolerance is the idea of radical solidarity, the alliance with other, similarly situated groups and peoples and unity with the most oppressed against imperialism and racism, often standing for the political interests of the metropolitan society itself. In many instances, the radical education acquired in the diaspora stands in complex, and not always concordant, relation with forms of radicalism as they exist in the home countries. **Nury**, **Isabel**, **Gabriela**, and others of that generation all exemplify this kind of enlightenment learning, where the diasporic agenda for change includes change in the established "left" in their home countries.

Finally, the philosophical learning characteristic of the most recent, current generation, marked off by hip hop and the globalizing shifts of contemporary society, centers on transnational cultural affinities. The sensitivity to diasporas and ethnoscapes, along the lines of race (notably the African diaspora and the Black Atlantic), environment, feminism, indigenous rights and traditions, among others, is dynamically enlivened in the current vocabulary. The "enlightenment" is happening, and being transmitted, primarily among youth, both in the diaspora and in home countries, young people like **Victoria**, **Wanda**, **Rodolfo**, and **Ursula**. Generally there is a political undertone or agenda guiding these forms of identification and education, a moral content that both continues and diverges from that of earlier periods. For instance, while the current generation takes for granted the trappings of modernity with which they have grown up in the diasporic setting, they often distrust and even disavow their attachments to those values and their symbolic expression in the dominant culture, since modernity in this sense so evidently goes to accompany the asymmetries established by imperial power. Such is certainly the tenor of testimonies like that of **Victoria**, or **Pedro**, or **Wanda**. Similarly, while the contemporary cultural currents align with earlier anti-imperialist and anti-racist agendas from the days of 1960s and 1970s movements like Black Power, the Young Lords Party and the Antonio Maceo Brigade, they carry a critical edge toward the limitations of those precedents by reaching more expansively in referring to Afro-Diasporic and environmental movements and those addressing gender and sexual injustice.

This third, contemporary project of diasporic "enlightenment" also points up a dimension of transnational cultural flows that was somewhat less pronounced in the previous periods. In addition to the new moral and political contents and the broader philosophical horizons that make up the substance of cultural remittances, there is then the lesson of "style," the form or manner in which these cultural contents find expression. In this sense, diasporic education is also a sentimental education, that is, a teacher of new aesthetic possibilities. The tales of **Lenny**, **Ursula**, **Victoria**, and **Rodolfo** are just the most powerful examples of this aesthetic learning and challenge, and provide telling evidence that the diaspora must be seen as a source of creative innovation and not just the repository of inherited national traditions. There is a new film about revolutionary hip hop in several Latin American countries; the young filmmakers (who include **Ursula)** who conducted all aspects of the work for this documentary decided to call it "Estilo Hip Hop," and in that way assure that attention is paid to the stylistic, creative aspect of this transnational cultural movement springing from diasporic realities. **Lenny**'s story of the contending and contesting cultural codes between the *guanguancó* drumming and vocal styles he learned in Central Park and the Puerto Rican *bomba* and *plena* traditions upheld by the masters of his native Mayagüez provide another memorable instance of mutual cultural education stemming from the diaspora-homeland contact zone. Once again, it is in large measure about style.

A closer look at aesthetic and stylistic flows requires an examination and interpretation of literary, musical, and other forms of cultural expression as they shuttle between homelands and diasporas, the subject of the third section of this present study. Before getting to that dimension of the process, however, read and re-read the "Tales of Learning and Turning," and add any further observations and lessons, and of course reservations, to those I have summarized in these pages.

PART 3:

STYLE TRANSFERS

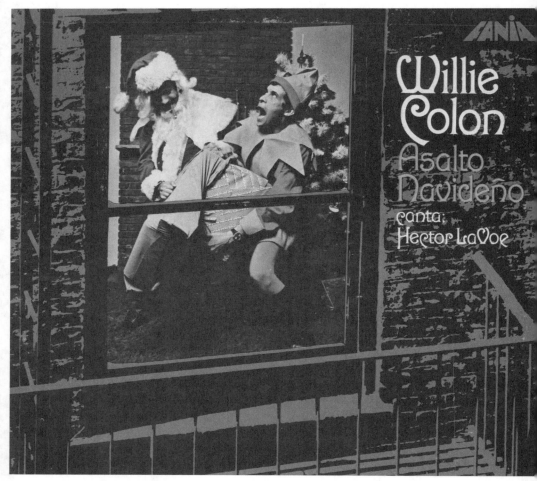

Asalto Navideño **album cover.**
Courtesy of Izzy Sanabria.

5 BRING THE SALSA

Diaspora Music as Source and Challenge

~~~~~~~~~

All Aboard the Air Bus

The flight attendant let out an icy scream of terror when she noticed a pair of hefty *jueyes*, native Puerto Rican land crabs, strutting down the center aisle of the plane. It was one of those infamous red-eye flights from San Juan to New York, filled to the last seat with Puerto Ricans from all walks of life, while the panicky flight attendant has the look of a stereotypical white-bread gringa, "angelical and innocent, a frigid blond like Kim Novak in her days as a frigid blond." What is this, a prank, or a hijacking? Who are these terrorist *jueyes*? The hysteria spread to the rest of the crew, and to the passengers, though among the *boricuas* there is an underlying but pervasive giggle, that familiar jocularity laced with irony that Puerto Ricans call *jaibería*, or "*el arte de bregar*," the art of dealing with the situation.[1] The stage is set for a dramatic cultural collision.

Students of contemporary Caribbean culture may well recognize this memorable scene from the opening sentences of the fanciful creative essay by Puerto Rican author Luis Rafael Sánchez entitled "La guagua aérea," "The Air Bus."[2] This highly entertaining and suggestive story set aboard the air shuttle known to the majority of his countrymen has become nothing less than canonical since its publication in 1983. In a few masterful pages Sánchez is able to capture the existential feel of a people caught up in a relentless process of circular migration and carrying their indelible cultural trappings back and forth between the beloved but troubled homeland and the cold and inimical but somehow also very familiar setting in the urban United States. The story struck such a chord that it has been republished countless times in a range of languages, is required reading in many schools and colleges on the Island, in the U.S., and in Latin America and the Caribbean, became the basis of a widely publicized movie, and serves as the guiding metaphor for two books about modern-day Puerto Rico, significantly titled *The Commuter Nation* and *Puerto Rican Nation on the Move*.[3] Its irresistible title alone, "La guagua aérea," has assured its place as perhaps the best-known work of recent Puerto Rican literature.

Present-day migration, no longer the momentous, once-in-a-lifetime trauma of earlier times, is now a commute, an everyday kind of excursion, like jumping on a bus or subway and arriving at an equally familiar destination. In the story, the feeling aboard that hilariously nervous flight is so matter-of-course that passengers even comment how they lose track which way they're headed, and whether they'll be landing in New York or San Juan. The two end-points become interchangeable, so much so that the *jueyes* caught and cleaned in Bayamón are sure to find their place in a stew-pot in the Bronx, no questions asked. No serious danger of losing the culture by being away from the Island, either, for the customs and sensibilities typical of the home culture are just as at home in New York, New Jersey, Chicago or Florida. How resilient, how immutable, that art of making do, how ineradicable that proverbial *mancha de plátano* (banana stain)! Any fears of a national schizophrenia, or cultural genocide, are assuaged thus by the comforting sense of trans-local equilibrium.

Yet, when looked at more closely, the story actually falls short of its promise: "la guagua aérea" only moves in one direction; the migratory voyage, presented as a commute, is still basically one-way. That is, the cultural baggage aboard the flight is entirely that of the Island, the homespun, almost stereotypical trappings of the national traditions, emblematized by the shocking sight of the land crabs but omnipresent in the gestures, humor, and gregarious, gossipy ways of the passengers. As for the other final stop of the commute, the New York City environment and its cultural life, mention is made of the Bronx and El Barrio and other familiar scenes, but only as sites for the playing out and preservation of traditional island ways of life, not as a place that is in fact home and the primary cultural base of half of those bi-national commuters. The rich liminal space between home culture and diaspora thus becomes nothing but a zone of cultural authentication, while the cultural and human salience of that "other" home is reduced to the anxieties of an up-tight gringa airline stewardess plagued by nightmares of King Kong atop the Empire State Building.

"La guagua aérea", then, begs a key question: what about the cultural baggage that goes the other way, the experience and expressions learned and forged in the diaspora that make their way back to the homeland, there to have their impact on those rapidly changing traditions and ways of life? With all the vast and burgeoning studies devoted to the cultural changes brought by modern migrations, transnational flows, and diaspora communities, and with the widespread understanding that these movements are most commonly circular and multi-directional, it is indeed striking how little attention has been paid to the cultural experience and consequences of the massive population of return migrants and their children who grew up in the diaspora. For too long, and too uncritically, I would suggest, it has been presumed that the main cultural flow, and notably the main line of cultural resistance, has been from the colonial or post-colonial point of presumed "origin" to the diaspora enclave in the metropolis. The flow in the other direction, on the other hand, from the metropolis to the colony/post-colony, appears to be strictly "from above," hegemonic, and reinforcing of the prevailing structure of cultural imposition and domination.

These abiding assumptions about the direction of cultural flows have also prevailed in discussions of Caribbean music. The idea that the only influence is from home islands to the metropolitan diaspora may go to perpetuate an at times misleading sense of the dynamic of Caribbean musical innovation and change, and therefore of the place and function of the music in contemporary Caribbean communities. I would suggest that concepts like "transnationalism from below" and "cultural remittances" carry a special relevance to our analysis of Caribbean music, historically and especially in our own times. I therefore invite you to get aboard the *guagua aérea* and head in the other direction, from the diaspora to the islands, and thereby glimpse some of the history of Caribbean music from a different aerial view than is commonly the case.

Salsa Invasion

One of the most frequent passengers on the cultural airbus is Willie Colón. The pioneering *salsero* and his music commute back and forth between his home turf in the Bronx and his ancestral Puerto Rico, with more than casual stop-offs in other musical zones of the Caribbean. His first albums, produced in the later 1960s at the threshold of the salsa era, attest to his very eclectic stylistic agenda; while comprised mainly of Cuban-based *sones* and *guaguancós*, the titles and cover images of *El Malo (Bad Boy)*, *The Hustler*, *Cosa Nuestra*, and *The Big Break/La Gran Fuga* proudly present the persona of the Latin superfly, the borderline criminal street thug. The music, too, veers boldly from its Afro-Cuban base by references to and samplings from styles from Puerto Rico, Colombia, Panama, and that "other" ancestral homeland, Africa, while also demonstrating the young Nuyorican's native familiarity with jazz, soul, and rock. Along with his partner in crime, celebrated vocalist Héctor Lavoe, Colón projects from the beginning of his influential salsa career the new musical mixes resounding in his beloved Nueva York barrios.

Of striking pertinence to our commute back and forth from the Caribbean is *Asalto Navideño*, Wille Colón's immensely and enduringly popular Christmas album released in 1971. For there he actually transports us on a musical airbus and makes the relation between diaspora and Caribbean homeland the central theme of his work. An undisputed classic of the salsa canon, this compilation puts the lie to the widespread notion that salsa is no more than an imitation of purely Cuban sources by mostly Puerto Rican exponents, and that Puerto Rican music and Nuyorican life have little or no significant presence. Rather, the listener recognizes immediately that the strongly accented *son*, *guaracha*, and *guaguancó* weave of the musical fabric is laced with vocal, instrumental and rhythmic qualities typical of Puerto Rican *seis*, *aguinaldo*, *bomba*, and *plena*. Most notably, aside from the decidedly *jíbaro* quality of Lavoe's vocals, Colón brings in the famed Yomo Toro on the *cuatro*, the quintessential string instrument of traditional Puerto Rican music. This "*popurrí navideño*" (Christmas medley), as one of the cuts is titled, is clearly intended as a dialogue with Puerto Rican culture. Even the album title, "*asalto*," makes reference to the age-old custom of Christmas-tide musical "invasions" of the houses of close friends and neighbors for the sake of partying and sharing in the holiday spirit, much in line with the primarily adoring, nostalgic tenor of that diaspora–island dialogue. But in light of the sequence of previous album titles, there is a thinly veiled double-entendre here: the more common meaning of "*asalto*" as "attack" or "mugging" lurks ominously close to the surface.

Two selections from that compilation, "Traigo la salsa" ("I bring you salsa") and "Esta Navidad" ("This Christmas"), are of most direct interest to our discussion, since both lyrically and musically they enact the diaspora addressing the Island culture in a complex, loving but at the same time mildly challenging way. At one level, "Traigo la salsa" is about "bringing" Latin music to the immediate New York or North American audience, and along with it holiday cheer from the warm tropics. Yet even here, it is not the usual salsa fare that is being offered; at one point the lyrics state, "Yo les traigo una rareza," "I bring you a rarity." The singer goes on to explain that on this special holiday occasion he is adding in the *cuatro*, an instrument atypical of salsa, "por motivo de Navidad" ("for the sake of Christmas"). The combination of salsa plus *cuatro* is clearly still a sign of the Island culture being "brought" to the New York scene as a delicious Christmas offering, or as an "*asalto*" or invasion on North American culture much like the land crabs aboard the airbus.

However, there is another dimension to this act of "bearing" or "bringing" the music at play here, and it refers to bringing New York salsa to the Island. Indeed, the opening words and body of the lyrics, beginning with "Oigame señor, préstame atención" ("Listen to me, sir, play close attention"), would seem to be addressing the personified Island itself, and to be saying that the singer is bringing salsa for him ("para tí"). The closing lines of the stanza, which say "como allá en la isla" ("like there on the Island"), make this geographical differentiation evident. That is, in addition to being a marker of Puerto Rican or Latino authenticity in the New York setting, salsa is at the same time, in Puerto Rico itself, a marker of diasporic Nuyorican authenticity, distinct from and originating externally to Island musical traditions. In other words, as has been pointed out, on the return trip aboard the air bus, "*traigo la salsa*" ("I carry or bring salsa").[4] Salsa is the musical baggage, the stylistic remittance of the diaspora on its return to the Island.

This ambivalence, or bi-directional meaning, is conveyed in the musical texture of the song as well, and in the album as a whole. Yomo Toro's *cuatro*, for example, with all its symbolic weight as an authentication of Puerto Rican culture, is deployed for both Christmas airs with the flavor of *la música típica* and for virtuoso riffs more resonant of jazz and rock than of the familiar cadences of *seis décimas* or *aguinaldos*. Another diaspora-based departure from the traditional Caribbean sources is of course Colón's trombone, a stylistic device introduced into the New York Latin sound by legendary *plenero* Mon Rivera, and firmly implanted by Barry Rogers, José Rodríguez and other trombone masters of Eddie Palmieri's pathbreaking "trombanga" band, La Perfecta, in the early 1960s. It is the improvisational trombone lines that are the most emphatic marker of the urban diaspora in Afro-Caribbean music, the herald of the friendly yet defiant musical "*asalto*" on territorially and nationally circumscribed tradition.

Let's not forget that as late as 1978 salsa was still referred to by some on the Island as "an offensive, strident, stupefying, intoxicating and frenetic music openly associated with the effects of sex, alcohol and drugs." As has been noted, for people of that mind-set upholding the idea of salsa as "typical Puerto Rican music" would be nothing short of explosive, like "planting a bomb in the foundation of the national culture."[5] It is ironic, though fully consonant with the logic of the music industry and a commodified cultural nationalism, that by the early 1990s salsa had been domesticated and comfortably re-patriated to the Island, to the point that it came to be equated with Puerto Rican identity as such. As signs of this reversal, the Puerto Rico pavilion at the 1992 Columbus Quincentenary celebrations in Madrid was emblazoned with the slogan "*Puerto Rico Es Salsa.*" Similarly, an independent documentary film of those same years, "*Roqueros y Cocolos,*" showed salsa fans on the Island justifying their preference for salsa over the advertently foreign, imposed rock music with the claim that "*salsa es de aquí,*" "salsa is from here." Aside from such claims that salsa is from Puerto Rico or from Cuba, a prevalent interpretation is actually a pan-Latino or Latin Americanist version of this nationalist appropriation. To that effect, salsa is being commonly identified as "tropical music" or, in the most influential book on the subject, *El libro de la salsa* by Venezuelan journalist César Miguel Rondón, as "music of the urban Caribbean" (*música del Caribe urbano*).[6]

In any case, the Christmas celebrated in *Asalto Navideño* is obviously not the usual holiday affair, but a very special one somehow askew of the expected and accepted customs. It is, in short, one that, rather than enforcing the comfort of a known and familiar identity, is riddled by contrasting, and to some degree clashing and contending, identity claims. It is, emphatically, "*esta navidad,*" "this Christmas." This complex, contradictory relation between diaspora and island cultures is addressed even more directly in the tune of that title, "Esta Navidad." There, the multiplicity of claims is dramatized in the frequent and varied naming of the enduring rural symbol of Puerto Rican identity, the peasant from the highlands, "*el jíbaro.*" Striking up a contagious *aguinaldo* air at the beginning, the typical *cuatro* parts sound in continual counterpoint with the mischievously playful trombone line, thus setting up an interplay that will run through the entire piece.

The lyrics tell of the attitude of the "*jíbaros*" who arrive from the United States only to look down on their island friends with "an air of superiority" ("*un aire de superioridad*") and of great wisdom. This is the theme of the song that is most remembered by the public, and is generally assumed to be its main message: that those from the diaspora have been corrupted by their experience away from the homeland and authentic national culture, and that they typically put on big-city airs while trying to pass themselves off as *jíbaros.* They are, in a tricky phrase, "*jíbaros guillados.*" But then, in an interesting twist, the lyrics continue with the speaker identifying himself as one of those would-be natives but one who is nonetheless, in a bold assertion, "*un jíbaro de verdad*" ("a *jíbaro* for real") ("*Hay jíbaros que saben más / y aquí queda demonstrado / soy un jíbaro guillado / pero un jíbaro de verdad*"; roughly, "There are *jíbaros* who know more / and here it's clearly shown / I am a would-be *jíbaro* / but a *jíbaro* for real.")

What entitles this returning diaspora Puerto Rican to feel confident about his knowledge and to claim "realness" after all? Evidently it is the song itself, as suggested in the phrase "*aquí queda demonstrado*" ("here it is shown"). Indeed, the vocal and instrumental improvisations with which it ends are very much in the *guaguancó*-based salsa style, the "*tumbaito,*" which in the course of the song come to replace the trappings and cadences of *música jíbara,* the proverbial *lei-lo-lai* with which it had begun. Or actually, in tune with that diasporic wisdom suggested in the lyrics, the lead voice draws the traditional holiday music into the eclectic, inclusive jam of this special Christmas celebration, even extending a special invitation to the prototypical *jíbaro* on strings, Yomo Toro: "*tambien invitaré a mi amigo, mi amigo Yomo Toro*" ("I'll also invite my friend, my dear friend Yomo Toro.")

Diaspora Music Comes of Age

The music known as salsa, then, which has become the quintessential marker of Spanish Caribbean expressive identity, is in its inception the stylistic voice and practice of the Puerto Rican and Latino diaspora concentrated in New York City. The story of Caribbean and "Latin" musical styles in New York is a long and largely uncharted one, extending as it does back to the early twentieth century when some of the earliest recordings and performances took place there and where many of the most illustrious musicians and bands came to live or perform. Caribbean Latino figures of the stature of Rafael Hernández, Antonio Machín, Pedro Flores and scores of others spent formative years in New York, their primary audiences being those of the diaspora. Ruth Glasser, whose book *My Music Is My Flag* documents and analyzes the experience of those early decades among Puerto Rican and Cuban musicians, demonstrates well the extent to which twentieth-century Puerto Rican popular music was actually composed and performed in New York City.[7]

Despite its prominent presence and voluminous output of influential work, however, this music of the early decades was still not diasporic in the full sense of the word. For though there was an unparalleled mastery of familiar Latin American song forms, like the *bolero*, *guaracha*, *danza*, and *son*, this period of the 1920s and 1930s did not witness the emergence of new genres and rhythms as a result of admixture and experimentation. Even when song lyrics make mention of life in New York, or when virtuoso instrumentalists like Alberto Socorrás or Juan Tizol find their place in jazz bands of the era, no radically new musical styles emerge. Such processes of hybridization and aesthetic fusion do not occur until the later 1940s, when New York Latin music saw the momentous innovations of Cubop and Latin jazz, which along with mambo were more strongly rooted in the North American urban diaspora than in the Caribbean. It is significant in this regard that "Machito and his Afro-Cubans," generally considered the greatest of all Latin bands, never even played in Cuba, and that of its fifteen "Afro-Cubans", all but two were New York Puerto Ricans.[8] Similarly, Dominican *merengue* enjoyed immense popularity among the mostly Puerto Rican communities in New York during the 1950s, as the recordings of Angel Beltrán, Angel Viloria, Luis Kalaff and others resounded at clubs and house parties alongside *plenas*, *boleros* and *música jíbara*. Indeed, the master Puerto Rican *plenero* Mon Rivera, whose albums often alternated among *pachangas*, *plenas*, and *merengues*, frequently played with bands and on recordings of New York *merengue* of the period. Yet here again, though internationally known, this music was barely familiar to audiences in the Dominican Republic, thanks in this case to the tightly restrictive cultural politics of the Trujillo regime.

It was not until the 1960s, with the appearance of fully Nuyorican styles culminating in salsa, that a fully active field of bi-directional musical flows begins to emerge. More than a mere extension or imitation of Cuban or native Puerto Rican styles, salsa is rather the source of a new, newly hybridized and creolized adaptation of those styles in their interaction and admixture with other forms of music-making at play in the diasporic environment. Even prior to the advent of salsa by that name, and in even more dramatic ways, Nuyorican and Cuban musicians and music publics had fused *son* and *mambo* sounds with vernacular African American styles such as rhythm and blues and soul music, as evidenced in the short-lived but wildly popular experiments of Latin soul and boogaloo.[9] Indeed, already at the beginning of the 1960s, New York-based *pachanga* signaled the breakthrough to a new stage of Latin music beyond the illustrious mambo era; Charlie and Eddie Palmieri, the early Ray Barretto, Johnny Pacheco, and a host of other musicians generally identified with what came to be called salsa, cut their teeth when they added *pachanga* and other diasporic styles to the *mambos, boleros,* and *cha chas* that had formed the repertoire for over a decade. As mentioned, Eddie Palmieri's band La Perfecta, which was formed in 1961, was the herald of the new era, introducing as it did a wholly new tempo and musical texture that captured the feel of the upcoming generation. It was not necessarily a new genre or rhythm of its own, but its eclecticism made for a new kind of music, a diasporic music in the sense that it could not have originated in the home country and its musicians and audience, or in the soil of its primary musical root, Cuba.

The salsa continuum is also diasporic in that it "returns" to those ancestral origins, and has a dynamic relation with musical and broader cultural life in the homelands. Mention must be made in this context of the towering accomplishment of percussonist and bandleader Rafael Cortijo, whose all-black "combo" had already effected a revolution in Puerto Rican music as of the mid-1950s, and whose Cubanized *bomba* and *plena* hits are generally considered part of the "salsa" repertoire. Cortijo and his unsurpassed vocalist Ismael Rivera wrought changes in musical taste and practice on the Island that were fully consonant with the challenges of New York "salsa" and, while immensely popular with audiences, also faced disregard or outright rejection from the cultural elite.[10] As exemplified and dramatized in Willie Colón's *Asalto Navideño* and other recordings, the initial arrival of 1960s Latin music to Puerto Rico was wrought with complex and ambivalent reactions, ranging from cultural nationalist and elitist repugnance to fascination and emulation among many others, especially the youth. The story of this dramatic encounter is told in personal terms by **Marielena**, who recounts how when she first returned to Puerto Rico everything about her—dress, hairstyle, language, musical taste—was frowned upon and ridiculed, and that included the boogaloo and 1960s Latin and rhythm and blues music she was raised on. It was of great personal importance to her that after she got acclimated and felt more comfortable hanging out with some of her schoolmates who had not lived in the diaspora, they started admiring her dance step and wanted her to teach them. Like the New York *jíbaros* in Willie Colón's Christmas *parranda*, **Marielena** brings them salsa, something new and fresh and hand-made by Puerto Ricans—but from over there.

Further, among the other tellers, **Quique** brings his record collection of New York sounds to the delight of his new neighbors and co-workers in Mayagüez; **Lenny** brings the *tumbao* from the jam sessions he was part of in Central Park during the same years; and on a slightly different, non-musical, note **Johnny** brings the "pizzazz" of inner-city schoolyard style to Puerto Rican basketball, with revolutionary consequences. Salsa in this sense is but the most conspicuous and salient instance of a general shift in the diaspora–homeland dynamic, signaling the force of cultural expressions forged in the diaspora when they land "home" and come to interact with the traditions from which they both spring, and diverge.

As of the later 1980s, this geocultural shift is also evident in the practice of the traditional or "folkloric" Afro-Puerto Rican musical genres, *bomba* and *plena*. While generally eclipsed over the decades, even among many Puerto Ricans, by Afro-Cuban rumba, mambo and other rhythms, the 1970s saw the formation of New York-based *bomba y plena* groups, starting with Victor Montañez and his Pleneros de la 110 and then followed by the ensemble that has set the standard through the decades, Los Pleneros de la 21. Since the early 1990s new groups or off-shoots began to emerge, such as Yerba Buena, Viento de Agua, and Los Instantáneos, many of them comprised of younger musicians. This movement has been characterized by two contrasting though intertwined tendencies, one toward preservation of the traditional forms in their "authenticity," the other experimentation and admixture of other styles found in the diasporic ambience, such as salsa, hip hop, *merengue*, and others. A remarkable fusion of these two tendencies at the highest level of musicianship was present in the all-star band of the mid-1970s, significantly named Grupo Folklórico y Experimental Nuevayorquino; Grupo's two albums, *Concepts in Unity* (1976) and *Lo Dice Todo* (1977), are considered by many aficionados worldwide as the champagne of music called salsa. All of these developments, both the preservationist and the experimental, have proceeded to have their impact on the Island; indeed, the musical director and founder of Viento de Agua Tito Matos, among others, argues that the revival of these musical practices, and the experimentation with new fusions, were an inspiration for similar movements on the Island in recent decades.[11]

Transnational Circuits

As the golden years of salsa begin to wane in the later 1970s, and at the verge of the hip hop explosion, *merengue* takes center stage in the Latin music scene and sets in motion another wave of Caribbean Latino transnational musical and cultural interaction. Times had changed since the earlier fever for *merengue* among Latino New Yorkers in the 1950s, when right-wing dictatorship and its paranoid nationalism prevented any possible resonance of such "foreign," tainted versions of the national music. The *merengue* boom of the 1970s and 1980s came as an announcement of the end of the dark Trujillo years, and of the exodus and diasporization of Dominican emigrants by the hundreds of thousands. It wasn't long before the burgeoning Dominican diaspora community in New York started generating influential groups native to the city, such as Millie, Jocelyn y los Vecinos, Gran Manzana, and New York Band.

Post-Trujillo superstars Johnny Ventura and Wilfrido Vargas broke *merengue* out of its long-held isolation and incorporated elements of salsa and rock and roll. This new, liberated, and hybridized *merengue* became an identifying symbol for the mushrooming Dominican diaspora, as was the long-disdained *bachata*, which had traditionally been dismissed as the music of the "lower classes." Dominicans everywhere were proud that their music was being enjoyed by Puerto Ricans, both on the Island and in the diaspora, and by other Latinos, and that it was blending so fruitfully with other Caribbean forms. Traditional, Island-based forms of *merengue* were stretched and fused in many directions, as bandleader Juan Luis Guerra introduced new stylization and experimentation to both *merengue* and *bachata*, which accounted for still further diffusion and unprecedented popularity among international audiences. Though he made his name as a founder of salsa and the Fania label, Dominican-born Johnny Pacheco became the first Dominicanyork to reach celebrity status, and even included a *merengue* on one of his most successful albums.

These developments had the effect of de-centering Dominican music production from the Island to the diaspora, or, perhaps more accurately, of converting New York *merengue* from what had been a "transplant" into a "transnational circuit."[12] The sharp separation between homeland and diaspora, bolstered in this case by political imposition and the prejudices of the national elite, faded rapidly and significantly, in particular with the incremental growth of the New York community in both size and clout. Though it is therefore difficult to determine the primary direction of cultural and musical flows, there is no doubt but that the huge diasporas in New York and in Puerto Rico are an indispensable part of the equation and constituent of a contemporary Dominican identity. The wars between *merengue* and salsa during the later 1970s were symptomatic in their own way, and definitive, and cannot be reduced to their primarily economic motivation. The two traditions vied not just for a proportionate share of the Latin music market, but also for pride of place as markers of Caribbean Latino identity.[13]

Only recently attention has begun to turn to the cultivation of Afro-Dominican percussion and spiritual traditions in the diaspora, and their transmission back to the Dominican Republic. Among the various groups involved in this interesting movement, the New York based bands Asadifé, led by Tony Vicioso, and La 21 División under the leadership of Bony Raposo, have been performing and giving workshops in traditional Afro-Dominican music. Music historian Paul Austerlitz has conducted preliminary studies among these groups, and reports on their reasons for coming to New York to advance their work: "Believing that no one is a prophet in his own land, several young Dominican musicians moved to New York in the early 1990s, hoping that inroads in the diaspora would eventually open doors at home."[14]

The process of musical remittances to Cuba from its diaspora communities is even more difficult to determine, primarily of course because of the severity of the political divisions between the two sides since the 1959 revolution. As previously mentioned, in the earlier decades little of the vast musical production and innovation made its way back to Cuba or influenced musical life there, and that includes giants of the stature of Machito, Mario Bauzá, and Arsenio Rodríguez. Celia Cruz of course remained a towering favorite in spite of the political blockade against her from the Cuban side, but she always toed the line of tradition very closely, and insisted till the end of her life and career that salsa for her is no more nor less than "part of Cuban folklore."[15] Though U.S. music from jazz to rock to pop has been an ubiquitous presence in Cuba for over a century, the remittance of diaspora-forged new styles has until very recently not been common or of major consequence in the history of music on the Island.

Salsa, though firmly rooted in *son montuno* and *guaguancó* traditions, was in important ways the result of the suddenly severed tie between New York and Havana after 1959, when New York Latin music was suddenly on its own and forced to create sui generis from the conditions in the diaspora itself. Indeed, it was for that reason often resented and ridiculed in Cuba during its early years, and considered a corruption of Cuban traditions. Only later, in the 1990s, did it gain acceptance and find exponents in Cuba, but the innovations of the major groups, like Irakere and Los Van Van, and the emergence of new rhythms like *mozambique* and *timba*, occurred for the most part independently of developments in New York or Miami. *Rumba guaguancó* and *santería* music have of course enjoyed a hearty life in the United States over the years, particularly in the period since the 1970s, but the overwhelming accent in those movements has been preservation of and fidelity to Afro-Cuban roots rather than innovative change and hybrid admixtures in accord with diasporic experience. The "return" of these styles and practices to Cuba has had some evident impact on race consciousness and the affirmation of blackness there, but decidedly less if at all on the music itself.[16] The transnational musical circuits between and among diasporas and homelands, though present and active over the decades, did not reach the power they were to experience in the decades to come.

The Hip Hop Challenge

It is only in the present generation, with the dramatic growth and increased diversity of the Caribbean Latino diasporas, and with decades of ongoing interaction among them and with Afro-American culture, that we witness the full force of diaspora as source and challenge in popular music history. In the post-salsa period, it is hip hop that has emerged as the most influential and innovative field of musical expression in most parts of the.Caribbean and its diasporas. In this case there can of course be no doubt as to the music's urban diasporic origins, though it is still less than accepted knowledge that Puerto Ricans, Jamaicans, Dominicans, and other Caribbean diaspora peoples and their musical styles played a formative role in the story of hip hop since its beginnings in the 1970s and early 1980s.[17] Purists and traditionalists from those background cultures are still bent on denying or minimizing the Caribbean-ness or *Latinidad* of hip hop in its many manifestations, and on regarding it as strictly African American. At times, as in the call to ban hip hop floats from the Puerto Rican Day Parade, this ethnocentric demarcation even takes on blatantly racist overtones. But in all cases it indicates a failure to understand the dynamic of contemporary diasporic cultural realities, particularly among the kind of diasporic youth who have taken part in the founding of hip hop. That is, to cite Vertovec again, "the youth of trans-national communities, whose initial socialization has taken place within the cross-currents of more than one cultural field, and whose ongoing forms of cultural expression and identity are often self-consciously selected, syncretized and elaborated from more than one cultural heritage."[18]

Fortunately, a book like Raquel Rivera's *New York Ricans from the Hip Hop Zone* is guided by just such an understanding, and helps identify the role and importance of diaspora youth in forging new stylistic possibilities without abandoning or turning their back on their inherited cultural background.[19] While it remains important thus to document and analyze the diasporic origins and social roots of emerging Caribbean music-making, close attention need also go to the diffusion of new styles and themes in the Caribbean home countries and the challenges they bring to traditional assumptions about national and regional musical traditions.

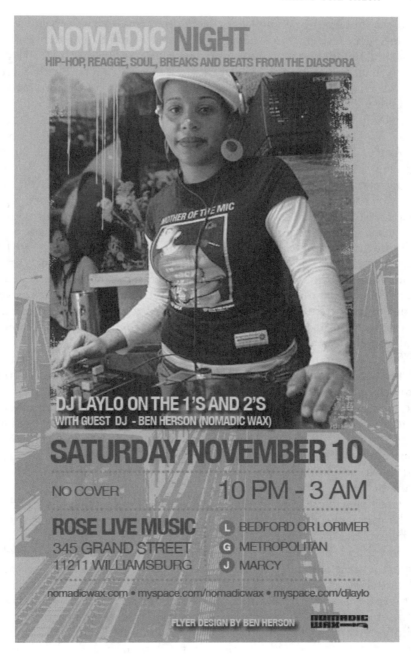

DJ Laylo ("Ursula") and Nomadic Wax, New York, 2007.

Flyer design Ben Herson (Nomadic Wax). Permission Ben Herson.

Before undertaking her pioneering work on Puerto Ricans in the New York hip hop scene, Rivera was studying the arrival of rap in her native Puerto Rico, and found herself confronting the avid resistance of cultural gate-keepers of all political stripes. In her Master's thesis, "Para rapear en puertor-riqueño: Discurso y política cultural" ("Rapping in Puerto Rican: Discourse and Cultural Politics"), she ascertained that it was return Nuyoricans who initiated hip hop styles and practices on the Island in the late 1970s and early 1980s. As she put it, "Rap, being a form of expression shared by Caribbeans and African Americans in the mainland ghettos, forms part of the cultural baggage of the young people who return or arrive on the Island. Being an integral part of the cultural life of the young [return] migrants, it therefore cannot be considered a mere foreign import."[20] Even Vico C., the first rapper to gain wide recognition, was born in Brooklyn, and teamed up with his partner Glenn from California to write his early rhymes, which gave voice to life in the working-class neighborhood of Puerto de Tierra in San Juan where he grew up. The style migrated from hood in the U.S. to hood on the Island, and even though it was quickly commercialized and domesticated in Puerto Rico by the mid-1980s, the underground scene continued to serve as a venue for the articulation of life in the marginalized and impoverished *calles* and *caseríos* (housing projects), themes which had been largely out of bounds for all other forms of artistic expression.

While the introduction of rap in Puerto Rico was first dismissed as a fad, and then more ominously regarded as still another instance of American cultural imperialism, history has it that hip hop went on to take firm root in its new location and in fact coalesced with important shifts already afoot in the national imaginary. The diasporic content provoked new sensibilities on issues of sex, gender, and race, while rap's social moorings among the urban poor raised uncomfortable problems of class and social inequality virtually absent in other forms of popular music and typically ignored by the cultured elite.

Interestingly, there was also a notable reverse in the direction of social desire for the geographical other: while traditionally the translocal Puerto Rican sensibility was characterized by the emigrant longing for the beauties of the long-lost island, in some rap texts and among street youth it was the urban diaspora settings of the Bronx and El Barrio that became places of fascination and nostalgia. Nuyoricans, commonly the object of public disdain and discrimination on the Island, became sources of admiration and solidarity among many Puerto Rican young people who had never left the national territory. Such radical challenges to traditional cultural values and assump-tions, largely associated with the hip hop invasion, have retained their appeal in subsequent decades, such that important young verbal artists like Tego Calderón and José Raúl González ("Gallego") continue to voice a fresh sense of what it means to be Puerto Rican in our changing times, in both cases with positive reference to the example set by their counterparts in the diaspora.

From being an isolated, subcultural phenomenon on the Island's cultural scene, rap has over the years established its place as a ubiquitous component of everyday life, vibrantly present in town festivals, religious events, and at activities on street corners, in schoolyards and neighborhood parks. It has also found its place in the country's musical soundscape, and been fused with more familiar styles like salsa, *bomba* and *plena*. Hip hop's presence in Puerto Rico also has its Caribbean dimensions, its introduction coinciding in significant ways with the inroads of reggae and *merengue*, with *merenrap* and *reggaetón* being but the best known of the varied fusions and crossovers present in the contemporary repertoire.

Dominicans and Cubans Represent!

Nor is Puerto Rico unique, of course, in its importation of rap via its return diaspora aboard the migratory air bus. The influence of its huge diasporas in New York and San Juan has been of dramatic note in the Dominican Republic, and again hip hop has been a crucial conduit. Dominican cultural critic Silvio Torres-Saillant has gone so far as to title his book *El retorno de las yolas* ("The Return of the Rafts"),[21] while a prominent historian has the following to say about the full-scale transformation of Dominican national identity resulting from the urban diaspora experience, making direct reference to the new musical sensibility:

> Social and racial discrimination as experienced by thousands of Dominicans in the urban ghettos of New York made them aware of their actual racial constitution, and taught them that they are not too different from their West Indian neighbors . . . . Many returned to Santo Domingo and their hometowns transformed both outwardly and inwardly in their thoughts, their clothes, their feelings, their language, and their music . . . . Afro-Caribbean music and dance were incorporated into Dominican folk dances and songs, particularly in the national merengue, while music groups expanded their repertoires . . ., showing, not always consciously, how much Afro-American culture had pervaded Dominican popular culture."[22]

The story of **Ursula** (DJ Laylo) is representative of the experience of many young diasporic Dominicans, for whom hip hop was the soundtrack of their upbringing in inner city New York and their link to Puerto Ricans and African Americans. Though not substantially present at the founding of that cultural movement, Dominicanyorks have played a major role in the development of rap, in New York, Puerto Rico, and the Dominican Republic. Building on the momentum of the *merengue* boom of the same years, they introduced the important fusion *merenrap*, which starting around 1990 then paved the way for the emergence of *reggaetón*. **Ursula** recounts in vibrant terms the key significance of rap in her quest for racial and gender identity, and in negotiating her relationship with Dominican culture. When she goes "home" to visit friends and family, she has the expected clashes and disappointments because of the sharp cultural and ideological differences, but finds that her skills and knowledge in the hip hop field help her in establishing positive interactions with young people there. While rap and bling and other trappings of commercial hip hop are often associated with the supposed crassness, violence, and criminality of those in the diaspora, as a form of expression it is no doubt the musical language with which much of the youth on the Island identify. It is also the conduit for the transmission of challenging new ideas about issues of race, class, and cultural change. **Ursula** is pleased to know that there are groups of rappers in Santo Domingo, like Lápiz Conciente, Vakero, and Toxic Crow, who are fully in tune with her both artistically and politically, and participants in what she regards as a hemispheric revolution of style and politics.

With *reggaetón* and its emergence into broad visibility since the later 1990s, Dominicans have been involved from the ground up. Starting with the catalytic role of production duo Luney Tunes, who stem from the Dominican Republic, spent formative years in Boston, and then settled in Puerto Rico, young Dominicans from both sides of the diaspora–homeland divide have been an instrumental and creative presence in this remarkably transnational musical creation. From initiators of *merenrap* Santi y sus Duendes and Proyecto Uno to the hip hop inflected *merengues* of Fulanito and the breakthrough success of the Bronx-based group Aventura around 2000, Dominicans have been "in the mix," as an extensive account of the subject is titled.[23] The resulting lines of interaction and solidarity with Puerto Ricans, in diaspora situations in New York and San Juan, have been profound and historically important in the face of the real and constructed hostilities between the communities. While, as with *merengue* history, it is difficult and at times less important to distinguish between Dominican youth culture in and outside of the Island, and cultural flows proceed in both directions, there is no doubt but that the primary influence is from diaspora to homeland. The direct and implicit messages with regard to issues of Black consciousness and rebellious defiance, though at times eclipsed by the sensationalist hype, have been an indispensable accompaniment to the challenge posed to the traditionally conceived and guarded national culture by the openings experienced in diaspora settings.

The story of hip hop in Cuba is of course a very different one than the Puerto Rican or Dominican case, but it carries equally revealing insights into the process of musical and cultural flows from the diaspora to the homeland, and their challenge to the national culture. The idea of cultural remittances is, at first impression, an unlikely stretch in the Cuban case, there being no equivalent diaspora to that of the other Caribbean Latino communities, or any pattern of migratory returns bearing diasporic cultural baggage. Indeed, there has hardly been talk of a Cuban diaspora other than the middle- and upper-class anti-revolutionary exile community centered in Miami. There is, however, a decidedly less visible but perhaps more numerous working-class and lower middle-class component of the Cuban diaspora, often with divergent political views and cultural orientation, that may take on increasing importance in the time ahead. Some of this other Cuban presence goes way back to the pre-revolutionary communities, while some has been forming out of the waves of less privileged arrivals to the United States. This dispersed community, which has had a historic center in the Union City and West New York area of New Jersey, may not be directly analogous to the Puerto Rican or Dominican diasporas; but compared to the Miami community it is closer, and perhaps more and more compatible over time. It has also been home to some Cuban American rap as well as the articulation of Afro-diasporic views. The stories of New Jersey Cubans **Pedro** and **Rodolfo** (among our tellers) are pertinent to these connections, as are the recordings of a young rapper like Alvare from Perth Amboy and Rahway.

But, again, in the Cuban case, diasporic cultural flows "home" have less to do with returnees from a diaspora community, nor even with a specifically Cuban diasporic culture. Hip hop is remitted to Cuba not primarily by Cubans on the basis of their Cuban American experience, but arrives as Afro-Latino or Afro-Diasporic, or Black, culture from the cultural meeting-grounds of Caribbean Latino diasporas. The identification is in this case not so much along national lines as politically and aesthetically along the lines of overlapping transnational diasporas, with a heavy grounding in African American music and culture. Hip hop in Spanish, or Spanglish, such as El General, Vico C., and Mellow Man Ace, is also very popular in the inception of hip hop in Cuba, and an incitement for young Cubans to actually create hip hop themselves. As **Toño** recounts in his tale, this cultural content and style are transmitted largely through illegal radio and television, Cuban merchant marine and dockworkers, and traveling athletes and musicians.

Toño's life-story brings us into the midst of the excitement and contention occasioned by the powerful embrace of hip hop in Cuba during the special period of the late 1990s. He describes the catalytic appeal of Black August and the Malcolm X Grassroots Organization in Brooklyn, and their central role along with radical rap groups like Dead Prez and Mos Def in the annual rap festivals held in Havana starting in 1996. Hip hop emerged in Cuba as part of a culture of resistance, comprised of youth of humble backgrounds who were as strongly anti-capitalist, patriotic, and socialist as they were critical of the bureaucracy and the hypocrisy so prevalent in Cuban society. But **Toño** also tells of the disappointment felt by many of those children of the revolution, and their sense of betrayal of the revolutionary ideals that they still uphold. The cynicism that then set in, and the situation that motivated him and others to leave in frustration, was due to the co-optation of this vibrant and challenging movement by the government. The quickly assembled "Agencia Cubana del Rap" turned out to be an attempt to hem it in and bring it into line with more acceptable attitudes on touchy issues of race, bureaucratic privilege, domestic violence, manipulation of the media, and police brutality.[24]

The musical impact of hip hop in Cuba is equally challenging, and is also suggestive of a new generation of youth culture allying itself with expressive forms arriving from outside the Island. To a large extent, of course, the appreciation for and emulation of hip hop is but one more link in the long and powerful chain of African American musical presence in Cuba. That lineage spans the entire history of jazz, and includes everything from show tunes to Tin Pan Alley and rock and soul music; indeed, an entire musical style or period in Cuban music history, "*filin*" or "feeling," is named in English because of the strong presence of jazz and blues in the arrangements of traditional boleros and love ballads. But hip hop is different in the sense that it is the first adoption of a "foreign" musical form that is itself so obviously diasporic in its constitution, and so explicitly political in a leftist sense, at least in the minds of its Cuban practitioners. What is perhaps most remarkable is the close articulation between this musical and cultural import on the one hand, and Afro-Cuban musical traditions and some of the pressing issues facing contemporary Cuban society on the other.

Significantly, this densely mediated presence of hip hop in Cuba has seen the emergence of some powerful groups, the best-known of which is Orishas. Combining intelligent lyrics, confident verbal delivery, able musicianship, and the strong Afro spiritual perspective suggested in their title, Orishas has released a series of impressive and highly successful recordings, starting with "A lo Cubano" in 1999. Less familiar to international audiences but even stronger in some ways as critical comments on Cuban society is the work of the groups Anónimo Consejo and Obsesión, the latter so named, according to **Toño**, because they felt "obsessed with making hip hop part of Cuban culture."[25]

The battle to establish a place for hip hop in the national cultures, and to assure its freedom to challenge the societies in fundamental ways, is similar in Cuba to parallel struggles in Puerto Rico and the Dominican Republic, but is perhaps even more daunting precisely because it is not being remitted from an ethnically grounded diaspora in the metropolis. In an ironic way the challenge of hip hop in Cuba may also be more significant in the end because that challenge is lodged directly to the nation state, or to the prevalent social reality, with far less mediation and distortion because of the commercialization so rampant in the Puerto Rican and Dominican hip hop scenes. In any case, it is clear that music making and the surrounding culture will never be the same again in any of the three countries since the hip hop "invasion." And the table was set for that momentous shift when someone decided to "bring the salsa."

Round Trip

Throughout their history Caribbean cultures have been traveling cultures, transformative departures and arrivals to and from, between and among, and en route. Caribbean musics are traveling musics best understood in their full range and complexity from the privileged vantage of *la guagua aérea*. In our times of mass and multidirectional migrations of people, styles, and practices, many new islands have been added to the archipelago, new sites of creolization and transculturation, unimagined in earlier periods of cultural definition and self-definition, and catalyzing unimagined changes in both lands of origin and places of arrival and settlement.

Paris, London, Toronto, Amsterdam, New York, and a range of other far-flung urban centers are now Caribbean islands, of sorts, or actually new poles of interaction and intersection among diverse Caribbean and non-Caribbean cultural experiences and traditions. The magnitude and structural implications of these contemporary diasporic formations are captured in provocative terms by Orlando Patterson when he says that,

> In structural terms, the mass migration of peoples from the periphery in this new context of cheap transportation and communication has produced a wholly different kind of social system . . . What has emerged is, from the viewpoint of the peripheral states, distinctive societies in which there is no longer any meaningful identification of political and social boundaries. Thus, more than half of the adult working populations of many of the smaller eastern Caribbean states now live outside of these societies, mainly in the immigrant enclaves of the United States. About forty per cent of all Jamaicans, and perhaps half of all Puerto Ricans, live outside of the political boundaries of these societies, mainly in America. The interesting thing about these communities is that their members feel as at home in the mainland segment as in the original politically bounded areas . . . . The former colonies now become the mother country; the imperial metropolis becomes the frontier of infinite resources . . . .

Patterson then concludes by observing,

> Jamaican, Puerto Rican, Dominican, and Barbadian societies are no longer principally defined by the political–geographical units of Jamaica, Puerto Rico, the Dominican Republic and Barbados, but by both the populations and cultures of these units and their postnational colonies in the cosmopolis."[26]

Caribbean societies, cultures, and musics cannot be understood today in isolation from the diasporic pole of their translocal realities, nor of course strictly from the vantage point of the diaspora alone. Rather, it is the relation between and among the poles of national and regional history and diasporic re-creation—what has been referred to, in a discussion of Haitian *konpas*, for example, as negotiation across the "insular–diasporic barrier"[27]— that provides a valuable key to present-day analysis of Caribbean expressive practices and possibilities. Thus the long march of Caribbean creolization proceeds apace in our time, but under radically altered geocultural circumstances. By now it is the diasporic settings, located well outside of national and regional territories, which make for the most intense "points of entanglement," to refer once again to Edouard Glissant's felicitous phrase about modern-day creolization. It is this "creolité in the hood," the infinitely inventive mingling and mixing of Caribbean experience and expressive ways in the urban centers of the metropolis, that is most radically re-fashioning what being Caribbean is about, and what Caribbean music sounds like. It is a process that becomes most clearly discernable when we remain attentive to the impact of this new mix as it reaches back to the historical region itself.

Of course this kind of reverse flow, if you will, from the metropolis to the colonial or postcolonial societies, is not new in Caribbean cultural and musical history. Nor should it be separated from the ongoing and forceful movement in the other direction which has wrought so much change, most of it unacknowledged, to the imperial societies themselves. Perhaps the key thing about this cultural migration is that it is and has been circular, as the age-old back-and-forth between jazz and Cuban music, or reggae and rhythm and blues, or the zig-zag stories of *merengue*, calypso or *konpas*, illustrate so well in the archive of Caribbean sounds and rhythms.[28] Throughout that history, creative innovations have resulted from the travels and sojourns of musicians themselves, and for over a century recordings, radio broadcasts, movies, and television, and the whole range of media have exposed musical practitioners and audiences to music-making from elsewhere, in great preponderance from the disproportionately endowed metropolitan centers, and very often as part of the imperial project.

But today's musical remittances are different; there has been a shift, as one study of the history of *merengue* in New York puts it, "from transplant to transnational circuit."[29] That is, these musical remittances are not just contemporary instances of traveling musics or of media-induced exoticist fascination, whether that fascination is based on healthy curiosity or on ideological or commercial persuasion. Rather, the return "home" of Caribbean music that has been re-cycled through the urban diaspora experience is a mass collective and historically structured process corresponding directly to patterns of circular migration and the formation of transnational communities. The musical baggage borne by return diasporas, while rooted in the traditions and practices of the Caribbean cultures of origin, is forged in social locations having their own historical trajectories and stylistic environments, and is thus simultaneously internal and external to the presumed parameters of national and regional musical cultures. It is this ambivalence which goes to explain the mix of consternation and adulation with which they are received on their entry, or re-entry, into the home societies: they can neither be repelled out of hand for being imposed by foreigners, nor do they square neatly with the musical and cultural dynamic at work in the societies from which they originally sprang.

Much of this work of transnational diffusion, of course, is performed by the corporate media, and aligns directly with the taste-making and trend-setting projects and hierarchies of imperial power. No doubt "transnationalism from above" remains a prominent if not the predominant driving power behind this uprooting and re-routing of styles and practices and their re-introduction into the societies of origin in diluted and bastardized form. But it is prevailing regimes of accumulation and the coercive management of flexible labor forces that impel patterns of circulatory migration and manage the shifting locations of transnational communities, which means that the formation and the re-location of diaspora musical cultures may also exemplify a non-hegemonic and to some degree counter-hegemonic transnationalism, that is, musical transnationalism from below. Caribbean music today, and its movement to and from its massive diasporas, thus remains popular music in the deepest and persistent sense, whether in the region or in its diaspora settings. In its migration back and forth between those dispersed but integrally connected locations, it lives on as the vernacular expression of people and communities seeking, and finding, their own voice and rhythm.

All of this, and more, are lessons to be learned aboard the "*guagua aérea*," but only if we take the time and effort to travel round-trip.

Bronx poet "Mariposa" (María Fernández) reciting her poem "Ode to a Diasporican" at the University of Puerto Rico in Mayagüez.

6 OPEN MIC

Poetry, Performance, Emerging Identities

In Your Face

There is a memorable scene in the movie *Piñero* where the iconic Nuyorican poet and playwright, the late Miguel Piñero, confronts the literary elite of the Island and gives them a piece of his mind. They are the kind often referred to as "los blanquitos" ("the whiteys"), which is more a class than a racial designation, or the confluence of the two. It's a stately but rather somber setting, at one of the Island's official cultural institutions, like the Ateneo Puertorriqueño or the Instituto de Cultura Puertorriqueña. The crowd is stiff and still, a lot of dead stares from the bespectacled *blanquitos* sporting Oxford shirts and intense incredulous glances.

"Reminds me of speaking to a parole officer," Piñero comments under his breath as he nods at some of his "own people" in the audience, notably his running buddy Miguel Algarín, and another guy in an Afro and a dashiki. It's a Q & A session after a poetry reading, and one of the blanquitos comes out with, "I'm not sure if you know about our internal problems here. What is it that you feel for Puerto Rico, other than nostalgic notions or sentimental attachments, like rum, music, dominoes on the sidewalk, and God knows what else you need to feed this anger?" Piñero keeps his cool: "You don't know?" Then another blanquito chimes in, "Even if well-intentioned, it is out of place when coming from a character that corrupts the language when you are calling yourself a Nuyorican, as if it were a race."

By then, Piñero can't hold it in any longer. "Well, check this out," he retorts, "I was born on the Island, in the town of Gurabo, 1948. Till the age of seven. My family moved to New York, not a trip I planned, nor wanted.

I am Puerto Rican. Now, I subsumed myself with a mother-fucking slang of a title, in this case, Nuyorican. And wherever I go, I am Puerto Rican, Rican, Nuyorican, 24 hours a day. If you are embarrassed about what you are, and where you come from, it's not my fault. Blame that Oxford shirt, or whatever prison you come from that you are wearing to fake something that you are not, that forces you to be something that you are not." Piñero looks around, spots Algarín chortling and his other henchmen doing what they can to fend off the icy tension. "You see," he adds, in a final stab, "even if I'm half and half, any one of those halves is much more whole than all of you, 'cause I know what I am, and I know when it hurts, and I'm still the same man, the same Puerto Rican 24 hours a day." And to the background airs of a courtly Puerto Rican *danza*, the Nuyorican guest closes the event by thanking everyone, and asking if anyone has any final "comments, questions, or literary criticisms." "Don't be afraid to speak up, you know. This is a free country, I think."

This brief "island" episode in the film, which is otherwise set in the "mean streets" of New York's Lower East Side, gains special poignancy because it captures so graphically a crucial moment in the emergence of a new, diasporic identity among Puerto Ricans born or raised in New York. Nuyorican, in that spelling and pronunciation, was in fact given currency by the two Miguels, Piñero and Algarín, back in the early 1970s when they named a poetry anthology and a café with that word. As the film suggests, the name came into more widespread usage as a response to the derogatory meaning it carried among many people on the Island, especially those of cultural privilege who had a stake in demarcating "authenticity" in the claim for national identity. In Spanish it was usually written "neorriqueño," or "neo-rican," generally in the plural and always indicating something negative, from traitors to fakers, from arrogant gringos to criminal low-lifes, but always with an overt or veiled class and racial subtext.

Algarín and Piñero and thousands of other New York-raised Puerto Ricans then re-signified the word, giving it a positive valence and spelling it in a truly hybrid, thoroughly bilingual way, Nuyorican. They were proud to be New Yorkers, and proud to be Puerto Ricans, and rather than adopt a hyphen they opted for their own name, thus marking off their own unique identity. Disdain for what they perceived as the oppressive, racist, crassly materialist nature of U.S. society was generally accompanied by a disdain for the condescending, racist, and self-serving attitude of the Island elite, who were felt to be the beneficiaries in some way of the hardship that the emigrant community was put through over the decades. "Nuyorican," then, became the name for a cultural identity fully shaped by diasporic realities and perspectives.[1]

That period, the early 1970s, was a time of major change in the history of Caribbean Latino presence on the U.S. scene, including its literary presence, and of the relations between diaspora expressive life and homeland traditions. Just as some Nuyorican writers were visiting the Island and recognizing the gulf separating them from their counterparts, the Young Lords Party was also there, setting up shop with the idea of recruiting and helping to lead the "Puerto Rican revolution," and facing similar frustrations and rejections. The lines were being drawn, not of definitive separation, but by way of redefining and remapping translocal cultural interactions, sources, and challenges. The Caribbean Latino participation in the general cultural and political effervescence of the 1960s and 1970s, while prevalently Puerto Rican in those years, had a catalytic and exemplary influence on Cuban and Dominican diasporas, who also came to mark off diasporic identities in subsequent years, with their own group nomenclature in terms like Dominicanyork, and in the Mexican case, Mexyorks.

Involvement by members of those diaspora communities, while numerically limited and at some variance with the Nuyorican example, set the stage for similar cultural self-definitions and re-alignments in more recent years. But in order to appreciate the momentous significance of that symbolic standoff between Piñero and the *blanquitos*, between the Caribbean Latino diasporas and their cultural homelands, it is helpful to locate it in the history of diaspora–homeland literary relations, with a focus on poetry. It will then be possible to more meaningfully examine the repercussions of those changes in the post-Nuyorican, hip hop era of the decades closer to the present, when signs begin to appear of a remarkable new stage in those relations. For by now, a full generation after Piñero's verbal rumble with the national elite, it is clear that diasporic forms and practices of poetic expression have begun to exert a strong influence on poetry in the home countries.

Early Literary Currents

Cuban exile writings of the nineteenth century comprise the first chapter in the story of Caribbean Latino literature in the U.S.[2] From José María de Heredia's canonical "Niágara" in the 1820s to the extensive journalism and poetry of José Martí in the 1880s and 1890s, this prose and lyrical work by Cuban and Puerto Rican anti-colonial intellectuals living along the Eastern seaboard played a formative role in the development of national literatures in those countries, and established New York and other U.S. cities as primary sites of diaspora life. Awe over the wonders of modernity and the sheer cosmic size and impact of U.S. life combine with a deep foreboding over the threat posed by the imposing giant to the north. The view from within "the belly of the beast," "desde las entrañas," carried special relevance in the Caribbean and Latin American imaginary, and nourished the sense that in some significant ways the center of national literary life is located in exile rather than in the home territory itself. Indeed, it is in the diaspora that the idea of "antillanismo," unity among Spanish Caribbeans, finds its strongest articulation; it is in Madrid, Paris, and especially New York, that "antillanos" come together more closely and often work in closer tandem than anywhere in the islands themselves. The outcome of this literary productivity, embodied in major writers like Martí, Cirilo Villaverde, Lola Rodríguez de Tió, "Pachín" Marín, and Eugenio María de Hostos, and their impact on the doings of their beloved homelands, may be considered an early prefiguration of what we today would call cultural remittances.

Nevertheless, despite the expansive and incisive reflections on U.S. life and culture in the writings of Martí and others, the main thematic focus and intellectual concern is no doubt the home country and its situation, as writers voice their unflinching patriotic love and their determination to fight for freedom and eventual return home. Understandably, there is as yet little sense of diasporic community nor a cultural or literary style reflective or expressive of life outside of rather than within the homeland. Diasporic settings are outposts, or way stations, for the thinking and writing of nascent national narratives, not for the forging of new cultural identities or creative modalities. Social organizations, publications, cultural activities—all are primarily oriented toward countries of origin more than toward building or maintaining group or community cohesion abroad. Those processes of community and identity formation, which have to do with establishing another pole of transnational cultural interaction located outside the national territory, would await developments of the twentieth century, when immigration and re-settlement come to supplant exile as the primary mode of Caribbean Latino diasporic life.

After 1898, with the conclusion of the Spanish–Cuban–American War, the nature of Caribbean Latino life in the U.S., and its literature, undergo a gradual but significant shift. Political and cultural attention turn from its urgent preoccupation with the fight against lingering Spanish colonial rule to establishing group presence in the U.S. in the face of hegemonic imperial control. While the Cuban population continues to grow, it is the Puerto Rican community that soon becomes the preponderant one among Caribbean Latinos, especially after the decreeing of citizenship for all Puerto Ricans in 1917. By 1930 Puerto Ricans far outnumber all other New York Latinos combined and the direct colonial relationship comes to define Latino immigration during those years. In general terms, one might say that if the nineteenth century was the Cuban era in this history, then certainly the twentieth stood as the Puerto Rican century, at least until the closing decades, when the Dominican presence begins to enter center stage. Perhaps the twenty-first century will be the Dominican one, or else the present century may come to see the coming-together of a pan-*antillano* identity within the larger composites of "Latinos," or Caribbeans, or Afrodiasporic peoples in the United States.

In any case, the first half of the twentieth century witnessed the consolidation of immigrant enclaves among Cubans and Puerto Ricans, with the Dominican presence still extremely limited until the floodgates opened in the later 1960s and 1970s. Literary concerns continue to center around affairs in the home countries, and more broadly Latin American and Caribbean social and cultural realities. Many of the major writers from each country choose to live permanently or for extended periods abroad, as is the case of the prestigious and prolific Henríquez Ureña family (Pedro, Salomé, and Camila)[3] and Pedro Mir from the Dominican Republic, Alejo Carpentier and Nicolás Guillén from Cuba, and a host of writers through the decades from Puerto Rico, including Manuel Zeno Gandía, Luisa Capetillo, José de Diego Padró, Clemente Soto Vélez, José Luis González, and Julia de Burgos. Of towering significance in this regard, though generally omitted from a narrowly literary discussion, are the composers of popular music, whose song lyrics rightfully belong in the anthologies of twentieth-century verse from the Spanish Caribbean. Rafael Hernández, Pedro Flores, Marcelino Guerra, Arsenio Rodríguez, Plácido Acevedo, and many of the other prolific composers of the standard songs of Latin music lived in New York City for a large part of their lives. Though the main tenor of this voluminous work is nostalgic longing for the tropical homeland and a sense of alienation and loss in a hostile social environment, increasingly over time the songs tell of life in the diaspora, and social relations established and issues confronted away from the country of origin.

When it comes to cultural remittances in the sense of literary and ideological values transmitted back to home countries from the perspective of diasporic communities (rather than from strictly individual sensibilities), two Puerto Rican figures stand out. In very different ways, both Luis Muñoz Marín and Bernardo Vega have been referred to as return migrants, but beyond that each drew major lessons from life in New York and brought them to bear in consequential ways on what it means to be Puerto Rican.[4]

Muñoz Marín is of course mainly known as the foremost political leader of Puerto Rico in the twentieth century, overseeing and guiding the whole modernization process on the Island as of the late 1930s and serving as elected governor in the crucial mid-century years through 1968. In recent interpretations of political and cultural history, greater note has been taken of Muñoz's formative years spent in New York City's Greenwich Village and his early incarnation as a bohemian poet with anarcho-socialist and *independentista* inclinations and associations. Of course much is made of how he changed his rhetorical tune in subsequent years, and committed a kind of ideological treason against his former comrades and allies. But it is evident that his early exposure to Yankee ways, and adoption of the proverbial "know-how," served to guide the ideology of capitalist progress and political gradualism that he applied with such acumen to the modernizing project in

Puerto Rico. Though his literary output is rarely given much attention, the cultural and ideological baggage that Muñoz brought with him to Puerto Rican life on the Island resonates to this day, and continues to haunt the embattled political scene. In his speeches and pronouncements, he also articulated an acommodationist vision of bicultural identity among Puerto Ricans in the diaspora that continues to hold sway, at least tacitly, among many of the community's elected officials and ethnic spokesmen. Beyond his rhetoric of paternalistic concern and inclusiveness toward his emigrant countrymen, this prestigious architect of the mass migration basically wrote them off, and urged them to just join in with U.S. society, even if as second-class citizens, while of course retaining their cultural allegiance to their long-lost island homeland.

Bernardo Vega, who lived in New York for fifty years from the late teens through the later 1960s, remains the main chronicler of the Caribbean Latino diaspora through the first half of the twentieth century. His *Memorias*, written around mid-century but not published until 1977 (1984 in English), document many aspects of community life and politics throughout that period, and range back into the later nineteenth century via the recollections of his long-lost Uncle Antonio. The book, which Bernardo Vega himself acknowledges contains its "dose of mythology," is of course a treasure-trove for historians from many fields, and still awaits inclusion in the narrative of New York City history. But it also provides an alternative vision of Puerto Rican history and national identity as it issues from a diaspora perspective. As recognized by important authors like José Luis González and César Andreu Iglesias (the original editor of the *Memorias*), Vega's working-class and socialist orientation compel a different understanding of migration under conditions of capitalist colonialism, a view from below and on the basis of diaspora social history and an astute class sensibility.[5] The chronicler's location among proletarian emigrants affords him a sharp, critical view of affairs "back home" in a way that would have eluded him had he not left and spent so many years on the outside looking in. Literarily, the *Memorias* helped establish the autobiographical chronicle and journalistic testimonial as the preferred genre for emigrant writing throughout those decades, while also turning the attention of major writers from the Island to take up the theme of the diaspora as an integral part of the national literature. (It is this period, the immediate post-war years through the mid-1960s, that is recalled by the eldest of our storytellers, notably **Andrés, Beatriz, Carmen**, and **David**.)

The powerful stories of José Luis González and Pedro Juan Soto stand out among the fictional renderings for the 1950s of Puerto Rican emigrant life, though the family drama *La carreta* by the Island's pre-eminent writer of the period, René Marqués, remains the protoypical representation of the experience through the eyes of the cultural elite of the Island. This emotionally wrenching station drama, written and performed in strong *jíbaro* dialect, portrays the migration of the impoverished peasant class as a tragic abandonment of the national soil, a mortal sin than can only be redeemed by return to the Island. The tendency among these "views from the Island," as I have elsewhere called them[6], is to observe and portray the experience from the outside, with little engagement with the society or its culture. The diasporic reality appears as strictly negative, alienating, foreign, dehumanizing, the only remedy being re-connection to the national territory and its presumed values. There is little if any sense of community or identity on the basis of that reality, and therefore no grounds for remittances of any kind from diaspora to nation of origin. The same may be said of the poetry of this period, by mainly forgotten writers having little bearing on later literary developments in the diaspora, the exceptions being Julia de Burgos, Clemente Soto Vélez and Jorge Brandon, all of whom came to be esteemed by the Nuyorican poets and literary public of the subsequent generation.

A fuller engagement with the diaspora setting can first be seen in the writings of Puerto Rican authors Jesús Colón and Guillermo Cotto-Thorner, both of whom in different ways present the New York community in its own terms, and therefore serve as anticipations of the literature to come. Colón continues the chronicling work of Bernardo Vega, but writes in English and keeps his attention riveted on issues in U.S. society, including the labor movement and questions of racism and black identity. Cotto-Thorner, a community-based pastor of a church in El Barrio, writes his novel, *Trópico en Manhattan*, in Spanish, but appends a bilingual glossary of "Neoyorquismos." Unlike the writers from the Island, he portrays the arrival and settlement as a historical process rather than an existential quagmire. Among the poets, none yet write in English (except for two short poems written by Julia de Burgos just before her death), and stylistic models generally remain Latin American and Spanish Caribbean, though Jorge Brandon's bold declamatory style made him something of a guru among Pedro Pietri, Tato Laviera, and other Nuyoricans in the 1970s.

Enter the Nuyoricans

The turning point came in the later 1960s, with Piri Thomas' autobiographical novel *Down These Mean Streets* and the poetry volumes of Victor Hernández Cruz, *Snaps* and *Mainland*. Though counterparts may be identified in the development of Chicano literature in the Southwest, there were as yet no precedents among Cuban or Dominican writers. The Caribbean Latino diasporic sensibility found its first literary articulation by Nuyorican writers, the children of the arrivals during the mass migration and industrialization program, Operation Bootstrap, of the post-war years. Here was a literature, primarily in poetic and dramatic genres, which bore no immediate or conscious relation to the Island tradition or contemporary styles or concerns. Pedro Pietri, Sandra María Esteves, Miguel Algarín, Tato Laviera, and many other young writers were strident in their claim to Puerto Rican identity, and dedicated to the theme and metaphor of Puerto Rican heritage. Yet they did so in English and Spanglish (rarely in Spanish), and with a social knowledge based entirely in the New York streets. The gap between the two literary worlds could hardly be wider; it came to be, as prose writer Nicholasa Mohr put it, a "separation beyond language."[7] Relations between authors from the two sides of the divide were rare, and what public encounters did occur tended to be anything from distant to icy, sometimes like the showdown between Piñero and the *blanquitos* of the Island's literary elite.

For most of the Nuyorican writers Spanish was a second language, and few had read any Puerto Rican writings, not even Bernardo Vega or Jesús Colón. Even the younger Spanish-language writers in New York served only occasionally, as in the case of Victor Fragoso or Manuel Ramos Otero, as effective bridges. With all their nostalgic reverence for the Island, most of the New York writers had rarely if ever been there for any extended length of time, and had little deep knowledge about it. On the other hand, writers and critics on the Island showed little regard for Nuyorican writing, when they even took the trouble to read it, and were dismissive at best of any claims to Puerto Rican identity or national belonging. In general, they were satisfied with stereotypes, as exemplified by Ana Lydia Vega's prize-winning story "Pollito Chicken," which demonstrated a superficial, clichéd view and little sensitivity for the very Nuyorican experience that the author publicly claimed to admire. Translations, symposia, readings, anthologies including authors from the two worlds were virtually non-existent, and what interaction there was tended to be all resentment on one side and all paternalism and hypocrisy on the other. The writing itself, with regard to both thematic interests and style, could hardly be different. In a word, the disconnect was all but complete, and the mutual distrust palpable.

As is evident in the Piñero scene, this distance has more to do with class differences than geography, and with the place and function of literature in the two settings rather than with literary quality or taste. In Puerto Rico, the writers generally belong to an established literary elite, buttressed as it is by an institutional infrastructure and periodical literature, so that access to publication and public acknowledgment rests on authorization and approval in accord with relations of power and privilege established over centuries of national formation and class hegemony. Literary recognition reproduces itself through the generations, and favors those who have undergone the requisite academic training or professional grooming. The nation's literary figures, including the contemporary cohort at any given period, tend to come from or to have achieved a status of privilege and accumulated cultural capital.

Literature in such a context generally serves the traditional role of aesthetic pleasure and education in the ways of society, often from the viewpoint of that elite sector.

The situation is radically different in diaspora contexts, especially working-class communities experiencing colonial power "from below." To begin with, there tends to be no such cultural infrastructure by way of institutes, academic posts or residencies, prestigious awards, or periodical reviews and public discussion. Writers generally have little formal education, stemming as they do directly and organically from conditions of poverty and working-class oppression where literature and the arts in any traditional sense are all but absent. On the other hand, popular forms of expression by way of oral traditions of poetry, songs, and storytelling are pervasive, and exert a strong influence on most of the aspiring writers. Published writing with established houses is not usually considered a feasible or in some cases even a desirable goal, so that the sense of marginality in this regard is widespread. In large measure the public life of the literary works depends on performance and oral delivery, which is the optimal, and sometimes the only, way to experience it. Some of the Nuyorican writers have books out, but the vast majority of them are in small presses, and some of the best known and most popular writers of over thirty years have only appeared in anthologies and magazines. Much of the poetry that does come out in print may be viewed, by official standards, as editorially incorrect at best, especially when deviations from academically established Spanish or English are so frequent and blatant.

Nuyorican and Chicano literatures have been the best examples of this Latino literary diaspora from below, though signs of a similar pattern have become evident in the Dominican and Cuban instances in subsequent decades. Already in the 1970s writers like the Dominican Chiqui Vicioso **(Gabriela)** and the Cuban Lourdes Casal took active part in the Puerto Rican and African American cultural and political movements of the times, and wrote forceful poems and prose commentaries in which they gave voice to many of the same radical ideals and principles of anti-imperialist, feminist and anti-racist movements. Casals' poem "To Ana Veldford" has become nearly canonical for radical Cuban and non-Cuban Latinas alike, especially because of its strong feminist and lesbian associations; its best-known stanza bears meaningful comparison with poems by other Latina writers of that and later generations, such as for example Chicana Gloria Anzaldúa or Nuyorican Sandra María Esteves. Casal's best-known lines read:

> That is why I will always remain on the margins,
> a stranger among the stones,
> even beneath the friendly sun of a summer's day,
> just as I will remain forever a foreigner,
> even when I return to the city of my childhood

> I carry this marginality, immune to all turning back,
> too habanera to be a newyorquina,
> too newyorquina to be
> —even to become again—
> anything else[8]

Chiqui Vicioso, while from a more privileged background in the Dominican Republic, was also deeply influenced by the Nuyorican cultural and
political movement of the early 1970s, and describes her personal transformation under the conditions of working-class diaspora life in New York
City.[9] Vicioso immerses herself in the realities of inner-city working-class
experience, and finds grounds for hope and renewal even in the most
wretched conditions; her poem "Perspectivas" ends with the lines: "Y se
empieza a sentir de otra manera / ese aire malo; a andar sobre los muertos, /
combatiendo contra la propia muerte, / para intentar hacer nueva la vida."
("And one begins to perceive differently / this bad air: to walk over the dead
/ fighting against death itself / to try to make a new life").[10]

But Casal and Vicioso were very early instances, and their transformative
diaspora experience predated the emergence of a new and more collective
sense of bicultural Dominican or Cuban identity by over a decade. It is
interesting that both of these women writers went on to return to their respective home countries, permanently in Vicioso's case, repeatedly as a leading
"dialoguera" in that of Lourdes Casal. Both of them exerted a challenging
and unsettling impact with their upholding of values and perspectives learned
in the diaspora. The point is that the early 1970s, when a "Nuyorican" identity
and poetic voice were being named and forged, constituted a landmark in
the history of Caribbean Latino experience, with wide-ranging repercussions.

Among our storytellers, most of them, indeed all from **Francisco** through
Quique, grew up and underwent formative changes in that historical context.
Whether in the field of writing, music, performance, basketball, political
activism, sexual, ethnic or gender relations, or just as a catalyst of enhanced
social or personal awareness, that period of rapid change is identified by all
of the tellers now in their later forties and fifties as a crucial autobiographical
turning point, the time when content was given to their diasporic sensibilities.
Even some of the older tellers, like **David** or **Ester**, also underwent major
changes in their personal viewpoints and actions during that time. But as all
of their stories reveal, the home cultures in Puerto Rico, Cuba or the
Dominican Republic were not ready to accept or engage their newfound sense
of values or interests, such that their renewed interaction with those cultures
invariably involved a clash or confrontation of some kind. Not as visceral
perhaps as that presented in Cuban American filmmaker Leon Ichazo's *Piñero*,
but one of palpable energy and defining personal consequence in all cases.

Poetry in the Hip Hop Zone

It is in the present generation, starting around the mid- to later 1980s, that the tables begin to turn. The last two decades have seen the beginning of an active and mutual engagement between homeland and diaspora literary and cultural perspectives. Among our storytellers, the lives of the final six, **Rodolfo** through **Wanda**, all were forged in that context, and the four who precede them, **Nury, Olga, Pedro**, and **Quique**, though slightly older, also overlap with that cultural conjuncture in significant ways.

Once again, the Puerto Rican example is the central case in point, but similar and intertwining processes are also evident among Dominican and Cuban youth now in their twenties and thirties. Writers in Puerto Rico more than ever came to take up urban themes and settings, and to address class, racial and gender relations and disparities. To some extent, as in the case of authors like Ana Lydia Vega and Edgardo Rodríguez Juliá, attention turned to the world of popular, community culture and black working-class life, with an acknowledgement of the importance and influence of Nuyorican and African American experience in thinking and representing contemporary Puerto Rican reality. Some of the Island authors, such as Alfredo Matilla, Angelamaría Dávila, Ché Meléndez, and Iván Silén, lent support and voiced admiration for Pedro Pietri and other Nuyorican voices, and translations and occasional readings and discussions brought the worlds together in more productive and respectful ways than in the past.

But it is the literary world after this so-called "*Generación del 70*," as that previous cohort of major writers from the Island is commonly called, that allowed for the initial signs of a deeper and more reciprocal rapprochement. Now for the first time in this long history of literary relations there exists an environment conducive to full translocal exchange and diasporic remittances in the form of new poetic styles and practices. A range of people and developments are directly instrumental in the emergence of this new situation, notably poet and novelist Mayra Santos-Febres, who has served as the doyenne of the young writers. Santos-Febres has provided support and broad public presence by means of television specials of which she is host, and where she has featured many of the Nuyorican writers and their Island counterparts. A Black Puerto Rican woman writer whose fictional and poetic work centers on issues of race, class, and sexuality in contemporary Puerto Rican society, she has gained wide acclaim in recent years. Her guiding role is attributable to those perspectives, and to her having spent some formative years in New York and befriended many of the writers in the diaspora. Her doctoral dissertation, entitled "Translocal Voices," is an early study of the themes I am addressing in this chapter.

In addition to that major personal presence, there were two influential publications in the 1990s; the book of interviews with diaspora writers,

Puerto Rican Voices in English (1997), compiled by the Island's foremost book reviewer, Carmen Dolores Hernández, and the anthology of Puerto Rican poetry in the U.S., *Papiros de Babel,* edited by New York-based poet Pedro López Adorno and published in Puerto Rico in 1991. Significantly, 1994 saw the opening of the Nuyorican Café in Old San Juan, which serves as a meeting-place for the new generation of poets and performers and continues to host events emulating the poetry slam nights at the historic café in the Lower East Side founded twenty years previously by Algarín and Piñero.

It is hip hop, and the attendant popularity of "spoken word" and solo performance, that is serving as the principle conduit for this emergent exchange among young writers. The idea of "open mic," "micrófono abierto," capsulizes well this orally based, performative, de-professionalized genre of poetic practice which is having the effect of bringing together creative young writers from both sides of the long-standing literary and cultural divide.

For that reason, Mayra Santos-Febres and I used that term, "Open Mic/ Micrófono Abierto," as the title of a special co-edited issue of the New York-based journal *Hostos Review,* where we assembled a sampler of work by nearly fifty poets from both locations. All of the included poets came onto the literary scene since 1990, and their thematic concerns and stylistic qualities, though widely diverse, appeared to us representative of the present generation. That collection, which we subtitled "Nuevas literaturas puerto/neorriqueñas/New Puerto/Nuyorican Literatures," appeared in 2005. The publication was followed in subsequent months by well-attended readings, in New York and in Puerto Rico, by many of the included writers. I myself accompanied a group of five of the diaspora writers on a tour of sites on the Island, and thereby gained a rare insight into the translocal interactions of the poets and their audiences in the "homeland." In the introduction to the anthology, Santos-Febres and I sought to define some of the features and historical contexts of this new generation of writers and their interactions, differences, and similarities. That brief, co-authored essay served as an early version of the present chapter, though here I am especially interested in the startlingly new receptivity and emulation of diaspora modes of expression by some young writers and audiences on the Island, and what I regard as a powerful example of cultural remittances from below.

One major reason for the new opening is that this "translocal chorus of griots–rappers–wordsmiths–oral performers," as we described the contributors to our collection, has pried open the box of the national literature by disengaging it, at least in part, from the elite institutional framework to which it has for so long been confined. The open, democratic format of readings and publications, inherited in significant ways from the diaspora example of the Nuyorican Café and other sites in the diaspora, makes for an inclusiveness and de-professionalization unprecedented in the established literary tradition. The "open mic" format bears a closer and sometimes conscious affinity to the improvisational styles of traditional popular songs and poetry along the lines of the *décima* and the *plena*; but that was generally bracketed as "folklore" and not considered to be "poetry" in the full literary sense. The association of poetry with other forms of expression, such as music, dance, performance, body movement, and even modes of dress and fashion, generally excluded from traditional and academic literary settings, has come to be taken for granted in the "open mic" practice. Also widely current is the idea of "spoken word" and "slamming," which came to the fore as part of the hip hop stylistic modality that has swept through Puerto Rico since the early 1990s, largely through the mediation of the diaspora in the United States.

As mentioned, aside from the practitioners of "folk" declamation and improvisation, exponents of literary creativity have traditionally stemmed from the nation's cultural elite, their prominence as established writers resting in large part on their class privilege and inherited inclusion in the cultural "family." While that status, and those ideological presumptions, still very much prevail, many of the young, rap-influenced writers of the current generation are from working- or lower-middle-class backgrounds, in this way more closely resembling their counterparts from the diaspora. Not exactly, since on the Island most of the aspiring writers and audiences are college students, but the same was also true of some of the original Nuyorican poets, and is even more commonly the case among the present generation of Puerto Ricans from varied geographical settings, no longer just New York, in the United States.

Thus the core of the writers from both locations is neither academically trained nor institutionally ensconced, and their involvement in literary practice does not generally issue from inherited cultural status or capital. The sociological reasons for this class shift in the Island context are many and varied, having mainly to do with such ongoing processes as urbanization, public education (however flawed), and circulatory migration patterns. "The result," as we say in the introduction to "Open Mic/Micrófono Abierto,"

is that the social conditions faced by the population in the two settings come to resemble each other more than ever. This new highly urban life gives precedence to the themes of migration, violence, a sense of loneliness and disorientation, transient identities, the cultures of the street, issues of race and racial identity, sexual preference, and other political and ecological questions. Thus, the bridges between the two contexts of Puerto Rican life and literary expression are more than geographic, but are based on common and converging social experience. Strikingly, in our times a writer or reader from the Island may feel a greater affinity with a contemporary Puerto Rican writer from the States than with what is offered him in the tradition of "high literature" from the Island itself.[11]

This sense of the compatibility and convergence between the two social realities finds forceful expression in the writings of "Gallego," the young poet José Raúl González (and teller **Samuel**), who is perhaps the prime example of cultural remittances in contemporary Puerto Rican poetry. His programmatic poem "Nantan-Bai," where Gallego offers the reasons for his own writing efforts, includes the lines: "I write because I too lived in New York city, / because there too they're killing each other for crack. / Because there too they're killing each other for heroine, / because there too there are jails, / because in jails there hundreds of Puerto Ricans / are also doing time" ("Escribo porque también viví en la ciudad de nuevayol, / porque también allá se están matando porel crack. / Porque también allá se están matando porla heroina, / porque también allá existen cárceles, / porque enlas cárceles de allá también hacen tiempo / cientos de puertorriquenos").[12] Seen from below, Puerto Rico and New York are like mirror images of each other, each having the same scenes of addiction, incarceration, alienation, and everyday violence as the same oppressive conditions of marginality bear down on the neighborhoods.

The word "nuevayol," always in this colloquial Puerto Rican spelling, is a constant in Gallego's poetic world, an integral part of everyday life in the Puerto Rican streets. One of his best-known poems, in part because it was used by *reggaetón* superstar Daddy Yankee, is "Chamaco's corner," a vintage Gallego rendering of the "boyz in the hood" scene; the guys ("los chamacos") talk about everything when they hang out, including, inevitably, about "nuevayol": "The guys talk about politics, of tricks and games, / of old-school salsa, about nuevayol, about graffiti and the ladies, / about the undercover cops who violated their rights last night" ("Los chamacos hablan de política, de trucos, / de salsa vieja, de nuevayol, de grafitis, de las mámises, / de los camarones que anoche les violaron los derechos").[13]

Gallego tells his story, among the tellers, as "**Samuel**." He tells how his stay in New York as a teenager was life-defining for him, and that the Nuyorican poets were an inspiration and helped him identify as a writer. In his poem "Y latina" he writes, "And poetry fell on me from a building in New York / on a summer night in 1984." ("Y la poesía me cayó de un building en Nueva York / en una noche del verano del noventicuatro"), and in his life-tale he identifies Pedro Pietri as the most important influence on his work. He saw in Pietri a different way to create and present poetry, and a model for the figure of the "poète maudit" that he himself was to become in the literary scene on the Island. Even his writing style often bears the clear imprint of Pietri's unmistakable ironic twists and uncanny understatement, as for example in the following stanza from "El grito": "Last night I dreamed that a hurricane uprooted the Capitol building / and that it landed in Central Park, in New York, / I dreamed that the guys with missing limbs / who went to Vietnam /

were hanging out in front of the Veterans' Hospital, / that my neighbor got divorced / and her husband asked for an order of protection against himself" ("Anoche soñé que un huracán arrancó el Capitolio / y que fue a parar al Central Park, en Nueva York, / soñé que los deambulantes / que fueron a Vietnam / jangueaban frente al Hospital de Veteranos, / que mi vecina se divorciaba / y su esposo pedía una orden de protección / contra sí mismo").[14]

De-centering Identities

Though Pietri and the whole Nuyorican scene in its original manifestation became a life-changing inspiration for Gallego since the later 1980s, his main personal contacts from the diaspora were his contemporaries, particularly Willie Perdomo and Mariposa (María Fernández), both of whom have emerged as groundbreakers of what might be termed the "post-Nuyorican" generation of the 1990s. Gallego has hung out with them and others, reading, touring and exchanging a lot of lessons and laughs. Their age and historical context is after all closer to that of Gallego than were those of Pietri, Algarín, Piñero, and others, as is their sense of the relation between "nuevayol" and the Island. With Perdomo he shares the street-wise conversational style and reflectiveness, while Mariposa's most famous lines, "I wasn't born in Puerto Rico, / Puerto Rico was born in me" ("no nací en Puerto Rico, / Puerto Rico nació en mí"), from her signature poem "Ode to the Diasporican," inspired his retort, as articulated in his new book, *The Fucking Map*, "I wasn't born in New York / New York was born in me" ("No nací en Nueva York, / Nueva York nació en mí"). The dialogue, the syncronicity, the reciprocity are all remarkable, such that at times it feels as though the diaspora and the Island constitute a single fabric of contemporary poetic expression.

What unites Gallego and other young Island poets with their counterparts in the diaspora more that with the original Nuyoricans is, among other historical specifics, the formative presence of hip hop. Aside from the lyrical style and performative delivery, hip hop is in many ways the cultural backdrop, the zeitgeist of the generation of the 1990s and into the new millennium. The emergence of rap, and its arrival and incorporation on the Island as of the early 1990s, set the tone for much of the new creativity of the period, whether the writers are especially taken with all of hip hop's stylistic trappings or not. It has become the air the young writers breathe, in a way that could not have been the case among the Nuyoricans of the 1970s, even though they are sometimes regarded as precursors.

Gallego himself remains something of an exception, of course, one of the few poets who is both outside of the traditional "lettered" circle of the national literature and has also published several books to a generally positive critical reception. He can name a few more, but not many, who share to some degree his creative project of writing socially critical poetry in the manner of the Nuyoricans. But he is hopeful, and confident, that change is under way, an optimism he gains from his role as MC for the open mic sessions at the Nuyorican Café in Old San Juan. There, every Sunday night, he introduces many aspiring new writers, younger than himself, writing and performing in the same vein, and sharing a poetic scene that differs in significant ways from the literary salons and recitals of earlier generations. The air at the Café is filled with a new sensibility, one that is clearly and explicitly nourished by the example of the ongoing Nuyorican cultural movement, which in the Island context constitutes a standing challenge to the traditional idea of what poetry is, and what being Puerto Rican is.

One of Gallego's best-known contemporaries, the poet Guillermo Rebollo-Gil, has complemented his dynamic poetic output with an analysis of these changes. Writing in 2004, Rebollo-Gil offers an extensive study of the writings of two New York poets, Pedro Pietri and Willie Perdomo, which he titles "The New Boogaloo: Nuyorican Poetry and the Coming Puerto Rican Identities." After a thoughtful and very knowledgeable introduction to the work of each poet, Rebollo-Gil concludes with a reflective chapter, "The Coming Puerto Rican Identities." He notes, and has himself experienced, the "increased exposure of Islanders to Nuyorican works," and it is clear that the resulting "clash" involves more than poetic styles or modes of performance but extends to concepts of cultural and national identity: "Traditional Island identity constructions are beginning to collide with Nuyorican formulations of Puerto Ricanness and may very well lead Islanders to question their long held views."[15] This "de-centering of Puerto Rican identity," as exemplified by the young writers on the Island turning more to their Nuyorican counterparts than to the canonical and even contemporary Island authors, implies an alternative philosophy and aesthetic, which the author characterizes as more "liberatory and multicultural" than the official cultural ideology. The "new vision of the Puerto Rican" based on the Nuyorican aesthetic allows for more positive interaction with other racial/ethnic communities, a "race-conscious revision of Puerto Rican history" that gives adequate due to the Black experience on the Island, a "more nuanced view of colonialism," and generally a more open, critical and "people-centered approach to political and social change."[16]

These are bold and wishful claims, of course, which perhaps pay inadequate heed to the less salutary aspects of the diaspora cultural package, or to the dynamics of change within Island society and culture. But the shifts underway in the Puerto Rican poetic landscape are no doubt serious, especially because they are motivated by the youth, and are also clearly part of a larger cultural "de-centering" engendered in some significant way by the new kinds of interaction with the diaspora experience. The work of young poets like Gallego and Guillermo Rebollo-Gil, publications like the bilingual student journal *Tonguas,* and the scene at the Nuyorican Café and other venues around the Island, show that the diaspora is now serving as a source of cultural innovation rather than a mere receptacle or extension. The contemporary poetic scene demonstrates that the "from below" cultural remittances arriving at the homeland, rather than being embraced in paternalistic fashion or dismissed as alien or inferior, are beginning to challenge the dominant values and philosophic orientations that prevail across the political spectrum.

Say It in Dominicanish

The experience of the Dominican diaspora and its complex relation to the island homeland has found powerful expression and representation in a rapidly emerging literature that includes the widely acclaimed novels and stories by Julia Alvarez, Junot Díaz, Nelly Rosario, Loida Maritza Pérez, and Angie Cruz, to name the best-known of them. Within a decade these and other English-language authors have had their work published by major publishers, translated quickly into Spanish, and even in some cases heralded in Santo Domingo. These works are by now an integral part of Latino literature in the U.S., and also, though of course more controversially, comprise an emerging component of Dominican literature. Aside from providing diverse portrayals of this new immigrant community, they also frequently bring to fictional life the dramatic relationship between this first generation of diasporic Dominicans and their ancestral homeland. The opening chapters of Alvarez's widely read novel, *How the Garcia Girls Lost Their Accents,* where we follow the very Americanized youngest of the sisters in her difficult visit "home," contains memorable episodes of the proverbial culture clash, as does the memorable title poem of her volume, *Homecoming.* In *Drown,* his acclaimed book of stories, and in his novel *The Brief Wondrous Life of Oscar Wao,* Junot Díaz captures stark scenes of Dominican life in post-industrial New Jersey in their sharp interaction with equally eerie people and events in the Dominican Republic. They leave no doubt but that the diaspora–homeland relation is an intense one in the Dominican case, and that the new writers are busy giving that relation vibrant literary expression.

What is perhaps most striking is how little time it has taken for the emergence of a literary output of this quantity, quality, and public recognition. While the history of Puerto Rican diaspora literature extends over a full century and comprises several generations and transitions through the decades, U.S. Dominican writing has cropped up in a matter of a single generation, only coming fully into view in the 1990s. This difference in historical longevity is a reminder that despite all the similarities the Puerto Rican and the Dominican migration and transnational experiences differ significantly. While Puerto Ricans would appear to have distinct advantages because of citizenship status and close proximity to imperial society, the indirect colonial condition of the Dominican Republic and the relatively better-off status of a significant portion of the Dominican emigrant population allow for somewhat greater social mobility and public visibility. These factors have also meant greater prestige of things diasporic in the home country.

Nevertheless, a similar sense of rejection and disdain as we witness in the case of Nuyoricans befalls diasporic Dominicans on their return or the remittance of their cultural values to the home country. Indeed, the term "Dominicanyork," though of much more recent coinage, has similar origins and a directly analogous semantic function to the concept of Nuyorican. Both emerged in the homeland as a derogatory reference to those from "over there," and the terms carry similar negative connotations of cultural loss and betrayal, antisocial and even criminal transgression against traditional national values and ways of life, as well as a distinctly class and racial relegation in multiple guises. And correspondingly, a positive, re-signified use of Dominicanyork, like "Nuyorican," then surfaces as the diaspora response of affirmation and defiance against this narrow, insular definition of the nationality. A congruent pattern seems to be at work, and for similar reasons. In both instances the diaspora sensibility recoils against a sense of marginalization and exclusion, and casts its re-centered and re-territorialized cultural lessons back in the face of the dominant national culture. In the Dominican case this re-signifying process entails even more radical challenges and repercussions.

Though there has been no Dominicanyork poetry movement compatible with that of the Nuyoricans in the 1970s, young Dominican poets have begun to surface in New York and other U.S. settings, often with linguistic and thematic issues directly compatible to those of their Nuyorican forebears. We have already considered the example of Chiqui Vicioso (storyteller **Gabriela**), her intense learning experience in the diaspora and her return in 1980 to a startled home culture, a trajectory she documents in her poem "Perspectivas," her memoir "Dominicanyorks," and her thoughtful story as rendered in our tales. In the 1980s there then emerges a group of young New York Dominicans who, writing mostly in Spanish but with English close at hand, give voice to the pains and trials of working-class immigrants and exiles whose homeland evokes an intense mix of nostalgia and disdain. Writers like Héctor Rivera, Guillermo Francisco Gutiérrez and others included in the anthology *Poemas del exilio y otras inquietudes / Poems of Exile and Other Concerns* (1988) directly precede the inclusion of hip hop, spoken word and performance among the range of expressive possibilities, and the first generation of English- and Spanglish-dominant Dominicans raised in the diaspora. Life-stories like those of **Ursula** and **Wanda**, and **Carmen**'s account of her daughters growing up in the Bronx, attest to the existence of a culturally vibrant Dominicanyork community strongly influenced by its proximity to Nuyorican and African American youth and cultural workers. The impact of this newly acquired cultural content, especially as it comes to collide with the dominant values and expressive forms on the Island, is proving nothing less than explosive, particularly as regards issues of race, class, gender, and sexuality.

An especially interesting example of Dominican diaspora creativity is that of poet and performance artist Josefina Báez (storyteller **Nury**). Though she came to New York when she was only 12, and as early as 1972, she has always paid frequent and sometimes extended visits to her large family in the Dominican city of La Romana, on the southeast coast of the Island. She writes and performs in colloquial Dominican Spanish and New York English, very much from the perspective of the New York experience, but always with a view toward and in dialogue with the cultural reality back home. Sometimes her poetic voice is located in La Romana, sometimes in New York, most of the time it is hard to tell for sure, or it jumps from one to the other. She cut her teeth as a performer in the later 1970s with the community-based street theater group Teatro 4 in Manhattan's Lower East Side, and has a long career with many other groups locally and internationally. Her turn to performance thus predates the hip hop era and its influence, though her work dovetails with much recent, spoken-word and solo work by Latina performance artists.

Perhaps her best-known published work is the performance text bearing the provocative title "dominicanish." In this highly eclectic, wildly multicultural "exercise" author/performer Báez guides us through a non-linear code-switching whirlwind of languages and images where her Dominican background makes an occasional unobtrusive appearance and is thereby enlivened by multiple contexts and relations with other germinal sources, ranging from jazz, Hindu dance and spirituality, to the Isley brothers, salsa, American commercial icons, and an unrelenting collage of bilingual jokes and word games. Nuyorican poets Pedro Pietri and Tato Laviera are everywhere present in the uncanny humor and ironic twists, and in the continual identification with Black identity and her response to racist indignities. A passage like the following gives a sense of the criss-crossing of Dominican and New York "home" settings, English and Spanish, and the complexities of diasporic self-presentation in public settings: "I went back there on vacation / There is La Romana / Here is 107th street ok / **Tú sabes ingles? / Ay habla un chin para nosotros ver si / tu sabes /** I was changed they were changed he she it / was changed too / Preterito pluscuamperfecto indicativo / imperativo / Back home home is 107 ok / Fell fridge full of morisoñando con minute maid / To die dreaming as a maid in a minute / Yesterday in the homeroom and today in the cafete- / ria the bilingual students me contaron los ojos. / They looked at me with the how-you-think- / you-are-bitch attitude. / And the North Americans laughed at my corny / vocabulary. / I ain't no bilingual nerd. I'm just immersed in / the **poetry of the senses. Poetry that / leads to acts of love . . . .**"[17]

The title, "dominicanish," intends to affirm and yet complicate diasporic identity with the suffix "-ish," which for one thing suggests that it is a language, like "Spanish," and at the same time serves to qualify the national reference along the lines of "sort of," as in coinages like "coldish" or "blueish." The idiosyncratic neologism does not mean to deny the word "Dominican-york"; on the contrary, Báez unequivocally and proudly calls herself by that better known term. In fact she uses it to draw class and cultural differentiations within the diaspora itself, that is, between the more middle-class, assimilationist, hyphenated usage "Dominican-American" and the inner-city, working-class, and black-identified "Dominicanyork," which also carries some valence of black identification and parallels to Nuyorican. The important thing is that Báez does not just name but performs her identity, both physically and verbally, by which means the poet/performer is able to straddle two and multiple worlds while allowing for a kind of fluidity among an endless range of expressive possibilities and cultural locations. One of her mottos is, "Here I am Chewing English and Spitting Spanish."

Another published work by Josefina Báez is even more directly pertinent to the theme of diaspora–homeland relations, as is clear even from the title, "Aquí ahora es Manhattan / Allá antes La Romana." This medley of poems is a veritable scramble of times and places, an intricate web of interlocking and clashing words and thoughts and movements between two very local points in her biography/history: the neighborhood in her hometown, La Romana, and 107th Street in her Manhattan Valley neighborhood on the Upper West Side where she grew up. As La Romana might not be familiar to some, she starts with an introduction, "La Romana 101," a three-page whirlwind of verbal and performative associations that bring vividly to life the streets where she grew up and where her huge family and her neighbors live. This very localized setting is brought into jarring relation to the national history and politics, and then with the contradictory lure of "allá," the other side of the Dominican quagmire. The poem ends: "Entonces nos fuimos. / Los que nos fuimos entretenemos los recuerdos / en el purgatorio / Regresamos con la muerte diaria que piensa / el pasado / 'Bienvenidos al mejor pais del mundo el tuyo' / Di tú tu verdad! / 'Todo lo que dejas te espera . . .' / said what? / mensaje de la presidencia / but of course."[18] In another poem from the medley, "Dominicaras Dominicosas Biografías," the Americanized, touristic La Romana stands in sharp contrast to the tropical, Caribbean feel of her New York City, as represented by the music of her compatriot, the Dominican salsa flutist and pioneer Johnny Pacheco. The opening lines read, "No fue KC and the Sunshine Band ni Gloria Gaynor / Donna Summer ni Bee Gees ni Chicago ni Nirvana / Alabama como en Hotel California en La Romana Pasaba / Aquí no/ / La 107 se arrullaba con Pacheco / Pacheco Tumbao anyejo / Pacheco flauta / Pacheco su nuevo tumbao . . ."[19] Easy listening in La Romana, *tumbao* afro on 107th Street: the contrast is resonant, perhaps intentionally, of Tato Laviera's challenging words to his beloved Puerto Rico in the poem "nuyorican," where the New York barrio is felt to be more alive with Puerto Rican culture than his Americanized homeland.

Among love poems and evocative snapshots of everyday life, Báez takes sharp critical aim at the virtual selling-off of her home country at the hands of imperialism and the mass exodus resulting from this absolute economic asymmetry. She toys with the phrase "divisas divisorias dividiendo" to indicate the divisive effects brought to bear by the political economy of U.S.–Dominican relations: "El país en venta / se vende esta mejora / se vende este Club Gallístico / For Sale / Por motivos de viaje vendo".[20] Her main strength, ultimately, is her creative use of poetic words and performative movement, and of course her solid foothold in the diaspora, and in cultural worlds outside of the frustrating enigma of transnational subordination and national complicity. Being Dominicanyork, in the sense given the designation by Josefina Báez, Chiqui Vicioso, and many other contemporary Dominicans, can be a huge asset in the "colonization in reverse" transpiring in present-day diasporic cultures. That term, attributable to Jamaican author Louise Bennet, has been very appropriately applied to Josefina Báez's creative project in the introduction to her book by literary historian Daisy Cocco de Filippis.[21]

Despite her impressive creative achievement at bridging and juxtaposing Dominican diaspora and homeland, Báez is still relatively unknown in either setting, especially in her homeland, despite her uninterrupted relation with that reality. Her mode of performance and poetic style do not jibe with what has traditionally taken place there, not to mention her irreverent point of view and idiosyncratic sense of being, after all, "una dominicana." But perhaps she has been slightly ahead of her time. As we see, many young Dominicanyorks, like **Wanda** and **Ursula** among our storytellers, whose formative field of cultural expression has been primarily hip hop and *reggaetón*, appear to bear some affinity to her political sensibility and forms of artistic creativity. Though "La Romana 101" seems totally out of place in an anthology of poetry from her home region in which it is included,[22] it would not be hard to imagine a group of young performance and spoken word artists in the Dominican Republic using her work for their own exercises in biting social criticism and provocation. All in Dominicanish!

DJ Flipper at annual hip hop festival, Alamar, Cuba, 2001.
Photo Angel Javier Machado Leyva. Permission Angel Javier Machado Leyva.

Cuban Openings

Despite the ideological and political differences from their Caribbean Latino counterparts, Cuban writers in the diaspora have also wrestled with the complexities of bicultural identity and the tortured relationship between their adopted society and their long-lost homeland. Those from families who have migrated to the U.S. since the 1959 revolution have tended to give expression to a middle-class exile condition rather than a working-class immigration like that of Puerto Ricans and Dominicans over the decades, which has made for a significantly different kind of diasporic culture. As there are very few permanent returns to Cuba, and many of the writers don't even visit, the evocation of the home country tends to be a purely nostalgic and even metaphysical one, with no noticeable interaction with contemporaneous literary life on the Island. No strong and at times defiant name, like Nuyorican or Dominicanyork, has emerged to identify the diaspora community and identity, which has for the most part assumed the assimilationist hyphen, Cuban-American. Despite this accommodation with mainstream U.S. culture there is surprisingly little about the interaction with other ethnic groups in the host country, even other Latinos, least of all with African Americans or Puerto Ricans. Nevertheless, especially in recent years, some openings have become evident, such that here again hip hop and other performative forms are playing a decisive role in transmitting expressive possibilities and thematic concerns of the Caribbean Latino diaspora to contemporary Cuba, with some markedly unsettling results.

Perhaps the best-known literary representations of the Cuban migratory and diaspora experience are the novels of Cristina Garcia, especially her masterful *Dreaming in Cuban* (1992), and Oscar Hijuelos' Pulitzer Prize winning *The Mambo Kings Play Songs of Love* (1989). In Hijuelos' work Cuba is a remote backdrop to the action, a place that has little or no physical reality or active thematic presence; Cubanness is all in and of the diaspora, with the homeland but a faint and distant metaphor. *Dreaming in Cuban*, on the other hand, brings the post-revolutionary society alive in a moving and at times gripping way, and the interestingly crafted plot moves us back and forth between the two social locations. While clearly opposed to the excesses of the revolution, the book's point of view has an ambiguity to it, and an ideological evenhandedness that is more pragmatic than overtly political. Other English-language fiction writers, like Virgilio Suárez and Roberto Fernández, also provide strong insights into diaspora life and its contradictions, but in none of this work is there the intense diaspora–homeland interaction evident in, say, Julia Alvarez or Junot Díaz.

Theatrical and performance work, such as that of Dolores Prida and Carmelita Tropicana, has also provided a vehicle for exposing the complexities of the Cuban–American experience, as has the writing by women in general. Interestingly, gender and sexuality differences evident among the writers have been especially significant in the Cuban case, with women's voices generally not characterized by the deep note of nostalgia and alienation that runs through the writings by male authors.[23] An especially strong and satirical dimension of Cuban-American literary production has been queer theater and performance, as exemplified by Carmelita Tropicana and Ela Troyano, which for obvious reasons has had no noticeable effective uptake on the Island, or in the conservative Miami exile community. Dolores Prida's long-standing presence in the New York Latina literary scene has allowed for an open-minded representation of some of the clashes and contradictions of life in exile, and of the close relations between many Cubans and other Latinos as a potential bridge to a more progressive and circumspect approach to the thorny issues of Cuban culture and politics.

As for poetry, little of any striking interest has emerged by way of thematizing the diaspora problematic, or creating new bilingual forms of expression. After the bold pronouncements of Lourdes Casal mentioned above, academic critic and poet Gustavo Pérez-Firmat has perhaps come closest, with his crafty and often entertaining lyrical reflections on and practice of bilingual punning and all that is gained, not lost, in translation. Despite its rather heavy ideological bent, his book of cultural criticism and history, *Life on the Hyphen* (1994), has become the most engaging study on the subject, and is made all the more attractive thanks to the neatly interspersed verse interludes, which he calls "mambos." Otherwise, though, English-language poets like Ricardo Pau-Llosa and Pablo Medina tend to wallow in a kind of pensive and undirected nostalgia to the point that their work offers little significant insight into the relation of their work, as Cuban-Americans, to any recognizable Cuban reality, past or present, and thus loses out on some of the creative energy made possible by intensely devised bilingual expression. Women writers, on the other hand, while noticeably less engulfed in traumas of loss and isolation, seem to have so severed any relation with the Cuban homeland that their writings, such as those of Berta Sánchez-Bello and Mercedes Limón, draw more attention for their righteous sense of erotic liberation than for any direct reference to the drama of national or ethnic confusion and self-discovery.[24]

Things have been changing, though, especially since the later 1990s, though no major poetic breakthroughs or challenges have yet come into view. A younger poet like Adrian Castro, born in Miami of Cuban and Dominican parents, writes strongly Afro-oriented poetry in the tradition of Nicolás Guillén and Luis Palés Matos, but is evidently unknown in Cuba. The primary diasporic baggage that is making its way "back" to Cuban society today, including in the form of poetic expression and performance, is not that which is generated specifically in the Cuban diaspora. Rather, expressive cultural remittances have been indirect, more by way of a Caribbean Latino and Afrodiasporic identity field shared by many young Cuban-Americans with their Puerto Rican and Dominican counterparts and associates.

The story of the arrival of hip hop to Cuba in the early 1990s and the consequences, as told for example by Ariel Fernández (storyteller **Toño**), is truly gripping, and shows how cultural remittances need not involve either physical return or even origins in that national diaspora. **Toño**, and the other Cuban teller **Rodolfo**, both recall how rapper Mellow Man Ace was especially popular in Cuba because he is Cuban-American and raps in Cuban Spanish to a Cuban *tumbao*. They also concur in telling how the Spanish-language hip hop that captured most interest in Cuba was by Panamanian El General and especially Puerto Rican Vico C. In memorable testimony, **Rodolfo** recounts how it was videos of Michael Jackson doing the moonwalk that caught his fancy and defined his entire life-course for years to come. His frequent returns to Cuba through the past decade have involved his sharing of salsa and hip hop, along with a diaspora brand of radical politics, with old friends and new acquaintances in his hometown. Similarly, on his visits to Cuba, teller **Pedro** has brought with him the strong strains of Black identity and heritage that he developed in New Jersey among Puerto Rican, Dominican, and African American friends and mentors.

Though the significance of hip hop in Cuba has drawn journalistic and scholarly attention in recent years, as in Eugene Robinson's *Last Dance in*

Havana (2004) and Sujatha Fernandes' *Cuba Represent!* (2006), most of the discussion has focused on its musical and broader cultural impact, and not on the new poetry movement that has arisen alongside it. Indeed, the movement known as Omni-Zonafranca and comprised of a large and active group of young poets, has its base in the same huge housing complex, Alamar, that was the birthplace and serves as the hub of Cuban rap, and was even the site of several of the annual rap festivals. The link and common identity of the rap and poetic experience is thus even more organic in Cuba than in Puerto Rico and the Dominican Republic. The anthology entitled *Alamar Express* provides an excellent introduction to eighteen of these new poetic voices, including the very vocal representatives Luis Eligio Pérez Meriño and Juan Carlos Flores. In addition, the centrally important rap producer Pablo Herrera is also a known poet of the present generation. Cultural remittances, in this case, have thus not involved cultural lessons borne or remitted primarily by other diasporic Cubans per se. However, as the testimony of all three younger Cuban tellers makes clear, the process does include the search for a new, post- or non-Miami kind of ethnic identity for U.S. Cubans, one which includes radical racial, gender, and anti-imperialist politics and a critically accepting or even supporting stance toward the revolution. And the result of these remittances, despite diametrically opposed ideological circumstances, has been similarly challenging to prevalent views and values in the home country, much like in the Puerto Rican and Dominican situations. If change is coming to today's Cuba, it is not only from within, nor strictly or most effectively in response to the reactionary exile pressure from Miami. Rather, it is being exerted, perhaps even more consequentially, by an Afro-Caribbean Latino diasporic perspective that is, here again, informed by a spirit of resistance and innovation. In Cuba, too, the microphone has opened to a new kind of spoken word, and new Cuban identities, previously unknown, are emerging, to the consternation of the homeland society.

RIGHT: **Official Seal of the Institute of Puerto Rican Culture, artist Lorenzo Homar, 1961.**

BELOW: **Jorge Soto, "Untitled" (interpretation of the seal of the Institute for Puerto Rican Culture), drawing, artist Jorge Soto.**

Courtesy by Centro de Estudios Puertorriquenos, Hunter College, CUNY.

CODA:
VISUAL CROSSINGS

The work of the well-known and provoc-
ative Nuyorican painter Jorge Soto (1947–1987) was about laying bare. In
his short, turbulent life, Soto set himself the task of unmasking, de-robing,
and anatomizing Puerto Rican reality and culture on the basis of the New
York diaspora experience. Perhaps his most famous work is his re-inter-
pretation of the canonical painting in Puerto Rican art history, Francisco
Oller's "El velorio" (1893), a huge canvas depicting the wake for an infant
and the ritual ceremony that accompanies that symbolic occasion among the
country folk of the Island. In his "El velorio de Oller en Nueva York" (1975),
Soto transposes the scene from the countryside to an urban tenement in New
York, and while maintaining the same layout proceeds to re-signify every
element by denuding everyone in attendance and inserting an intricate array
of indigenous and African symbols and motifs. Given the unchallenged
prominence that Oller's nineteenth-century original occupies in the annals
of Puerto Rican art, Soto's serigraph is nothing short of irreverent, and
suggestive of a total transformation of the sacred and solemn iconography of
the national culture.[1]

Somewhat less known but even more direct was Soto's reworking of the
official seal of the Institute of Puerto Rican Culture by the Island's foremost
visual artist of the twentieth century, Lorenzo Homar (1913–2004). Homar's
logo, which was conceived and commissioned by the Institute's founding
director Ricardo Alegría shortly after its founding in 1955, juxtaposes three
male figures who stand for the three main roots of Puerto Rican culture
according to the standard, official version: the Spanish *caballero*, the
indigenous Taíno, and the African slave. The conservative and patriarchal
iconographic agenda is obvious from the very positioning of the three
allegorical figures, with the Spaniard in the foreground center bearing a book
and the other two flanking him, bare chests exposed and carrying a stone
carving and a drum and machete respectively. Though in its time the
mere inclusion of the indigenous and the African might have been considered
an advance over the long-reigning Hispanophile cultural ideology, the

privileging of the Spanish "trunk" of the culture, and marginalization and undervaluing of the "other" roots, was still blatantly Eurocentric. Indeed, such a hierarchy had been a tradition in the dominant intellectual tradition since the time of Salvador Brau in the later eighteenth century and very pronouncedly in the foundational 1934 essay *Insularismo* by Antonio S. Pedreira.

Jorge Soto is merciless in his surgical transformation of this officialist concept, and of the rather atypical and widely criticized work of Homar. In his "Untitled", the master Nuyorican iconoclast not only denudes all three figures, but centers the Spaniard as a skeleton and agent of death bearing the severed skull of the other colonizer, Uncle Sam. To his left is the muscular body of the African, with multiple visages and exposing the severed head of the Spaniard; instead of a drum and machete for cutting cane he bears a rapier, which evidently served him in the act of decapitation of the colonial overlord. But the most prominent presence is that of the indigenous figure, who is here a hermaphroditic double personage with huge thighs and fecund sexual corporeality, clearly the counterpart to the African in representing life against the Spaniard's identification as the carrier and emblem of death. The overall image is rich with Taíno and African symbology and a range of other inversions of the official representation. But the most significant other element is of course the lettering: instead of "INSTITUTO DE CULTURA PUERTORRIQUEÑA" Soto writes "NOOJALK CULTURA PUERTORRIQUENA," so as to leave no doubt that the geo-cultural perspective of this re-vision of the heritage stems from the diaspora location of New York City. On the very bottom he replaces the traditional lamb, the Christian symbol that has come to stand for the supposed docility of the Puerto Rican people, with the idiosyncratic tree-frog, "*el coquí*," and the lizard. Less perceptibly, just below the feet of the indigenous figure, he inscribes the initials U.S.A., and on the right side of the logo he replaces the Catholic crosses that had surrounded the head of the Spaniard with the cross used by the Nationalist Party and its iconic leader Pedro Albizu Campos.

Jorge Soto's pointed Nuyorican retort to the national tradition, though unparalleled in its directness and stridency, is actually part of an extended history of visual crossings between diaspora and homeland going back to the nineteenth century and continuing to the present. Oller himself, like so many of his contemporaries, spent his formative years in Rome, Madrid, and Paris before returning to Puerto Rico bearing the lessons learned from the European realists and impressionists, especially in his case Gustave Courbet. In the twentieth century many of the major artists spent time living and learning in the United States; among the masters of the so-called Generation of the 1950s, three of the most prominent of them, Carlos Osorio, Rafael Tufiño, and Lorenzo Homar, were either born or spent extended periods in New York City. Homar, in fact, lived in New York from 1928 through 1950, arriving at age 15 and gaining most of what he knew about graphic techniques from lengthy apprenticeships in New York; indeed, an extensive and extremely valuable essay on Homar by cultural historian Arcadio Díaz-Quiñones is subtitled "Betweeen San Juan and New York" ("Entre San Juan y Nueva York").[2] All three then returned to Puerto Rico in the 1950s to take part in the active workshops and exhibits there, coinciding with the founding of the Institute of Puerto Rican Culture. Though rebellious in their political persuasions and bohemian lifestyle, the tendency among them was to work with the more official, institutional effort to establish and affirm the national culture under the accommodationist populist government of the Muñoz Marín era. It was in this context that Homar followed Ricardo Alegría's instructions in creating the controversial Eurocentric seal for the newly founded *Instituto*.

In the early 1970s Osorio and Tufiño then found themselves back in New York, their return coinciding with the emergence of the Nuyorican generation and the founding of its arts workshop organization, Taller Boricua, in 1971. Though not among the immediate founders, Jorge Soto soon emerged as the most vocal and unmistakable among the close-knit group, speaking, writing, and painting what came to be known as the "Afro-Taíno aesthetic" of the boisterous, diaspora-born generation. The young Turks invited "los maestros" to join them at the Taller, and Tufiño and Osorio in fact offered important workshops in many aspects of artistic technique as well as some of the radical iconography prevalent among Island-based artists of the preceding generation. The development of an arts movement springing directly from the diasporic setting was of supreme importance in the history of the community, and by extension, in the history of Puerto Rican art.

It is of some note that more recently, on the occasion of a major retrospective of Rafael Tufiño's work at New York's Museo del Barrio in 2003, this founding narrative is reversed, and credit for the creation of Taller Boricua is attributed to the Island masters themselves. In the catalogue to that exhibit, written by then-Director of the Institute of Puerto Rican Culture Teresita Tió, it is claimed that "Along with Osorio, [Tufiño] founded the Taller Boricua where they offered workshops to the boys from El Barrio" ("los muchachos del Barrio").[3] Needless to say, the "boys from El Barrio," the members of Taller Boricua, were infuriated by this revisionist version of their creative accomplishments. The episode demonstrates cogently that the complex artistic crossings between diaspora and homeland, as evident in the combative iconography of Jorge Soto, were not always harmonious. With all their ardent patriotism in the face of racism and colonial domination, and their reverence for masters like Osorio, Homar, and Tufiño, the organic, working-class artists of Taller Boricua were about burning their own path and uncovering the elitist and patriarchal prejudices of the national traditions.

* * *

According to Marcos Dimas, the only still-active founding member of the Taller, it is "difficult to gauge" how much influence the art produced in the New York diaspora has had among Island artists or public. More so than in the case of music or literature, the world of visual art is so heavily conditioned by political and market exigencies that an evident "flow" of iconographic or stylistic remittances may be minor at best, or at least not one readily acknowledged by the artistic elite on the Island. The generally recognized "maestro" of the present generation, Antonio Martorell, has played a major intermediary role since the early 1970s, circulating frequently between the two worlds while having his main base on the Island. He has often thematized the diaspora–Island interaction in his work, as in his visual rendition of "La guagua aérea" included in the installation titled "La Casa de Todos Nosotros," which was featured in New York's Museo del Barrio in 1993. Though there is no clear sign of any direct influence of the Nuyorican artists on his voluminous and varied output, it is possible that the U.S. Black Power movement and its emphasis on blackness and African descent may have made its way into Martorell's iconographic repertoire in his well-known depiction of the great nineteenth-century leader Ramón Emeterio Betances with its very strong African features.[4]

The diaspora–Island artistic interactions continue in more recent years, as in the widely admired installation "Transboricua" by Pepón Osorio, an internationally known artist who was raised on the Island but has spent most of his adult life in New York and Philadelphia. "Transboricua" drew broad attention for its suggestive contextualization of Puerto Rican culture and identity within a pan-Latino and transnational framework. Diógenes Ballester, like Osorio an Afro-Puerto Rican artist born on the Island, has gone on to international renown while keeping El Barrio, New York as his home. Nitza Tufiño, the prolific daughter of master Rafael Tufiño, has also been active as a muralist in New York City after early years on the Island. Versatile conceptual artist Nestor Otero was also born on the Island and raised in New York City, where he was active with the Taller Boricua and other groups through the 1980s and 1990s; Otero then chose to return to Puerto Rico in the later 1990s, where he has been struggling to incorporate himself into the artistic world. Juan Sánchez and José Morales, on the other hand, both grew up in New York City, and while gaining some recognition on the Island have kept New York as their base. Among the youngest generation, though born on the Island Miguel Luciano was raised in a variety of settings in the United States and has now settled in New York City. His playful and at times satirical representations of aspects of Puerto Rican iconography and popular culture have drawn lively interest both in the diaspora and on the Island.

An instance of this transnational crossing in the visual arts world that I had occasion to witness more closely is the case of Carmelo Sobrino. Having been active on the Island for over three decades, including the co-founding of the important Taller Alacrán with Martorell in 1969, Sobrino felt impelled to spend some time in New York because some contact with the diaspora experience seemed to him necessary in order to attain a more complete knowledge of Puerto Rican culture. I spoke with him at great length when he arrived in the early 1990s, and recall his strong conviction that without a familiarity with diaspora life he could not be a "full Puerto Rican." He took up very humble quarters in Harlem and was off each day to the streets of the city in order to gain inspiration from the neighborhoods which had been home to so many of his countrymen through the decades. He would tell me of all he was learning, and painted prolifically right there in the streets. One of his paintings in particular caught my eye: an impressionist scene of a crowded intersection in midtown, with a large image of two classroom desks hovering over it. He titled the piece "Salón de calle" ("Classroom in the Street"), and has been so kind as to allow me to use it as the cover image for this book. That image, and the moving story of my dear friend Carmelo Sobrino, seemed an apt representation of what I mean by "tales of learning and turning."

Again, as Taller Boricua mainstay Marcos Dimas reminds us, it is hard if not impossible to ascertain what if any stylistic influence Nuyorican visual art styles and practices have had on the robust tradition on the Island, and whether it is even meaningful to speak of "art remittances" in the case of graphic arts expression. The lines simply seem to go in too many directions to allow for any easy generalizations. My instructive conversations with New York-based Dominican painter Freddy Rodríguez indicated that the same is true of the visual arts in that case. And, as expected, the Cuban scene is even more complicated still, such that identifying the influence in Cuba of the work of such U.S.-based Cuban artists as Luis Cruz Azaceta or the late Afro-Cuban Juan Boza, who came as part of the Mariel boat exodus, would also be elusive at best.

On the other hand, one does notice a profusion of New York-style graffiti lettering in all three *antillano* homelands, often mixed with more native public iconographies and evidencing a hip hop presence paralleling that of rap, spoken word, and breakdance. That kind of lettering and imagery is of course visible in many parts of the world in our times, and there is no necessary or obvious reason to attribute it to the remittances from diasporas in urban U.S. settings where the style originated. Not that such instances of public visual expression are seen as much more than vandalism in the more formal art scenes in those countries. But again, as in the other genres of hip hop practice, graffiti writing may be exerting a similar subterranean effect not so much on prevailing styles as on the very concept and function of graphic art per se.

As we have seen when considering the musical and poetic forms of stylistic transfer, remittances from below tend to occur under the radar screen of the established, institutional cultural forums and take time to overcome their staunch dismissal and derogation on the part of the nations' cultural gatekeepers.

Thus the examples of Jorge Soto's irreverent iconoclasm and Marcelo Sobrino's apprenticeship in the "salon de calle" do attest to the workings of the challenging, unsettling effects of diasporic cultural experience. Here too, in the expressive practices opened up by the hybridic, self-affirming expressions of marginalized immigrant and exile communities, we can see that "the diaspora strikes back."

* * *

Finally, a word about the title, "The Diaspora Strikes Back." Twenty-five years ago the immediate association would have been the movie *Star Wars*: Episode V of that blockbuster was *The Empire Strikes Back*, a phrase that, along with "May the force be with you," was in the air everywhere in those years. But as you now know, the heroes of my book are not Darth Vader or Luke Skywalker, and my use of "strikes back" hopes only to evoke the excitement of that term and nothing of the plot, special effects or accompanying histrionics.

However, in those years there was a book that did take its title from Episode V and which I am directly and deliberately echoing here. In 1982, the Centre for Contemporary Cultural Studies in Birmingham, England published *The Empire Strikes Back: Race and Racism in 70s Britain*, a collection of essays by Bill Ashcroft and a group of young scholars in England who were all of either Caribbean or Indian background. Here they were, educated English citizens from the former colonies of the British Empire writing critical analysis of race relations in the metropolis and addressing the momentous changes, indeed the crisis, wracking English social realities and national identity as a result of their own presence in that society. Black British cultural critic Paul Gilroy wrote the preface to the collection, and then five years later published his own book, *"There Ain't No Black in the Union Jack": The Cultural Politics of Race and Nation*, which, along with the path-breaking work of Stuart Hall and his own subsequent book *The Black Atlantic* (1993), put the issue of race and post-colonialism on the agenda of cultural studies. A further, related resonance is the book *The Empire Writes Back*, a collection on post-colonial literatures edited by a group of Australian cultural studies critics.

The main idea behind this notion of the empire "striking back," which gained broader international currency with the appearance of Salman Rushdie's phrase "the Empire within" in his collection of essays *Imaginary Homelands* (1991), is that the chicken has come home to roost on the colonial empires with the immigration of millions of natives from the former colonies, who take up citizenship over the course of several generations in the metropolitan center. Aside from the transformative impact of this black, post-colonial presence within the society, the studies of post-colonial literatures assert that the center of English literary production has shifted from England itself to those former outposts of the empire. As in the case of the French colonies and decades earlier the former Spanish colonial holdings, the most interesting and original cultural creativity comes to be based in areas where it had been least expected for centuries: the presumably backward, uncultured backwaters of Asia, Africa, Latin America, and the Caribbean. This remarkable ground-shift has had the effect of redrawing the cultural map on a world scale, a change clearly issuing from the economic and political conditions known as globalization.

The "diaspora strikes back" takes this line of thinking one step further, or points out another angle to the double-take involved in this radical rethinking of the workings of imperial power. My idea is that the presence of colonial and post-colonial diasporas in the metropolis bring new challenges and potential change not only to those advertently "advanced" societies, but that this diasporic, hybridic sensibility forged in the new communities makes its way back to the home societies themselves, there to exert dramatic pressures for change as well. It is a kind of double-whammy on the outworn ideas of periphery and center, with the empire coming home to roost once again, as the massive migrant communities forced upon millions of lives and stemming from long-term colonial asymmetries, go on to haunt and undermine the legitimacy of the very national elites who had conspired in and benefited from their expulsion in the first place. It is an insight voiced strongly by Nuyorican poet Tato Laviera in the lines: "I am your son, / of a migration, / a sin forced on me, / you sent me to be born a native of other lands. / why? Because we were poor, right? / because you wanted to empty yourself of poor people. / Now I return, with a *boricua* heart . . . ." Again and again, in the many testimonies and in the cultural histories of diasporic Puerto Ricans, Dominicans, and Cubans presented here, we have seen this same process of the return of the cultural repressed and the real or potential subversion of traditional values when the working-class emigrants, exiles, and refugees come home to roost.

Perhaps the core of what I mean here by "the diaspora strikes back" is captured in the cogent observation by Orlando Patterson, quoted earlier in the book, when he says, "The former colonies now become the mother country; the imperial metropolis becomes the frontier of infinite resources." Thus despite its ancient ring, diaspora in our times does have something futuristic about it. Maybe "the diaspora strikes back" has the makings of a new episode of *Star Wars* after all.

NOTES

1 Thinking Diaspora from Below

1   See Brent Edwards, "The Fact of Diaspora," *Social Text* 19:1 (2001), 45–73.

2   See Earl Lewis, "To Turn as on a Pivot: Writing African Americans into a History of Overlapping Diasporas," *American Historical Review* 100 (1995), 765–798; and Robin Cohen, "The Diaspora of a Diaspora: The Case of the Caribbean," *Social Science Information* 31 (1992), 159–169.

3   See Arjun Appadurai, *Modernity at Large: Cultural Dimensions of Globalization* (Minneapolis: University of Minnesota Press, 1996); Stuart Hall, "Diaspora and Cultural Identity," in *Colonial Discourse and Post-Colonial Theory*, ed. Patrick Williams and Laura Chrisman (New York: Columbia University Press, 1994), 392–403.

4   Robin Cohen, *Global Diasporas* (Seattle: University of Washington Press, 1996).

5   See Khachig Tölölyan, "The Nation-State and Its Others: In Lieu of a Preface," *Diaspora* 1:1 (1991), 3–8.

6   James Clifford, *Routes: Travel and Translation in the Late Twentieth Century* (Cambridge: Harvard University Press, 1997), 250.

7   Ibid., 253.

8   Ibid., 371.

9   William Safran, "Diasporas in Modern Societies: Myths of Homeland and Return," *Diaspora* 1:1 (1991), 83–99.

10   It is thus far unclear what the conceptual relationship is between diaspora and transnational community. While Van Hear considers diaspora a kind of subset of transnational community, and Kim Butler refers to transnational community as exemplified by the work of Roger Rouse as a kind of "micro-diaspora," the discussion by Levitt and Waters in *The Changing Face of Home* appears to set up a contrast but is unclear as to where the main differences actually lie. See Kim Butler, "Defining Diaspora, Refining a Discourse," *Diaspora* 10:2 (2001), 8, and Peggy Levitt, and Mary C. Waters, eds. *The Changing Face of Home: Transnational Lives of the Second Generation* (New York: Russell Sage Foundation, 2002), 6–8.

11   Nicholas Van Hear, *New Diasporas: The Mass Exodus, Dispersal and Regrouping of Migrant Communities* (Seattle: University of Washington Press), 1998, 6.

12   Alejandro Portes, "Global Villagers: The Rise of Transnational Communities," *The American Prospect* 7:25 (1996), 3.

13   See Levitt and Waters, "Introduction," *The Changing Face of Home*, 8.

14   Ibid., 8.

15   Michael Peter Smith and Luis Eduardo Guarnizo, eds. *Transnationalism from Below* (New Brunswick: Transaction, 1998), 23.

16   Arjun Appadurai, "Grassroots Globalization and the Research Imagination," in Arjun Appadurai, ed., *Globalization* (Durham: Duke University Press, 2001), 1–21.

17   Pnina Werbner, "Vernacular Cosmopolitanism," *Theory, Culture & Society* 22:2–3, 497. See also Homi K. Bhabha, "Unsatisfied: Notes on Vernacular Cosmopolitanism," in Laura Garcia-Moreno and Peter C. Pfeiffer, eds., *Text and Nation: Cross-Disciplinary Essays on Cultural and National Identities* (Columbia: Camden House, 1996), 191–207.

18   Tölölyan, "The Nation State and Its Others," 3.

19   Cohen, *Global Diasporas*, 128.

20   Stuart Hall, "Creolization, Diaspora, and Hybridity in the context of Globalization," in Okwui Enwezor, Carlos Basualdo, Ute Meta Bauer, Susanne Ghez, Sarat Maharaj, Mark Nash, and Octavio Zaya, eds., *Créolité and Creolization: Dokumenta11_Platform3* (Ostfildern-Ruit, Germany: Hatje Cantz, 2002), 190.

21   Okwui Enwezor, Carlos Basualdo, Ute Meta Bauer, Susanne Ghez, Sarat Maharaj, Mark Nash, and Octavio Zaya, eds., *Créolité and Creolization: Dokumenta11_Platform3* (Ostfildern-Ruit, Germany: Hatje Cantz, 2002).

22   Orlando Patterson, "Global Culture and the American Cosmos," *Andy Warhol Foundation for the Visual Arts: Paper Series on the Arts, Culture, and Society* (1994), 7.

23   Glissant, *Caribbean Discourse*.

24   Jean Bernabé, Patrick Chamoiseau, and Raphäel Confiant, *Eloge a la Créolité/In Praise of Creoleness* (Paris: Gallimard, 1993). See also Lucien Taylor, "Créolité Bites: A Conversation with Patrick Chamoiseau, Raphäel Confiant, and Jean Bernabé," *Transition* 74 (1998), 124–161.

25   Appadurai, *Modernity at Large*, 178–179.

26   Ibid., 204.

27   Patterson, "Global Culture and the American Cosmos," 6.

28   See David Palumbo-Liu and Hans Ulrich Gumbrecht, eds., *Streams of Cultural Capital* (Stanford: Stanford University Press, 1997).

29   Cohen, "Diasporas and the Nation-State". Also in Steven Vertovec, and Robin Cohen, eds. *Migration, Diasporas and Transnationalism* (Cheltenham, UK: Edward Elgar Publishing, 1999).

2 Of Remigrants and Remittances

1   George Gmelch, *Double Passage: The Lives of Caribbean Migrants Abroad and Back Home* (Ann Arbor: Univerity of Michigan Press, nd), 285.

2   Ernest George Ravenstein, "The Laws of Migration," *Journal of the Statistical Society of London* 48:2 (June 1885), 167–235.

3   See, for example, Bimal Ghosh, *Return Migration: Journey of Hope or Despair?* (Geneva: International Organization for Migration and the United Nations), 2000 and Robert B. Potter, Dennis Conway, and Joan Phillips, *The Experience of Return Migration: Caribbean Perspectives* (Hants, England: Ashgate, 2005).

4   See Russell King, ed. *Return Migration and Regional Economic Problems* (London: Croom Helm, 1986); Ghosh, *Return Migration*; Jean-Pierrre Casarino, "Theorizing Return Migration," *International Journal of Multicultural Societies* 6:2 (2004), 253–279

5   See Mark Wyman, *Round-Trip to America: The Immigrants Return to Europe, 1880–1930* (Ithaca: Cornell University Press, 1993).

6   See Anders H. Stefansson, "Homecomings to the Future: From Diasporic Mythographies to Social Projects of Return," in Fran Markowitz and Anders H. Stefansson, eds., *Homecomings: Unsettling Paths of Return* (Oxford: Lexington Books, 2004), 3.

7   Francesco Cerase, "Expectations and Reality: A Case Study of Return Migration from the United States to Southern Italy," *International Migration Review* 8:2 (1974), 245–262; see also Francesco Cerase, "Nostalgia or Disenchantment: Considerations on Return Migration," in *The Italian Experience in the United States*, ed. S.M. Tomasi and M.H. Engel (New York: Center for Migration Studies, 1970), 217–239.

8   Cerase, "Expectations and Reality," 258. See also Jean-Pierre Cassarino, "Theorising Return Migration: The Conceptual Approach to Return Migrants Revisited," *International Journal on Multicultural Societies* 6:2 (2004).

9   See Robert B. Potter, "'Tales of Two Societies': Narratives of Adjustment," in Robert B. Potter, Dennis Conway, and Joan Phillips, eds., *The Experience of Return Migration* (Aldershot: Ashgate, 2005) 49–67.

10   See, for example, Cassarino, "Theorising Return Migration," 254, and Michael Kearney, "From the Invisible Hand to Visible Feet: Anthropological Studies of Migration and Development," *Annual Review of Anthropology* 13 (1986), 331–361.

11   See, for example, George Gmelch, "Return Migration," *Annual Review of Anthropology* 9 (1980), 150. See also Frank Bovenkerk, *The Sociology of Return Migration: A Bibliogaphic Essay* (The Hague: Martin Nijhof, 1977), 33–35.

12   See, for example, Iain Chambers, *Migrancy, Culture, Identity* (London: Routledge, 1994); Nigel Rapport and Andrew Dawson, eds. *Migrants of Identity: Perceptions of Home in a World of Movement* (Oxford and New York: Berg, 1998), as well as Appadurai, *Modernity at Large* (1996) and Homi Bhabha, *The Location of Culture* (London: Routledge, 1994).

13   See Cerase, "Expectations and Reality," 258 ff.

14   Gmelch, *Double Pasage*, 305. See also Mary Chamberlain, *Narratives of Exile and Return* (New York: St. Martin's, 1997).

15   See Constance Sutton and S. Makiesky, "Migration and West Indian Racial and Political Consciousness," in *Migration and Development: Implications for Ethnic Identity and Political Conflict*, ed. Helen Safa and B. DuToit (The Hague: Mouton, 1975), 113–144.

16   Fran Markowitz and Anders H. Stefansson, eds., *Homecomings: Unsettling Paths of Return* (Oxford: Lexington Books, 2004).

17   Ibid., 10ff.

18   Ibid., 10–11.

19   Ibid., 12. See Carol Stack, *Call to Home: African Americans Claim the Rural South* (New York: Basic Books, 1996).

20   In addition to *Homecomings*, see for example Ghosh, *Return Migration*; Nigel Rapport and Andrew Dawson, eds., *Migrants of Identity: Perceptions of Home in a World of Movement* (Oxford: Berg, 1998); Potter et al., *The Experience of Return Migration*; and Lynellyn D. Long and Ellen Oxfeld, eds., *Coming Home: Refugees, Migrants, and Those Who Stayed Behind* (Phildelphia: University of Pennsylvania Press, 2004).

21   See, for example, Luin Goldring, "Rethinking Remittances: Social and Political Dimensions of Individual and Collective Remittances," CERLAC (Centre for Research on Latin America and the Caribbean) Working Papers, York University, February, 2003.

22   Ibid., 3. See also Steven Vertovec, "Rethinking Remittances," University of Oxford and ESRC Research Programme in Transnational Communities.

23   See Vertovec, "Rethinking Remittances."

24   See Goldring, "Rethinking Remittances," 3ff.

25   Peggy Levitt, "Social Remittances: A Local-Level, Migration-Driven Form of Cultural Diffusion," *International Migration Review* 32 (1999), 926–949.

26   Levitt, *The Transnational Villagers*, 54.

27   See my article "The Diaspora Strikes Back: Reflections on Cultural Remittances," in *NACLA: Report on the Americas* 39:3 (November/December 2005), 21–26.

28   Chiqui Vicioso, "An Oral History (Testimono)," in Miriam DeCosta-Willis, ed., *Daughters of the Diaspora: Afra-Hispanic Writers* (Kingston: Ian Randle Publishers, 2003), 313–318.

29   Frank Moya Pons, "Dominican National Identity in Historical Perspective," *Punto 7 Review* (1996), 23–25.

3 *Caribeño* Counterstream

1   Cohen, *Global Diasporas*, 127–154.

2   Ibid., 144.

3   Ibid.

4   Sutton and Makiesky, "Migration and West Indian Racial and Political Consciousness"; also in Constance R. Sutton and Elsa M. Chaney, eds. *Caribbean Life in New York City: Sociocultural Dimensions.* New York: Center for Migration Studies, 1987.

5   See Gmelch, "Return Migration."

6   Betty Davidson, "No Place Back Home: A Study of Jamaicans Returning to Kingston, Jamaica," *Race* 9:4 (1968), 499–509.

7   See Orlando Patterson, "The Emerging West Atlantic System: Migration, Culture, and Underdevelopment in the United States and the Circum-Caribbean Region," in William Alonso, ed., *Population in an Interacting World* (Cambridge: Harvard University Press, 1987), 227–260.

8   Nina Glick-Schiller and Georges Fouron, *Georges Woke Up Laughing: Long Distance Nationalism and the Search for Home* (Durham: Duke University Press, 2001), and Michel S. Laguerre, *Diasporic Citizenship: Haitan Americans in Transnational America* (New York: St. Martin's Press, 1998).

9   See Patterson, "The Emerging West Atlantic System."

10   Two helpful studies are Gerald Poyo, *"With All, and for the Good of All": The Emergence of Popular Nationalism in the Cuban Communities of the United States, 1848–1898* (Durham: Duke University Press, 1989), and Susan D. Greenbaum, *More Than Black: Afro-Cubans in Tampa* (Gainesville: University of Florida Press, 2002).

11   Bernardo Vega, *Memoirs of Bernardo Vega*, ed. César Andreu Iglesias (New York: Monthly Review, 1984), 43.

12   Pedro Mir, *Countersong to Walt Whitman and Other Poems* (Washington, D.C.: Azul Editions, 1993). Translation by Jonathan Cohen and Danald D. Walsh.

13   Evelio Grillo, *Black Cuban, Black American* (Houston: Arte Público, 2000).

14   Ruth Glasser, *My Music Is My Flag: Puerto Rican Musicians and Their New York Communities* (Berkeley: University of California Press, 1995), 101.

15   Gustavo Pérez-Firmat, *Life on the Hyphen: The Cuban-American Way* (Austin: University of Texas Press, 1994).

16   See, for a discussion of Schomburg and Colón, Winston James, *Hold Aloft the Banner of Ethiopia: Caribbean Radicalism in Early Twentieth-Century America* (London: Verso, 1998), 195–231.

17   Glasser, *My Music is My Flag*, 149.

18   Cited in Virginia Sánchez-Korral, *From Colonia to Community: The History of Puerto Ricans in New York City, 1917–1948* (Westport: Greenwood, 1983), 147.

19   Ramón Grosfoguel and Chloe S. Georas, "'Coloniality of Power' and Racial Dynamics: Notes Toward a Reinterpretation of Latino Caribbeans in New York City," *Identities* 7:1 (2000), 1–41. Also published as "Latino Caribbean Diasporas in New York," in Agustín Laó and Arlene Dávila, eds., *Mambo Montage: The Latinization of New York* (New York: Columbia University Press, 2001), 97–118.

20   See, for example, Eugenia Georges, *The Making of a Transnational Community: Migration, Development, and Cultural Change in the Dominican Republic* (New York: Columbia University Press, 1990); Sherri Grasmuck and Patricia Pessar, *Between Two Islands: Dominican International Migration* (Berkeley: University of California Press, 1991); Luis E. Guarnizo, "The Emergence of a Transnational Social Formation and the Mirage of Return Migration among Dominican Transmigrants," *Identities* 4:2 (1997), 281–322; Jorge Duany, *Quisqueya on the Hudson: The Transnational Identity of Dominicans in Washington Heights* (New York: Dominican Studies Institute, City University of New York, 1994); and Levitt, *The Transnational Villagers*.

21   See Appadurai, *Modernity at Large*, 3 passim, and Hall, "Cultural Identity and Diaspora."

5 Bring the Salsa

1   See Arcadio Díaz Quiñones, *El arte de bregar* (San Juan: Ediciones Callejón, 2000). On *jaibería*, see Frances Negrón Muntaner and Ramón Grosfoguel, eds., *Puerto Rican Jam* (Minneapolis: University of Minnesota Press, 1997).

2   Luis Rafael Sánchez, *La guagua aérea* (San Juan: Editorial Cultural, 1994).

3   See Carlos Torres, Hugo Rodríguez, and William Burgos, eds. *The Commuter Nation: Perspectives on Puerto Rican Migration* (Rïo Piedras: Editorial de la Universidad

de Puerto Rico, 1994), and Jorge Duany, *The Puerto Rican Nation on the Move: Identities on the Island and in the United States* (Chapel Hill: University of North Carolina Press, 2002).

4   See Juan Otero Garabís, "Terroristas culturales: en 'guagua aérea' 'traigo la salsa'," unpublished manuscript. See also, Otero Garabís, *Nación y ritmo: "descargas" desde el Caribe* (San Juan: Ediciones Callejón, 2000).

5   Cited in Garabís, *Nación y ritmo.*

6   César Miguel Rondón, *El libro de la salsa: Crónica de la música del Caribe urbano* (Caracas: Editorial Arte, 1980). See also, Angel Quintero Rivera, *Salsa, sabor y control: Sociología de la musica tropical* (Mexico: Siglo XXI, 1998), and Félix Padilla, "Salsa Music as a Cultural Expression of Latino Consciousness and Unity," *Hispanic Journal of Behavioral Sciences* 2:1 (1989), 28–45.

7   Glasser, *My Music Is My Flag.*

8   I wish to thank Paul Austerlitz and René López for their valuable insights.

9   See my essay "'Cha Cha With a Backbeat': Songs and Stories of Latin Boogaloo" in *From Bomba to Hip-Hop: Puerto Rican Culture and Latino Identity* (New York: Columbia University Press, 2000), 79–112.

10   On Cortijo, see Edgardo Rodríguez Juliá, *El entierro de Cortijo* (Río Piedras: Ediciones Huracán, 1982), and my introduction to the translation of that work, *Cortijo's Wake/El entierro de Cortijo* (Durham: Duke University Press, 2004), 1–14. See also my essay "Cortijo's Revenge: New Mappings of Puerto Rican Culture," in *Divided Borders: Essays on Puerto Rican Identity* (Houston: Arte Público, 1993) 92–107.

11   I thank Tito Matos for a helpful personal interview in New York in 2005.

12   See Paul Austerlitz, "From Transplant to Transnational Circuit: Merengue in New York," in Ray Allen and Lois Wilcken, eds., *Island Sounds in the Global City: Caribbean Popular Music and Identity in New York* (Brooklyn: Institute for Studies in American Music), 1998, 44–60.

13   See Francisco Rodriguez de León, *El furioso merengue del norte* (New York: n.p., 1998), 71–81.

14   See Paul Austerlitz, "Urban Maroons: Music as a Counter-Narrative of Blackness in the Dominican Republic and the Dominican Diaspora," Paper presented at the annual convention of the Caribbean Studies Association, 2007.

15   I refer to the public interview with Celia Cruz held at the Smithsonian Institution on October 16, 1997.

16   I thank René Lopez and Leonardo Acosta for their suggestions.

17   See my essay "Puerto Rocks: Rap, Roots and Amnesia," in *From Bomba to Hip-Hop: Puerto Rican Culture and Latino Identity* (New York: Columbia University Press, 2000), 115–139, and Raquel Rivera, *New York Ricans from the Hip Hop Zone* (New York: Palgrave, 2003).

18   Cited in Cohen, *Global Diasporas,* 128.

19   Rivera, *New York Ricans from the Hip Hop Zone.*

20   Raquel Rivera, "Para rapear en puertorriqueño: Discurso y política cultural" (M.A. thesis, 1996).

21   Silvio Torres-Saillant, *El retorno de las yolas: Ensayos sobre diáspora, democracia y domincanidad* (Santo Domingo: Ediciones Librería La Trinitaria, 1999).

22   Moya Pons, "Dominican National Identity in Historical Perspective," 23–25.

23   Deborah Pacini Hernandez, "Dominicans in the Mix: Reflections on Dominican Identity, Race and Reggaeton," unpublished manuscript, forthcoming in Raquel Rivera, Deborah Pacini Hernández, and Wayne Marshall, eds., *Reading Reggaeton* (Durham: Duke University Press, 2008).

24   Margot Olavarria, "Rap and Revolution: Hip-Hop Comes to Cuba," *NACLA: Report on the Americas* 35:6 (2002), 28–30.

25   Personal conversation with Ariel Fernández Díaz, August 5, 2007.

26   Orlando Patterson, "Ecumenical America: Global Culture and the American Cosmos," in Peter Kivisto and Georganne Rundblat, eds., *Multiculturalism in the United States* (Thousand Oaks: Pine Forge Press, 2000), 465–480.

27   See Gage Averill, "Moving the Big Apple: Tabou Combo's Diasporic Dreams," in Ray Allen and Lois Wilcken, eds., *Island Sounds in the Global City: Caribbean Popular Music and Identity in New York* (Brooklyn: Institute for Studies in American Music, 1998), 152.

28   For helpful and informative discussions of some of these interactions, see Averill, "Moving the Big Apple."

29   Austerlitz, "From Transplant to Transnational Circuit."

6 Open Mic

1   On the term Nuyorican, see my entry in the *International Encyclopedia of the Social Sciences*, ed. William A. Darity, Jr., Vol. 5, 2nd ed. (Detroit: Macmillan Reference USA, 2008), 552–553. See also, *Notes of Neorican Seminar*, ed. Robert L. Muckley (San Germán, Puerto Rico: n.p., 1972).

2   For a useful overview of "Latino Caribbean Literature Written in the United States," see William Luis, *Dance Between Two Cultures* (Nashville and London, Vanderbilt University Press, 1997). See also my essay "Islands and Enclaves: Caribbean Latinos in Historical Perspective," in Marcelo M. Suarez-Orozco and Mariela M. Páez, eds., *Latinos Remaking America* (Berkeley: University of California Press, 2002).

3   For an overview of early Dominican writing in the U.S., see *Literatura dominicana en los Estados Unidos: Presencia temprana 1900–1950*, ed. Daisy Cocco De Filippis and Franklin Gutierrez (Santo Domingo: Editora Búho, 2001).

4   For discussions of Muñoz Marín as a return migrant, see Erna Kerkof, *Contested Belonging: Circular Migration and Puerto Rican Identity* (Utrecht: n.p., 2000). For interpretive assessments of Bernardo Vega, see Eugene Mohr, *The Nuyorican Experience* (Westport: Greenwood, 1982), and Efraín Barradas, *Partes de un todo: Ensayos y notas sobre literaturea puertorriqueña en los Estados Unidos* (San Juan: Editorial de la Universidad de Puerto Rico, 1998).

5   See the introductions by José Luis González and César Andreu Iglesias to the Spanish-language edition of the *Memorias* (Río Piedras: Ediciones Huracán, 1977), 9–33. See also Arcadio Díaz Quinones, *Conversación con José Luis González* (Río Piedras: Ediciones Huracán, 1976).

6   I use the phrase "views from the Island" in my essay "Puerto Rican Literature in the US: Stages and Perspectives," *Divided Borders* (Houston: Arte Publico Press, 1993), 142–153. This section of the present chapter summarizes the main lines of analysis of that earlier essay.

7   Nicholasa Mohr, "Puerto Rican Writers in the United States, Puerto Rican Writers in Puerto Rico: A Separation Beyond Language," in Denis Lynn Daly Heyck, ed., *Barrios and Borderlands: Cultures of Latinos and Latinas in the United States* (New York: Routledge, 1994), 264–269.

8   On Lourdes Casal, see in Miriam DeCosta-Willis, ed., *Daughters of the Diaspora: Afra-Hispanic Writers* (Kingston: Ian Randle Publishers, 2003), 177–201.

9   See Vicioso, "An Oral History."

10   Chiqui Vicioso, "Perspectives," in Daisy Cocco de Filippis and Emma Jane Robinett, eds., *Poems of Exile and Other Concerns/Poemas del exilio y de otras inquietudes* (New York: Ediciones Alcance, 1988).

11   Juan Flores and Mayra Santos Febres, eds. "Open Mic/Micrófono abierto: Nuevas literaturas Puerto/neorriqueñas / New Puerto/Nuyo Rican Literatures," *Hostos Review /Revista hostosiana*, 2 (2005), p. xxi.

12   José Raúl González (Gallego), *Barrunto* (San Juan: Isla Negra, 2000), 15.

13   Ibid., 65.

14   José Raúl González (Gallego), *Residente del lupus* (San Juan: Isla Negra, 2006), 36.

15   Guillermo Rebollo-Gil, "The New Boogaloo: Nuyorican Poetry and the Coming Puerto Rican Identities," MA Thesis, University of Florida, 2004, 48.

16   Ibid., 51–53.

17   Josefina Báez, *Dominicanish: Performance Text* (New York: I Ombe, 2000), 31–32.

18   Josefina Báez, *Aquí ahora es Manhattan. Allá entonces La Romana* (New York: Ediciones Alcance, 1999), 6.

19   Ibid., 11.

20   Ibid., 21.

21   See ibid., 3.

22   See Isael Pérez, ed., *A la sombra del cañaveral: Antología de poetas de Este* (Santo Domingo: Edicones Ferilibro, 2006).

23   See, for example, Luis, *Dance Between Two Cultures*, 171ff.

24   See Ibid., 175–185.

Coda: Visual Crossings

1   See Yasmín Ramírez, "Nuyorican Visionary: Jorge Soto and the evolution of an Afro-Taíno aesthetic at Taller Boricua," *Centro* 12 (2005), 22–41, and Diógenes Ballester, "Aesthetic Development of Puerto Rican Visual Arts in New York as Part of the Diaspora: The Epitaph of the Barrio," in *Homenaje Alma Taller Boricua XXX Aniversario* (San Juan: Museo de las Américas, 2001), 30–35. I am also grateful for extended discussions with Marcos Dimas on these issues.

2   See Arcadio Díaz-Quiñones, "Imágenes de Lorenzo Homar: Entre Nueva York y San Juan," in Díaz-Quiñones, *El art de bregar* (San Juan: Ediciones Callejón, 2000), 124–181.

3   Teresita Tió, "Ensayo – No es lo mismo ser que estar," *Rafael Tufiño: Pintor del Pueblo, Painter of the People* (Museo de Arte de Puerto Rico, 2003), 100.

4   I thank Arcadio Díaz-Quiñones for this reference.

BIBLIOGRAPHY

Al-Ali, Nadje, and Khalid Kose, eds. *New Approaches to Migration? Transnational Communities and the Transformation of Home*. London: Routledge, 2002.

Algarín, Miguel, and Miguel Piñero, eds. *Nuyorican Poetry: An Anthology of Puerto Rican Words and Feelings*. New York: Morrow, 1975.

Alvarez, Julia. *Homecoming*. New York: Plume, 1996.

Alvarez, Julia. *How the Garcia Girls Lost Their Accents*. Chapel Hill: Algonquin Books, 1991.

Anderson, Benedict, "Long-Distance Nationalism: World Capitalism and the Rise of Identity Politics," *New Left Review* 193 (1992), 3–13.

Appadurai, Arjun, "Grassroots Globalization and the Research Imagination," in *Globalization*, ed. Arjun Appadurai. Durham: Duke University Press, 2001, 1–21.

Appadurai, Arjun. *Modernity at Large: Cultural Dimensions of Globalization*. Minneapolis: University of Minnesota Press, 1996.

Aranda, Elizabeth M. *Emotional Bridges to Puerto Rico: Migration, Return Migration, and the Struggles of Incorporation*. Lanham: Rowman & Littlefield, 2006.

Areíto, Grupo, *Contra viento y marea*. Havana: Casa de las Américas, 1978.

Ariet, Grupo, ed., *Contra viento y marea: Jovenes cubanos hablan desde su exilio en Estados Unidos*. Mexico: Siglo Veintiuno, 1978.

Ashcroft, Bill, Gareth Griffiths, and Helen Tiffin, eds. *The Empire Writes Back: Theory and Practice in Post-Colonial Literatures*. London: Routledge, 1989.

Austerlitz, Paul. *Merengue: Dominican Music and Dominican Identity*. Philadelphia: Temple University Press, 1997.

Austerlitz, Paul. "From Transplant to Transnational Circuit: Merengue in New York," in *Island Sounds in the Global City: Caribbean Popular Music and Identity in New York*, eds. Ray Allen and Lois Wilcken. Brooklyn: Institute for Studies in American Music, 1998, 44–60.

Austerlitz, Paul. "Urban Maroons: Music as a Counter-Narrative of Blackness in the Dominican Republic and the Dominican Diaspora," paper presented at the annual convention of the Caribbean Studies Association, 2007.

Averill, Gage. "Moving the Big Apple: Tabou Combo's Diasporic Dreams," in *Island Sounds in the Global City: Caribbean Popular Music and Identity in New York*, eds. Ray Allen and Lois Wilcken. Brooklyn: Institute for Studies in American Music, 1998.

Báez, Josefina. *Aquí ahora es Manhattan. Allá antes La Romana*. New York: Ediciones Alcance, 1999.

Báez, Josefina. *Dominicanish: Performance Text.* New York: I Ombe, 2000.

Ballester, Diógenes. "Aesthetic Development of Puerto Rican Visual Arts in New York as Part of the Diaspora: The Epitaph of the Barrio," in *Homenaje Alma Taller Boricua XXX Aniversario.* San Juan: Museo de las Américas, 2001, 30–35.

Barradas, Efraín. *Partes de un todo: Ensayos y notas sobre literaturea puertorriqueña en los Estados Unidos.* San Juan: Editorial de la Universidad de Puerto Rico, 1998.

Basch, Linda, Nina Glick-Schiller, and C. Szanton, eds. *Nations Unbound: Transnational Projects, Postcolonial Predicaments, and Deterritorialized Nation-States.* Switzerland: Gordon and Breach, 1994.

Berger, Ronald J., and Richard Quinney, eds. *Storytelling Sociology: Narrative as Social Inquiry.* Boulder: Lynne Rienner, 2005.

Bernabé, Jean, Patrick Chamoiseau, and Raphaël Confiant, *Eloge a la créolté/In Praise of Creoleners.* Paris: Gallimard, 1993.

Besserer, Federico. *Topografías transnacionales.* Mexico: Universidad Autónoma Metropolitana Unidad Iztapalapa, 2002.

Besson, Jean, and Karen Fog Olwig, eds. *Caribbean Narratives of Belonging: Fields of Relations, Sites of Identity.* Oxford: Macmillan, 2005.

Bhabha, Homi K., *The Location of Culture.* London: Routledge, 1994.

Bhabha, Homi K., "Unsatisfied: Notes on Vernacular Cosmopolitanism," in *Text and Nation: Cross-Disciplinary Essays on Cultural and National Identities,* ed. Laura Garcia-Moreno and Peter C. Pfeiffer (Columbia: Camden House, 1996), 191–207.

Bovenkerk, Frank. *The Sociology of Return Migration: A Bibliogaphic Essay.* The Hague: Martin Nijhof, 1974.

Bovenkerk, Frank, "Why Returnees Generally Do Not Turn Out to Be 'Agents of Change': The Case of Surinam," in *Nieuwe West Indische Gids* 55 (1981), 154–173.

Boyd Caroli, Betty. *Immigrants Who Returned Home.* New York: Chelsea House Publishers, 1990.

Brah, Avtar. *Cartographies of Diaspora: Contesting Identities.* London: Routledge, 1997.

Brecher, Jeremy, John Brown Childs, and Jill Cutler, eds. *Global Visions: Beyond the New World Order.* Boston: South End Press, 1993.

Butler, Kim, "Defining Diaspora, Refining a Discourse," *Diaspora* 10:2 (2001), 1–31.

Campbell, James T. *Middle Passages: African American Journeys to Africa, 1787–2005.* New York: Penguin, 2006.

Cassarino, Jean-Pierre, "Theorising Return Migration: The Conceptual Approach to Return Migrants Revisited," *International Journal on Multicultural Societies* 6:2 (2004), 253–279.

Centre for Contemporary Cultural Studies, *The Empire Strikes Back: Race and Racism in 70s Britain.* London: Hutchinson, 1982.

Cerase, Francesco, "Nostalgia or Disenchantment: Considerations on Return Migration," in *The Italian Experience in the United States,* ed. S.M. Tomasi and M.H. Engel. New York: Center for Migration Studies, 1970, 217–239.

Cerase, Francesco, "Expectations and Reality: A Case Study of Return Migration from the United States to Southern Italy," *International Migration Review* 8:2 (1974), 245–262.

Césaire, Aimé. *Collected Poetry.* Berkeley: University of California Press, 1983.

Chamberlain, Mary. *Narratives of Exile and Return*. New York: St. Martin's Press, 1997.

Chamberlain, Mary, ed. *Caribbean Migration: Globalised Identities*. London: Routledge, 1998.

Chambers, Iain. *Migrancy, Culture, Identity*. London: Routledge, 1994.

Chow, Rey. *Writing Diaspora: Tactics of Intervention in Contemporary Cultural Studies*. Bloomington: Indiana University Press, 1993.

Clifford, James. "Diasporas," *Cultural Anthropology* 9:3 (1994), 302–338.

Clifford, James. *Routes: Travel and Translation in the Late Twentieth Century*. Cambridge: Harvard University Press, 1997.

Cocco de Filippis, Daisy, and Emma Jane Robinett, eds. *Poems of Exile and Other Concerns: A Bilingual Selection of Poetry Written by Dominicans in the United States*. New York: Ediciones Alcance, 1988.

Cocco de Filippis, Daisy, and Franklin Gutiérrez, eds. *Literatura dominicana en los Estados Unidos: Presencia temprana 1900–1950*. Santo Domingo: Editora Búho, 2001.

Cohen, Robin. "The Diaspora of a Diaspora: The Case of the Caribbean," *Social Science Information* 31 (1992), 159–169.

Cohen, Robin. "Diasporas and the Nation-State: From Victims to Challengers," *International Affairs* 72:3 (1996), 507–520.

Cohen, Robin. *Global Diasporas: An Introduction*. Seattle: University of Washington Press, 1997.

Constant, Amelie, and Douglas Massey. "Return Migration by German Guestworkers: Neoclassical versus New Economic Theories," *International Migration* 40:4 (2002), 5–38.

Cotto-Thorner, Guillermo. *Trópico en Manhattan*. San Juan: Editorial Cardillera, 1960.

Davidson, Betty. "No Place Back Home: A Study of Jamaicans Returning to Kingston, Jamaica," *Race* 9:4 (1968), 499–509.

De la Campa, Román. *Cuba on My Mind: Journeys to a Severed Nation*. London: Verso, 2000.

De la Garza, Rodolfo and B. Lindsay Lowell, eds. *Sending Money Home: Latino Remittances to Latin America*. Boulder: Rowman & Littlefield Publishers, 2002.

De Los Angeles Torres, María. "Encuentros y encontronazos: Homeland in the Politics and Identity of the Cuban Diaspora," *Diaspora* 4:2 (1995), 211–238.

Decena, Carlos, and Margaret Gray. "Putting Transnationalism to Work: An Interview with Filmmaker Alex Rivera," *Social Text* 24:3 (2006), 131–138.

Diouf, Mamdou. "The Senegalese Murid Trade Diaspora and the Making of a Vernacular Cosmopolitanism," *Public Culture* 12:3 (2000), 679–702.

Díaz-Quiñones, Arcadio. *Conversación con José Luis González*. Río Piedras: Ediciones Huracán, 1976.

Díaz-Quiñones, Arcadio. *El arte de bregar*. San Juan: Ediciones Callejón, 2000.

Duany, Jorge. *Quisqueya on the Hudson: The Transnational Identity of Dominicans in Washington Heights*. New York: Dominican Studies Institute, City University of New York, 1994.

Duany, Jorge. *The Puerto Rican Nation on the Move: Identities on the Island and in the United States*. Chapel Hill: University of North Carolina Press, 2002.

Duany, Jorge. *A Transnational Migrant Crossroads: The Circulation of People and Money in Puerto Rico*. San Juan: Report for the Center for the New Economy, 2007.

Edwards, Brent Hayes. "The Uses of Diaspora," *Social Text* 19:1 (2001), 45–73.

Edwards, Brent Hayes. *The Practice of Diaspora: Literature, Translation, and the Rise of Black Internationalism*. Cambridge: Harvard University Press, 2003.

Ellis, M., D. Conway and A. J. Bailey. "The Circular Migration of Puerto Rican Women: Towards a Gendered Explanation," *International Migration* 34 (1996), 31–64.

Enwezor, Okwui, Carlos Basualdo, Ute Meta Bauer, Susanne Ghez, Sarat Maharaj, Mark Nash, and Octavio Zaya, eds. *Créolité and Creolization: Documenta11_Platform3*. Kassel: Hatje Cantz, 2003.

Evans Braziel, Jana, and Anita Mannur, eds. *Theorizing Diaspora*. Malden, Mass.: Blackwell, 2003.

Fernandes, Sujatha. *Cuba Represent!: Cuban Arts, State Power, and the Making of New Revolutionary Cultures*. Durham: Duke University Press, 2006.

Fernández Díaz, Ariel R. "Rap Cubano: ¿Poesía urbana o la Nueva Trova de los noventa?" *Cayman Barbudo* 296 (2000), 4–16.

Flores, Juan. *Divided Borders: Essays on Puerto Rican Identity*. Houston: Arte Público, 1993.

Flores, Juan. *From Bomba to Hip-Hop: Puerto Rican Culture and Latino Identity*. New York: Columbia University Press, 2000.

Flores, Juan, "Islands and Enclaves: Caribbean Latinos in Historical Perspective," in *Latinos Remaking America*, ed Marcelo M. Suárez-Orozco and Mariela M. Páez (Berkeley: University of California Press, 2002), 59–74.

Flores, Juan, "The Diaspora Strikes Back: Créolite in the Hood," in *Creolité and Creolization: Dokumenta11_Platform3*, eds. Okwui Enwezor *et al.*, Kassel: Hatje Cantz, 2003, 165–175.

Flores, Juan, *Cortijo's Wake/El entierro de Cortijo*. Durham: Duke University Press, 2004.

Flores, Juan, "The Diaspora Strikes Back: Reflections on Cultural remittances," *NACLA: Report to the Americas* 39 (2005), 21–26, 40.

Flores, Juan, "Creolité in the Hood: Diaspora as Source and Challenge," in *Contemporary Caribbean Cultures and Societies in a Global Context*, ed. Franklin W. Knight and Teresita Martínez-Vergne. Chapel Hill: University of North Carolina Press, 2005, 117–129.

Flores, Juan, "Nuyoncan," in *International Encyclopedia of the Social Sciences*, ed. William A. Darity, Jr., Vol. 5, 2nd ed. Detroit: Macmillan Reference USA, 2008, 552–553.

Flores, Juan and Mayra Santos Febres, eds. "Open Mic/Micrófono abierto: Nuevas literaturas Puerto/neorriqueñas/New Puerto/Nuyo Rican Literatures," *Hostos Review/Revista hostosiana*, 2 (2005).

Foner, Nancy, "What's New About Transnationalism? New York Immigrants Today and at the Turn of the Century," *Diaspora* 6:3 (1997), 355–375.

Gaillard, Anne Marie. *Migration Return: A Bibliographical Overview*. New York: Center for Migration Studies, 1994.

García Zamora, Rodolfo. *Migración, remesas y desarrollo local*. Mexico: Doctorado en Estudios del Desarrollo, México: UAZ, 2003.

Georges, Eugenia. *The Making of a Transnational Community: Migration, Development, and Cultural Change in the Dominican Republic.* New York: Columbia University Press, 1990.

Ghosh, Bimal, ed. *Return Migration: Journey of Hope or Despair?* Geneva: International Organization for Migration and the United Nations, 2000.

Gill, Hannah E. "*Querido Emigrante*: Musical Perspectives of Dominican Migration," Transnational Communities Programme Working Papers Series, ISCA, n.d.

Gilroy, Paul. *The Black Atlantic: Modernity and Double Consciousness.* London: Verso, 1993.

Gilroy, Paul. '*There Ain't No Black in the Union Jack*': *The Cultural Politics of Race and Nation.* Chicago: University of Chicago Press, 1991.

Glasser, Ruth. *My Music Is My Flag: Puerto Rican Musicians and Their New York Communities, 1917–1940.* Berkeley: University of California Press, 1997.

Glick Schiller, Nina and Georges Fouron. *Georges Woke Up Laughing: Long Distance Nationalism and the Search for Home.* Durham: Duke University Press, 2001.

Glick Schiller, Nina, Linda Basch, and Cristina Blanc-Szanton. "From Immigrant to Transmigrant: Theorizing Transnational Migration," *Anthropological Quarterly* 68:1 (1995), 48–63.

Glissant, Edouard. *Caribbean Discourse.* Charlottesville: University of Virginia Press, 1999.

Gmelch, George, "Return Migration," *Annual Review of Anthropology* 9 (1980), 135–159.

Gmelch, George. *Double Passage: The Lives of Caribbean Migrants Abroad and Back Home.* Ann Arbor: University of Michigan Press, 1992.

Goldring, Luin, "Re-thinking Remittances: Social and Political Dimensions of Individual and Collective Remittances," Centre for Research on Latin America and the Caribbean, University of York, Working Paper Series (2003), 1–26.

González, José Luis, and César Andreu Iglesias. "Introduction," *Memorias.* Río Piedras: Ediciones Huracán, 1977, 9–33.

González, José Raúl (Gallego). *Barrunto.* San Juan: Isla Negra, 2000.

González, José Raúl (Gallego). *Residente del lupus.* San Juan: Isla Negra, 2006.

Grasmuck, Sherri, and Patricia Pessar. *Between Two Islands: Dominican International Migration.* Berkeley: University of California Press, 1991.

Greenbaum, Susan. *More Than Black: Afro-Cubans in Tampa.* Gainesville: University of Florida Press, 2002.

Grillo, Evelio. *Black Cuban, Black American.* Houston: Arte Público, 2000.

Grosfoguel, Ramón, and Chloe S. Georas, "'Coloniality of Power' and Racial Dynamics: Notes Toward a Reinterpretation of Latin Caribbeans in New York City," *Identities* 7:1 (2000), 1–41.

Guarnizo, Luis E. "'Los Dominicanyorks': The Making of a Binational Society," *Annals of the American Academy* 533 (1994), 70–86.

Guarnizo, Luis E. "The Emergence of a Transnational Social Formation and the Mirage of Return Migration among Dominican Transmigrants," *Identities* 4:2 (1997), 281–322.

Gupta, Akhil, and James Ferguson, eds. *Culture, Power, Place: Explorations in Critical Anthropology*. Durham: Duke University Press, 1997.

Hall, Stuart. "Cultural Identity and Diaspora," in *Identity: Community, Culture, Difference*. London: Lawrence & Wishart, 1990, 222–237.

Hall, Stuart. "Diaspora and Cultural Identity," in *Colonial Discourse and Post-Colonial Theory*, ed. Patrick Williams and Laura Chrisman. New York: Columbia University Press, (1994), 392–403.

Hall, Stuart. "Creolization, Diaspora, and Hybridity in the Context of Globalization," *Creolité and Creolization: Dokumenta11_Platform 3*, ed. Okwui Enwezor, *et al.* Ostfildern-Ruit, Germany: Hatje Cantz, 2002.

Hall, Stuart, and Paul du Gay, eds. *Questions of Cultural Identity*. London: Sage Publications, 1996.

Hannerz, Ulf. *Transnational Connections: Culture, People, Places*. London: Routledge, 1996.

Hernández, Carmen Dolores. *Puerto Rican Voices in English: Interviews with Writers*. Westport: Praeger, 1997.

Hernández Alvarez, José. *Return Migration to Puerto Rico*. Westport: Greenwood Press, 1967.

Hoffnung-Garskof, Jesse. "The Prehistory of the *Cadenú*: Dominican Identity, Social Class, and the Problem of Mobility, 1965–78," in *Immigrant Life in the U.S.: Multidisciplinary Perspectives*, eds. Donna R. Gabacia and Colin Wayne Leach. London: Routledge, 2004, 30–50.

Hutchinson, Sydney. "*Merengue Típico* in Santiago and New York: Transnational Regionalism in a Neo-Traditional Dominican Music," *Ethnomusicology* 50:1 (2006), 37–72.

Ishkanian, Armine. "Home-Coming and Goings," *Diaspora* 13:2 (2001), 111–120.

James, Winston. *Hold Aloft the Banner of Ethiopia: Caribbean Radicalism in Early Twentieth-Century America*. London: Verso, 1998.

Johnson, Roberta Ann. "The Newyorican Comes Home to Puerto Rico: Description and Consequences," in *Return Migration and Remittances*, ed. William F. Stinner, *et al.* 129–156.

Kearney, M. "From the Invisible Hand to Visible Feet: Anthropological Studies of Migration and Development," *Annual Review of Anthropology* 13 (1986), 331–361.

Kearney, M. "The Local and the Global: The Anthropology of Globalization and Transnationalism," *Annual Review of Anthropology* 24 (1995), 547–565.

Kerkhof, Erna. *Contested Belonging: Circular Migration and Puerto Rican Identity*. Utrecht: n.p., 2000.

King, Russell, ed. *Return Migration and Regional Economic Problems*. London: Croom Helm, 1986.

King, Russell, and John Connell, eds. *Small Worlds, Global Lives: Islands and Migration*. London: Pinter, 1999.

Koptiuch, Kristin. "Third-Worlding at Home," *Social Text* 28 (1991), 87–99.

Kornblum, William. "Discovering Ink: A Mentor for an Historical Ethnography," *Annals (AAPSS)*, 595 (2004), 176–189.

Kubat, Daniel, ed. *The Politics of Return: International Return Migration in Europe.* Rome: Centro Studie Emigrazione, 1984.

Laguerre, Michel. *Diasporic Citizenship: Haitian Americans in Transnational America.* New York: St. Martins, 1998.

Lamming, George. *The Pleasures of Exile.* Ann Arbor: University of Michigan Press, 1960.

Laue, Barbara. *Identitätsprobleme spanisher Remigrantenkinder: Leben im Spannungsfeld zwischen zwei Welten.* Cologne: Böhlau Verlag, 1990.

Lavie, Smadar and Ted Swedenburg, eds. *Displacement, Diaspora, and Geographies of Identity.* Durham: Duke University Press, 1996.

Lee, B. and E. LiPuma. "Cultures of Circulation: The Imaginations of Modernity," *Public Culture* 14:1 (2002), 191–213.

Lesser, Jeffrey, ed. *Searching for Home Abroad: Japanese Brazilians and Transnationalism.* Durham: Duke University Press, 2003.

Levitt, Peggy. "Social Remittances: Migration-Driven Local-Level Forms of Cultural Diffusion," *International Migration Review* 32:4 (1998), 926–948.

Levitt, Peggy. *The Transnational Villagers.* Berkeley: University of California Press, 2001.

Levitt, Peggy, and Mary C. Waters, eds. *The Changing Face of Home: Transnational Lives of the Second Generation.* New York: Russell Sage Foundation, 2002.

Lewis, Earl. "To Turn as on a Pivot: Writing African Americans into a History of Overlapping Diasporas," *American Historical Review* 100:3 (1995), 765–787.

Long, Lynellyn D., and Ellen Oxfeld, eds. *Coming Home? Refugees, Migrants, and Those Who Stayed Behind.* Philadelphia: University of Pennsylvania Press, 2004.

López Adorno, Pedro, ed. *Papiros de Babel: Antología de la poesía puertorriqueña en Nueva York.* Río Piedras: Editorial de la Universidad de Puerto Rico, 1991.

Luis, William. *Dance Between Two Cultures: Latino Caribbean Literature Written in the United States.* Nashville: Vanderbilt University Press, 1997.

Mariposa, *Born Bronxeña.* New York: Bronxeña Books, n.d.

Markowitz, Fran, and Anders H. Stefansson, eds. *Homecomings: Unsettling Paths of Return.* Oxford: Lexington Books, 2004.

Marshall, Paule. *Brown Girls, Brownstones.* New York: Random House, 1959.

Martínez-San Miguel, Yolanda. *Caribe Two Ways: Cultura de la migración en el Caribe insular hispanico.* San Juan: Ediciones Callejón, 2003.

Miller Mathei, Linda, and David A. Smith. "'Boyz 'n the 'Hood'? Garifuna Labor Migration and Transnational Identity," in *Transnationalism from Below*, ed. Michael Peter Smith and Luis Eduardo Guarnizo. New Brunswick: Transaction, 1998, 270–290.

Mintz, Sidney. "The Localization of Anthropological Practice," *Critique of Anthropology* 18 (1998), 117–133.

Mir, Pedro. *Countersong to Walt Whitman and Other Poems.* Washington, DC: Azul Editions, 1993.

Mohr, Eugene. *The Nuyorican Experience.* Westport: Greenwood, 1982.

Mohr, Nicholasa. "Puerto Rican Writers in the United States, Puerto Rican Writers in Puerto Rico: A Separation Beyond Language," in *Barrios and Borderlands: Cultures of Latinos and Latinas in the United States*, ed. Denis Lynn Daly Heyck. New York: Routledge, 1994, 264–269.

Moya Pons, Frank. "Dominican National Identity in Historical Perspective," *Punto 7 Review* (1996), 23–25

Muckley, Robert L., ed. *Notes of Neorican Seminar.* San Germán, PR: n.p., 1972.

Mudimbe, V.Y. *Nations, Identities, Cultures.* Durham: Duke University Press, 1997.

Mullings, Leith. "Race and Globalization: Racialization from Below," *Souls* 6:2 (2004), 1–9.

Muñoz, José. *Disidentifications: Queers of Color and the Performance of Politics.* Minneapolis: University of Minnesota Press, 1999.

Muntaner, Frances Negrón and Ramón Grosfoguel, eds. *Puerto Rican Jam.* Minneapolis: University of Minnesota Press, 1997.

Olavarria, Margot, "Rap and Revolution: Hip-Hop Comes to Cuba," *NACLA: Report on the Americas* 35:6 (2002), 28–30.

Olwig, Karen Fog. *Global Culture, Island Identity: Continuity and Change in the Afro-Caribbean Community of Nevis.* Chur, Switzerland: Harwood, Academic Publishers, 1993.

Ong, Aihwa. *Flexible Citizenship: The Cultural Logics of Transnationality.* Durham: Duke University Press, 1998.

Otero Garabís, Juan "Terroristas culturales: en 'guangua aérea' 'traigo la salsa'," unpublished manuscript.

Otero Garabís, Juan. *Nación y ritmo: Descargas desde el Caribe.* San Juan: Ediciones Callejón, 2000.

Pacini Hernández, Deborah. *Bachata: A Social History of a Dominican Popular Music.* Philadelphia: Temple University Press, 1995.

Pacini Hernández, Deborah. "Dominicans in the Mix: Reflections on Dominican Identity, Race and Reggaeton," in *Reading Reggaeton: Historical, Aesthetic and Critical Perspectives*, eds. Raquel Z. Riviera, Deborah Pacini Hernandez, and Wayne Marshall, Durham: Duke University Press, forthcoming 2008.

Padilla, Félix. "Salsa Music as a Cultural Expression of Latino Consciousness and Unity," *Hispanic Journal of Behavioural Sciences*, 2:1 (1989), 28–45.

Palumbo-Liu, David, and Hans Ulrich Gumprecht, eds. *Streams of Cultural Capital.* Stanford: Stanford University Press, 1993.

Patterson, H.O. (Orlando). "West Indian Migrants Returning Home: Some Observations," *Race* 10:1 (1968), 69–77.

Patterson, Orlando. "The Emerging West Atlantic System: Migration, Culture, and Underdevelopment in the United States and the Circum-Caribbean Region," in *Population in an Interacting World*, ed. William Alonso. Cambridge: Harvard University Press, 1987, 227–277.

Patterson, Orlando. "Global Culture and the American Cosmos," *Andy Warhol Foundation for the Visual Arts: Paper Series on the Arts, Culture, and Society* (1994), 1–16.

Patterson, Orlando. "Ecumenical America: Global Culture and the American Cosmos," in *Multiculturalism in the United States*, eds. Peter Kivisto and Georganne Rundblat, Thousand Oaks: Pine Forge Press, 2000, 465–480.

Pausides, Alex, Pedro Antonio Valdéz, and Carlos R. Gómez Beras, eds. L@s nuev@s caníbales v. 2: Antología de la más reciente poesía del Caribe hispano. San Juan: Editorial Isla Negra, 2003.

Pérez, Gina M. *The New Northwest Side Story: Migration, Displacement, and Puerto Rican Families.* Berkeley: University of California Press, 2004.

Pérez, Isael, ed. *A la sombra del cañaveral: Antología de poetas de Este.* Santo Domingo: Ediciones Ferilibro, 2006.

Perez Firmat, Gustavo. *Life on the Hyphen: The Cuban-American Way.* Austin: University of Texas Press, 1994.

Pessar, Patricia, ed. *Caribbean Circuits: New Directions in the Study of Caribbean Migration.* New York: Center for Migration Studies, 1997.

Pessar, Patricia, and Sarah Mahler. "Transnational Migration: Bringing Gender In," *International Migration Review* 37:3 (2003), 812–838.

Portes, Alejandro. "Global Villagers: The Rise of Transnational Communities," *The American Prospect* 7:25 (1996), 1–8.

Portes, Alejandro, Luis E. Guarnizo, and Patricia Landott. "Introduction: Pitfall and Promise of an Emergent Research Field," *Ethnic and Racial Studies* 22 (1999), 463–478.

Potter, Robert B. "'Tales of Two Societies': Narratives of Adjustment," in *The Experience of Return Migration: Caribbean Perspectives*, ed. Robert B. Potter, Dennis Conway, and Joan Phillips. Hants, England: Ashgate, 2005.

Potter, Robert B., Dennis Conway, and Joan Phillips, eds. *The Experience of Return Migration: Caribbean Perspectives.* Hants, England: Ashgate, 2005.

Poyo, Gerald, *"With All, and for the Good of All": The Emergence of Popular Nationalism in the Cuban Communities of the United States, 1848–1898* (Durham: Duke University Press, 1989).

Quiroga, José. *Cuban Palimpsests.* Minneapolis: University of Minnesota Press, 2005.

Radhakrishnan, R. *Diasporic Meditations: Between Home and Location.* Minneapolis: University of Minnesota Press, 1996.

Ramírez, Yasmín. "Nuyorican Visionary: Jorge Soto and the Evolution of an Afro-Taíno aesthetic at Taller Boricua," *Centro* 12 (2005), 22–41.

Rapport, Nigel, and Andrew Dawson, eds. *Migrants of Identity: Perceptions of Home in a World of Movement.* Oxford: Berg, 1998.

Ravenstein, Ernest George, "The Laws of Migration," *Journal of the Statistical Society of London*, 48 (1985), 167–235.

Rebollo-Gil, Guillermo. *Sonero.* Río Piedras: Editorial Isla Negra, 2003.

Rebollo-Gil, Guillermo. "The New Boogaloo: Nuyorican Poetry and the Coming Puerto Rican Identities." MA Thesis, University of Florida, 2004.

Rimer, Sarah. "Finally, Back to the Island for a Summer at Home," *New York Times*, August 22, 2005, B1, B5.

Rivera, Angel Quintero, *Salsa, sabor y control: sociología de la musica tropical.* Mexico: Siglo XXI, 1998.

Rivera, Raquel "Para rapear en puertorriqueño: Discurso y politica cultural," M.A. thesis 1996.

Rivera, Raquel. *New York Ricans from the Hip Hop Zone*. New York: Palgrave, 2003.

Robinson, Eugene. *Last Dance in Havana: The Final Days of Fidel and the Start of the New Cuban Revolution*. New York: Free Press, 2004.

Rodríguez de León, Francisco. *El furioso merengue del Norte: Una historia de la comunidad dominicana en los Estados Unidos*. New York: n.p., 1998.

Rodríguez Juliá, Edgardo. *El entierro de Cortijo*. Río Piedras: Ediciones Huracán, 1982.

Rondón, César Miguel. *El libro de la salsa: Crónica de la música del Caribe Urbano*. Caracas: Editorial Arte, 1980.

Rouse, Roger. "Mexican Migration and the Social Space of Postmodernism," *Diaspora* 1:1 (1991), 8–23.

Rushdie, Salman. "Imaginary Homelands," in *Imaginary Homelands: Essays and Criticism 1981–1991*, London: Granta, 1992, 9–21.

Safran, William. "Diasporas in Modern Societies: Myths of Homeland and Return," *Diaspora* 1:1 (1991), 83–99.

San Juan, E. "Configuring the Filipino Diaspora," *Diaspora* 3:2 (1994), 117–133.

Sánchez, Luis Rafael. *La guagua aérea*. San Juan: Editorial Cultural, 1994.

Sánchez-Korral, Virginia. *From Colonia to Community: The History of Puerto Ricans in New York City, 1917–1948*. Westport: Greenwood, 1983.

Santos Febres, Mayra. "Translocal Voyages: Migration and the Globalization of Culture," Unpublished manuscript, Departamento de Estudios Hispánicos, Universidad de Puerto Rico, n.d.

Shain, Yossi. *Marketing the American Creed Abroad: Diasporas in the U.S. and Their Homelands*. Cambridge: Cambridge University Press, 1999.

Shain, Yossi. "The Mexican-American Diaspora's Impact on Mexico," *Political Science Quarterly* 114:4 (1999), 661–691.

Smith, Carolyn, ed. *Strangers at Home: Essays on the Effects of Living Overseas and Coming "Home" to a Strange Land*. Bayside: Aletheia Publications, 1996.

Smith, Michael Peter, and Luis Eduardo Guarnizo, eds. *Transnationalism from Below*. New Brunswick: Transaction, 1998.

Smith, Robert C. "Transnational Localities: Community, Technology and the Politics of Membership within the Context of Mexico and U.S. Migration," in *Transnationalism from Below*, ed. Michael Peter Smith and Luis Eduardo Guarnizo. New Brunswick: Transaction, 1998, 196–238.

Smith, Robert Courtney. *Mexican New York: Transnational Lives of New Immigrants*. Berkeley: University of California Press, 2005.

Sørensen, Ninna Nyberg. "Narrating Identity Across Dominican Worlds," in *Transnationalism from Below*, ed. Michael Peter Smith and Luis Eduardo Guarnizo, eds. New Brunswick: Transaction, 1998, 241–269.

Stack, Carol. *Call to Home: African Americans Reclaim the Rural South*. New York: Basic Books, 1996.

Stefansson, Anders H. "Homecomings to the Future: From Diasporic Mythographies to Social Projects of Return," in *Homecomings: Unsettling Paths of Return*, ed. Fran Markowitz and Anders H. Stefansson. Oxford: Lexington, 2004, 2–20.

Stinner, William F., Klaus de Albuquerque, and Roy S. Bryce-Laporte, eds. *Return Migration and Remittances*. Washington, D.C.: Research Institute on Immigration and Ethnic Studies, 1982.

Suárez-Orozco, Marcelo M., and Mariela M. Páez, eds. *Latinos Remaking America*. Berkeley: University of California Press, 2002.

Sutton, Constance R., and Elsa M. Chaney, eds. *Caribbean Life in New York City: Sociocultural Dimensions*. New York: Center for Migration Studies, 1987.

Sutton, Constance R. and Susan Makiesky, "Migration and West Indian Racial and Ethnic Consciousness," in *Migration and Development: Implications for Ethnic Identity and Political Conflict*, ed. Helen I. Safa and Brian M. Du Toit. The Hague: Mouton, 1975, 113–144.

Tallaj, Angelina, "'A Country That Ain't Really Belong to Me': Dominicanyorks, Identity and Popular Music," *Phoebe* 18:2 (2006), 1–14.

Taylor, Lucien. "Créolité Bites: A Conversation with Patrick Chamoiseau, Raphäel Confiant, and Jean Bernabé," *Transition* 74 (1998), 124–161.

Thomas, Piri. *Down These Mean Streets*. New York: Vintage, 1967.

Thomas-Hope, Elizabeth. "Globalization and the Development of a Caribbean Migration Culture," in *Caribbean Migration*, ed. Mary Chamberlain. London: Routledge 1998, 188–199.

Tió, Teresita. "Ensayo—No es lo mismo ser que estar," *Rafael Tufiño: Pintor del Pueblo, Painter of the People*. Puerto Rico: Museo de Arte de Puerto Rico, 2003.

Tölölyan, Khachig. "The Nation-State and Its Others: In Lieu of a Preface," *Diaspora* 1:1 (1991), 3–8.

Tölölyan, Khachig. "Rethinking Diaspora(s): Stateless Power in the Transnational Moment," *Diaspora* 5:1 (1996), 3–36.

Torres, Carlos Antonio, Hugo Rodríguez and William Burgos, eds. *The Commuter Nation: Perspectives on Puerto Rican Migration*. Río Piedras: Editorial de la Universidad de Puerto Rico, 1994.

Torres-Saillant, Silvio. *El retorno de las yolas: Ensayos sobre diáspora, democracia y dominicanidad*. Santo Domingo: Ediciones Libreria La Trinitaria, 1999.

Torres-Saillant, Silvio, and Ramona Hernández. *The Dominican Americans*. Westport: Greenwood Press, 1998.

Torres-Saillant, Silvio, Ramona Hernández, and Blas R. Jiménez, eds. *Desde la orilla: Hacia una nacionalidad sin desalojos*. Santo Domingo: Editora Manatí, 2004.

Tsuda, Takeyuki. "From Ethnic Affinity to Alienation in the Global Ecumene," *Diaspora* 9 (2000), 53–92.

Tsudas, Takeyuki. *Strangers in the Ethnic Homeland: Japanese Brazilian Return Migration in Transnational Perspective*. New York: Columbia University Press, 2003.

Tsuda, Takeyuki. "When Home Is Not the Homeland: The Case of Japanese Brazilian Ethnic Return Migration," in *Homecomings: Unsettling Paths of Return*, ed. Fran Markowitz and Anders H. Stefansson. Oxford: Lexington, 2004, 125–145.

Tuan, Yi-Fu. *Space and Place: The Perspective of Experience.* Minneapolis: University of Minnesota Press, 1977.

Van Hear, Nicholas. *New Diasporas: The Mass Exodus, Dispersal and Regrouping of Migrant Communities.* Seattle: University of Washington Press, 1998.

Vega, Bernardo. *Memoirs of Bernardo Vega,* ed. César Andreu Iglesias. New York: Monthly Review, 1984.

Vertovec, Steven. "Conceiving and Researching Transnationalism," *Ethnic and Racial Studies* 22:2 (1999), 447–462.

Vertovec, Steven. "Rethinking Remittances," ESRC Transnational Communities Research Programme Working Papers 2K–15 (2000).

Vertovec, Steven. "Migrant Transnationalism and Modes of Transformation," *International Migration Review* 38 (2004), 970–1001.

Vertovec, Steven, and Robin Cohen, eds. *Migration, Diasporas and Transnationalism.* Cheltenham: Edward Elgar Publishing, 1999.

Vicioso, Chiqui. "Perspectives," in *Poems of Exile and Other Concerns/Poemas del exilio y de otras inquietudes,* eds. Daisy Cocco de Filippis and Emma Jane Robinett. New York: Ediciones Akance, 1988.

Vicioso, Chiqui. "An Oral History (Testimono)," in *Daughters of the Diaspora: Afra-Hispanic Writers,* ed. Miriam DeCosta-Willis. Kingston: Ian Randle Publishers, 2003, 313–318.

Waldinger, Roger. " Between Here and There: How Attached are Latino Immigrants to Their Native Country?" Pew Hispanic Center, October 25, 2007.

Werbner, Pnina. "Global Pathways: Working Class Cosmopolitans and the Creation of Transnational Ethnic Worlds," *Social Anthropology* 7:1 (1999), 17–35.

Werbner, Pnina. "Introduction: The Materiality of Diaspora—Between Aesthetic and 'Real' Politics," *Diaspora* 1 (2000), 3–20.

Werbner, Pnina. "Understanding Vernacular Cosmopolitanism," *Anthropology News* 47:5 (2006a), 7–11.

Werbner, Pnina, "Vernacular Cosmopolitanism," *Theory, Culture & Society* 23 (2006b), 496–498.

Westwood, Sallie, and Annie Phizacklea. *Trans-nationalism and the Politics of Belonging.* London: Routledge, 2000.

Wilson, Rob, and Wimal Dissanayake, eds. *Global/Local: Cultural Production and the Transnational Imaginary.* Durham: Duke University Press, 1996.

Wyman, Mark. *Round-Trip to America: The Immigrants Return to Europe, 1880–1930.* Ithaca: Cornell University Press, 1993.

INDEX